AUTUMN AND EVERYTHING AFTER

THE MURDER OF JOHN LENNON, EVOLUTION OF BRUCE SPRINGSTEEN & THE BIRTH OF THE REAGAN ERA

MIKE DERRICO

Copyright © 2020 by Mike Derrico

Paperback ISBN: 978-1-7354767-0-4
eBook ISBN: 978-1-7354767-1-1.

Author's disclaimer: The following numbered citations contain material from books, magazines, newspapers and television interviews serving as vital examples and reinforcement of significant points in this publication. The limited use of this content with full consideration and acknowledgment of the authors and copyright owners is cited under Section 107 of the Copyright Act 1976. (3. 4, 9. 10, 11, 13, 14, 20, 21, 28, 49, 54, 55, 56, 57, 61, 63, 85, 86, 145,178, 181, 210, 218, 228, 229, 230, 234, 261, 268, 269)

*To Mom and Dad for their patience and support,
and to all those who continue to fight for a more equitable
civilization in the face of obstruction*

CONTENTS

INTRODUCTION VII

PART ONE: YOU SAY YOU WANT A REVOLUTION 1
    1   COME TOGETHER, JOIN THE PARTY 3
    2   JUST A PRISONER 27
    3   LADIES AND GENTLEMEN, RONALD REAGAN 49
    4   STOP SCARING THE HELL OUT OF PEOPLE 68
    5   STARTING OVER 85
    6   STATE OF THE UNION 105

PART TWO: THIS IS GOING TO SHAKE UP THE WHOLE WORLD 127
    7   THE TIES THAT BIND 129
    8   CLEANUP TIME 145
    9   HEAD-ON COLLISION 158
    10   DECEMBER 8, DAYTIME 177
    11   DECEMBER 8, NIGHTTIME 191
    12   THIS LAND IS YOUR LAND 209

PART THREE: CROSSED SWORDS ON THE KILLING FLOOR **225**

    13 INAUGURATION DAY 227
    14 LET ME TAKE YOU DOWN 244
    15 BORN IN THE U.S.A. 264
    16 A MEANNESS IN THIS WORLD............................. 281
    17 REVOLUTION FROM THE TOP DOWN 293
    18 LAST GASPS (AFTERMATH) 318

BIBLIOGRAPHY **331**
CHAPTER NOTES **349**
ENDNOTES **357**

INTRODUCTION

I was standing in front of the Dakota Building in New York City one time and this kid looking to be in his early twenties came walking around the corner after just having come out of the subway. He was wearing a John Lennon New York City t-shirt. He was a tourist, looked confused and asked me in what sounded like an Eastern European accent where Times Square was. I asked him if he knew where he was and he said no, he was lost. I told him that wasn't what I meant. I acknowledged that he was lost and that he was looking for Times Square and proceeded to direct him where he had to go and how he might get there. Then, for the second time, I asked him, but I phrased the question a little differently.

"You have John on your shirt," I pointed out.

"Yes," he nodded, smiling.

"Are you aware of where you're standing right now?"

He shrugged, smiled and threw his hands up.

"I...I...I am lost."

So I told him where he was and his eyes lit up in astonishment. He looked up at the building and I pointed to the arch over the driveway.

"Oh yeeaahh," he exclaimed in recognition.

We walked as close as we could and stopped at the closed gate.

"Right here, no?" he asked.

"Right over there," I said, pointing about twenty feet ahead of us.

It was one of many times I'd stood outside that driveway...trying to figure it out...trying to envision it.

For years, I'd hang out in the Metropolitan Museum of Art on Friday nights and most of Saturday. I'd drive uptown via the West Side Highway and exit at Seventy-Ninth Street and then shoot down to Seventy-Second. I'd park illegally and go stand outside the Dakota, peering into the driveway...often just staring. The guards knew why. They left me alone. They left everybody alone, and there were always people standing there at any given time of the day. Then I'd get in my car, cut across the park to the East Side and get on with my day. That was something that happened for years.

I've spent much of my adult life trying to solve the mysteries of my childhood. *What was that movie I saw in the fall of 1977 at my aunt's house with the violent shootout in a church during the last scene? Whose house was I in at the age of four when I'm holding a Rolling Stones Hot Rocks album and proudly showing it to people? I don't recognize any of those people. Who the hell were they? Who was that kid Danny who used to ride around the neighborhood who everyone was afraid of? Where did he go? Is he in prison? Is he dead? Why does nobody remember him? What was really going on when I was in kindergarten and saw the principal of my school walking around the mall with one of the teacher's aides?* Questions that always nagged at me that never really went away. They exist all over my early childhood, and because I'm one of those people with Superior Autobiographical Memory, those mysterious events are highlighted in bold print. By coincidence, the last months of 1980 remain an obsession, and by doing this book, I've come to realize that the main reason for me writing it is as a personal exorcism in the hopes that maybe some of these ghosts I retrace year after year will finally go away.

INTRODUCTION

During his concerts in the 1980s, Bruce Springsteen often prefaced a song with a somber instrumental intro underneath a monologue that usually recounted a childhood memory that would eventually circle back to the song he was about to perform. His introduction to a song called "Spare Parts" often told about domestic violence and recalling overhearing the married couple next door fighting. In one of his more profound observations of early childhood, he remarked how there is nothing more frightening for a child than hearing grown-ups arguing. "Your house is your world," he'd say.[1] And when you're a kid, living in that sort of instability can make the world seem very unsafe. That was in 1988, around the time when I first began to fully get into John Lennon's music which coincided with the release the *Imagine* documentary, which was also close to the eighth anniversary of John's death. The fact that I had spent those past eight years haunted by the death of John Lennon had much more to do with the world's reaction to his death than with my own personal connection to him in 1980. I was ten when it happened, and understood very little of why he meant so much to people. His music didn't hit me personally until later on in my teens. I only knew something big and very bad had happened, and everyone was upset about it. But Springsteen's words brought full realization into what initially triggered those bad memories of Lennon's death. His suggestion that hearing grown-ups arguing as one of the most frightening aspects of being a child made me remember how seeing adults crying had the same effect on me. ...adults on TV crying, the babysitter crying, teachers crying, people all over the world crying. Why was everybody crying?

Being a lifelong Springsteen fan, I, like so many others, ventured into bootleg territory and collected all of those live recordings that were never authorized as well as the studio outtakes that never made the official albums. While the consensus among diehards was that the 1978 Darkness on the Edge of Town Tour was Springsteen's absolute peak, I was always fascinated much more by the River Tour of 1980-81...particularly the first leg, which ran from October through December. By that time, Springsteen had already established himself as the best performer in rock music, but it was this period that really sealed his legend in terms of his concerts...the never-ending marathons they became...these superhuman tests of endurance for those who lived to tell about them...the beginning of those myths that Springsteen played all night...sometimes until morning...five, six-hour shows, etc...The truth is, Springsteen never played six hours. In fact, he didn't even actually play four-hour shows until 2016. The *River* shows and beyond were at a time when he played with an intermission, and the total time between two sets, an encore and an intermission usually exceeded anywhere from three and a half to four hours total. But the legend was that he played *all night*. Still, at the time, what he did on the concert stage was unprecedented, and rarely, if ever, equaled by anyone dead or alive in the decades since. I guess my first obsession was with the Thanksgiving Madison Square Garden show that I was too young to attend, although my mother called Ticketron several times to no avail. I've used the word *obsession* several times already, and it is an accurate word because that first leg of The River Tour became an obsession for me.

I always visualize the view from my seat in my fifth grade classroom. Last desk, second row from the door. I sat next to a girl named Kelly. She was a big Led Zeppelin fan, as was I. We always talked about music. Back then, it's what fifth graders did. Rock music was still a thing back then for kids. But I remember a few weeks after the school year started she came in one day and went right up to me to ask if I'd heard that John Bonham had died. So we talked about that a lot in the days that followed. In fact, the publication of this book will probably coincide with the fortieth anniversary of all of these things. A few weeks later, Springsteen's new album, *The River* came out, and my dad got it on cassette. He had recently purchased this hi-tech Kenwood cassette deck and stopped buying vinyl records for a while. So I absorbed *The River* over the next few months. In that time period, Ronald Reagan was elected President of the United States and then John Lennon was murdered. Those two things alone are a permanent stamp on my memory of that school

INTRODUCTION

year. So when I think of those two events, I think of fifth grade, and when I think of fifth grade, I think of those two events.

The indelible Lennon memory begins on the afternoon of Friday, December 5, 1980. It was the final hour of the school day and our teacher let the class outside on the playground for a kickball game. Late in the game, I was running from second base to third base when I collided very badly with someone, sending me flying back onto the concrete where I bashed the back of my head on a sharp rock. I blacked out for maybe a minute, waking up with my entire class surrounding me and blood gushing from my head. Needless to say the teacher freaked out but couldn't leave the class by itself so she asked for someone to walk me to the nurse. Two girls who will remain nameless volunteered, so off I went with each of them on one side of me as I staggered toward the Main Unit building. I remember being dizzy and walking very slowly, holding my head with blood trickling through my hair. When we got to the building, one of the girls opened the door for me and I walked through. I vividly remember the sound of the power scrubber washing the floor in the cafeteria and the clanking sounds of tables being slammed shut and pushed against the wall. It was the sound of Friday afternoon. The girls dropped me off in the nurse's office and I could hear the sound of Bruce Springsteen's "Hungry Heart" playing on the radio next door in the teacher's room. I remember the principal coming in and looking at my head, literally holding it in his hands. He was remarking to the nurse how profusely the human scalp will bleed when given the right kind of blow. Inside the teacher's room, John Lennon's new song "Starting Over" came on. The part that sticks with me most is the band teacher walking out into the hall. He was talking to someone, looking back at them and he stopped directly in front of the nurse's office. "John Lennon…" he said. Whatever the other person said back to him was unclear. "John Lennon," he said again. And then a third time…"Yeah…John Lennon…the Beatles. This is his new song." Then he walked away. In the nurse's office, I waited for my dad to pick me up after the nurse called home. It wasn't a good way to start the weekend. Three days later, John Lennon was dead. My teacher played "Give Peace a Chance" in class and talked about Lennon everyday that week. A month later, TVs were wheeled into every classroom for kids to watch the inauguration of Ronald Reagan, and on a split screen was an airplane carrying American hostages ready to take off back to the United States. The hostage crisis in Iran had lasted 14 months and it was never far from our discussions at any time during those months. Fifth graders are very impressionable. You're much too young to think about the political implications of things, so you take everything at face value. I remember it being a great day for America. That's what they told us. I remember the feeling around school being pretty celebratory. I remember watching the hostages being released as Reagan was being sworn in, and I remember how the whole thing made him seem like a hero. And then years later, it hit me...that's exactly how they intended it to be.

Several decades went by before I realized that three of my major historical obsessions all took place in the last months of 1980. On top of that was this idea I had regarding Springsteen and the River Tour. It had pretty much been common knowledge that Springsteen wasn't happy with the election results on the night of November 4, 1980, and after five albums and nearly a decade of being a non-political artist, announced his displeasure and concern about Reagan in front of his audience the next night. This major detail has been a part of Springsteen's concert history over the past 40 years and although it has been mentioned by writers and critics over the years, not much has been made of it or explored any further. I've always felt there was an entire book in such an exploration. Things happened to Springsteen on that tour. He didn't come out of it the same artist or the same person. Everything we would see of him as an artist and activist over the next three decades had its roots in the 1980-81 tour, although he would later say that his parents, Douglas and Adele Springsteen also helped shape his politics. When Springsteen released the deluxe box version of *The River* in 2015 commemorating the record's thirty-fifth anniversary, he went on tour playing the full album in celebration of the most pivotal collection of songs of his entire career. At the outset of every show, he'd tell his audience: "*The River* was a record where I was trying to figure out where I fit in. By the time I got to that record, I had taken notice of the things that bond people in their lives. There's work, commitments, families…I wanted to imagine and I wanted to write about those things, and I figured if I could write about them, maybe I'd get one step closer to realizing them in my own life. I wanted to make a record that was big enough so it felt like life…or like an E Street Band show. I wanted the record to contain fun, dancing, jokes, good comradeship, love, faith, sex, lonely nights and of course tears. And I figured if I could make a record that was big enough to contain all of those things, maybe I'd get a little closer to the home I was searching for. So tonight I want you to come along with us as we go down to the river."[2]

What that 2016 celebration didn't really acknowledge, nor did critics at the time, was that the 1980-81 River Tour also marks the beginning of Springsteen's active role in the political process, activism and an overall sense of using his voice on a much larger scale than what the average rock star's reach entailed. It begins with the election of Ronald Reagan and snowballs into Springsteen's personal excavation of history and America's past. Springsteen wasn't always the opinionated liberal who the political right loves to hate simply for supporting Democratic candidates and speaking out against social injustices. That's been the stigma assigned by Republicans for decades now, though a massive part of his audience is made up of conservative Republicans who are increasingly torn between their love of Springsteen's music and their allegiance to the Republican Party. But Springsteen has always had the unique distinction of being both the most loved rock artist and probably the most hated rock artist on the planet. Decade after decade saw people who loathed the guy just for existing…the liberal scumbag who can't keep his political opinions to himself. Before he publically endorsed politicians, the same people complained that he was a hypocrite for being a millionaire while singing songs about working class values. So it was long before politics that they hated him. Before that, he was stereotyped as the guy who wrote songs about the beach and fast cars and all of those universal elements of youth and freedom that are encapsulated in the most quintessential rock and roll songs. And something about *that* made them hate him. And the one constant through the decades that ran parallel to the haters was the fact that his audience and ticket sales only grew larger over time. With regard to Springsteen's political awakening, courtesy of the 1980 election, it's been occasionally mentioned by writers here and there over the years, but never fully investigated…nor has the River Era, despite the anniversary celebration in 2016. We can't go through *Born in the U.S.A.* and *Nebraska* without going through *The River* first. And so, while there were dozens of books written on Bruce Springsteen over the years, nobody was writing *this* one.

In the case of Lennon, his story during the last months of 1980 provides a sharp contrast to Springsteen's. Springsteen, who had not gotten involved in politics or used his platform until then, was nine years younger than Lennon, not married, and did not have any kids yet. Lennon had just spent five years being a father and house husband, completely rejecting the rock star life and ignoring his role as an artist. His new album *Double Fantasy* was a step forward in that it was an *adult* album. It tackled themes of marriage, parenting and domestic life. But Lennon was self-conscious about his role going forward…how people looked at him as an artist in terms of relevancy and what he felt was expected of him verses what he really wanted to do… which he doesn't really seem to be too sure of anyway. We know he wanted to move forward…possibly even tour…and that sentiment was quickly jump-started when he returned from a vacation in Bermuda in the summer of 1980. *Double Fantasy* climbs the charts at the same time as *The River* is at the top of the charts. Lennon and Springsteen are neck and neck in the Top Ten with their respective hit singles, though they are both at different stages of their career. Lennon is a hero to Springsteen. Lennon is also very aware of Springsteen, admires him as an artist and voices concern about how he will handle the media, the fans and the fame monster itself. Though it could not

INTRODUCTION

be confirmed, it is rumored that *The River* was on Lennon's turntable at the time of his death.

John Lennon was one of the most documented people in history. He kept journals and recorded hours and hours of tape and video. Yet we know very little about his murder...probably because he hadn't pressed *record* to capture it...even though he was holding a tape recorder as he was shot. We know he was shot by Mark David Chapman although conspiracy theorists would like us to believe that the government had him killed and that Boogeyman Reagan was behind it. The problem with writing a book that connects Lennon with Reagan is that the initial thoughts of the conspiracy people will be "Finally! Someone has written a book exposing this!" So at the outset, let me say the following: As there is not one shred of evidence to support the conspiracy nonsense, this book does not for one second or sentence give credence to any of it. Mark David Chapman shot and killed John Lennon. Period. What happens in this book, however, examines in detail the questions that were left hanging on the night of December 8, 1980...the details that we have forgotten about as the story has strangely evolved over the years about John Lennon being shot in the back outside his apartment in New York City. That's the version we've come to know.

Except of course for one detail.

John Lennon was never shot in the back.

And so, while there were dozens of books written on John Lennon over the years, nobody was writing *this* one.

Ronald Reagan was initially going to be the backdrop of this book, whereby I told three simultaneous stories that take place during the last months of 1980. The light bulb that went on inside by head was more like a nuclear explosion. "I get to talk about all three obsessions at the same time while weaving a whole new story that nobody has ever told before!" But seriously though...who in their right mind writes a book connecting John Lennon and Bruce Springsteen to Ronald Reagan? And while much can be made in terms of Lennon's death coinciding with the election of Reagan be-

XV

ing symbolic of the true death of the 1960s, what further connections can be made in such a publication as this?

It's all been said before.

Hasn't it?

So as I began this project during the Christmas holidays of 2016, I went into it knowing that a thesis would eventually have to emerge somewhere… not confidently knowing at that point whether one would emerge at all, aside from the tired and obvious "death of the dream" analogy. And then, a few weeks later, Donald Trump moved into the White House.

I spent much of 2017 researching Ronald Reagan…his parents, childhood, college years, Hollywood years, years with General Electric, military service, marriages, children, governorship, presidency, critics, supporters, influence, legacy, and the criticism of such a legacy. 2017 was also a big year for my *Rock Under Fire* podcast because I started to score some pretty cool guest interviews and I spent the summer of that year producing shows that examined the pop cultural impact of all things 1977, marking the year's fortieth anniversary. So while I was mentally living in 1977 during 2017, Ronald Reagan was never far from my mind…not even during those shows. But with Donald Trump in the White House, America's story began to transform literally before our eyes in ways we never saw coming. It changed everything, including the work I was doing on this publication. As the country became increasingly rocked by chaos and turmoil, and a shameless Republican Party constantly tried to associate itself with the legacy and name of Ronald Reagan, the direction and purpose of this book began to take on another shape. And so, while there were dozens of books written on Ronald Reagan over the years, nobody was writing *this* one.

Three widely-documented famous people are more than enough to take on at once. Any one of these figures alone would be daunting. And so, what I was really doing in a way, was writing three books at the same time. In writing this book, I stayed close to a very specific period of time that is contained in the space of autumn 1979 to autumn 1981, although it goes far beyond this period of concentration. Many names come in and out of these pages as one would expect while taking on such high-profile figures. I've tried to remain economical in my approach to people in and around my subjects...meaning, I delve into the things that are relevant to the story I am telling, but stay away from details that would be and have been much better-served in other books. For example, I get into the Lennon/Ono marriage much more than I get into Bruce Springsteen's personal life which I avoid, primarily because Springsteen was unmarried at the time, and his relationship with actress Joyce Hyser is inconsequential to the story we are looking at...whereas John's marriage to Yoko Ono in many ways for better or worse, consumed and somewhat defined him during the last five years of his life. For further example, I stayed away from details related to Ono's life pre-Lennon, such as her daughter Kyoko and prior marriage... for the same reason...it bears no significance to the book...so at the risk of Yoko appearing rather one-dimensional, there are certain areas that I just did not go into. Regarding Springsteen's relationships, he bounced on and off different women over the years until his marriage to Julianne Phillips in 1985 and then Patti Scialfa in 1991. Though the complexities of relationships became a constant theme of his work, even to a certain degree on *The River*, the 1980-81 period was a time when Springsteen really had no place to go after the show. His marriage was to rock and roll, and every drop of energy and commitment went into each and every concert he did. These voids in his life would come to the surface many years later, and as they presented problems, he would deal with them accordingly...but again, they serve no real purpose here, as this book prefers to stick primarily to the assessment of Springsteen's development as an artist during these years.

Finally, on the subject of politics that will inevitably arise from aligning two well-known liberal figures with a well-known conservative, my own progressive liberal beliefs are undoubtedly on my sleeve. At present time as I complete this introduction, America has seen the verticality of the First Amendment, Congress, checks and balances, law enforcement, the Department of Justice, Federal Bureau of Investigation, Central Intelligence Agency, United States Supreme Court, United States Postal Service, education, science, healthcare and the electoral process as well as American democracy itself, all undermined by the highest level of government and his enablers. As I write this, machines in post offices that sort mail are being shut down, with mail boxes locked or confiscated in an effort to stop Americans from voting in the 2020 election in the event that a second wave of a pandemic happens on Donald Trump's watch. As I finish this introduction, it is the big news story of the week. It is August, and news happens fast these days and things change so frequently that it is impossible to know how it will all pan out. But I'm going to make an assumption based on what I have gathered from the character of Ronald Reagan and history itself, and suggest that what has happened here in this place called America in the years since Donald Trump took office, would have Reagan (a man who Republicans have deified) turning over in his grave. With that, anyone who picks up this book expecting a bunch of Reagan-bashing will be extremely disappointed. If anything, I aimed at an objective and fair approach to a much-misunderstood figure in American history…obviously long-misunderstood by the political left, and most of all, sorely and dangerously misunderstood by the political right, especially Republicans who seem to have a delusional belief that they have some ideological hereditary claim to him. Long story short, they don't. Let this be their wakeup call.

Mike Derrico
August 2020

PART ONE

YOU SAY YOU WANT A REVOLUTION

"The 1980s have been born in turmoil,
strife, and change."

— President Jimmy Carter

1

COME TOGETHER, JOIN THE PARTY

I know what it's like to be dead.
    Peter Fonda wasn't all that well-known yet when he walked up to John Lennon uttering this line as the Beatle peaked on an acid trip in the middle of a bright and sunny afternoon in Los Angeles. The Beatles were on a break from touring and were hanging out with some girls and members of the Byrds. Bob Dylan turned the band on to marijuana one year earlier, and by the time 1965 rolled into 1966, Lennon had entered his psychedelic phase, as did many artists of creative and artistic importance in that era. Fonda had not yet made *Easy Rider*, nor had he even made *The Trip* or *Psych-Out*. Yet, he was a cat who was literally living the characters he'd play. Fonda in those roles didn't even need to act. Lennon described him as boring, however, and he didn't need the negativity. In fact, he found it scary when he recounted the incident to David Sheff years later. He was blunt.
    "I don't want to know what it's like to be dead!"[3]

John Lennon and Paul McCartney walked into the newly opened Indica Books and Gallery in March 1966, the same place where Lennon would meet his second wife, artist, Yoko Ono later in the year. The Beatles were in the process of an ongoing artistic evolution that would profoundly alter pop music. In pursuit of some new philosophical and intellectual influences, Lennon wanted to score a copy of *The Portable Nietzche*. Instead, he grabbed something a little more conducive to his recent exploration of hallucinogens, and walked out with *The Psychedelic Experience*, a handbook for LSD use written by Timothy Leary, Ralph Metzner and Richard Alpert… all three, PHDs, and all involved in psychology or psychotherapy in some fashion. Leary and Alpert had previously both lost prominent and respected positions at Harvard University where they had done research on psilocybin and LSD-25, as well as experiments involving students at the Harvard School of Divinity. Alpert, who had spent a great deal of time meditating in India had returned under the spiritual name Ram Dass and was serving as a sort of countercultural guru of Eastern mysticism and the sacramental psychedelics in vogue. While Alpert managed to stay under the radar and avoid as much public scrutiny, Leary, whose phrase "turn on, tune in, drop out," had become a reviled figure to old fashioned traditionalists who despised the change and dissent that the counterculture of the 1960s represented. *The Psychedelic Experience*, a book Leary, Alpert and Metzner had based on the *Tibetan Book of the Dead* became an underground bible to the world of hallucinogens in connection with Eastern spirituality, and Lennon was able to carve two songs out of such inspiration for the upcoming Beatles album, *Revolver*. "Tomorrow Never Knows" was born straight out of Leary's message, although the title came from one of Ringo Starr's malapropisms, and "She Said, She Said" borrowed from Lennon's psychedelic encounter with Fonda, and the *line I know what it's like to be dead.*

    Among conservatives horrified over the younger generation's courage to say "fuck you" to its own government, was Ronald Reagan, an ex-actor turned politician. He was also an ex-union man, ex-Democrat and an ex-liberal. By the time Reagan's political ambitions were fully realized, his ideological transformation was complete, and in the early stages of his first term as Governor of California, ordered the National Guard out to bust up student demonstrations at Berkley, and made his contempt for protest known. Although no friend to the concerns of the Baby Boomers, then in their late teens and early twenties, he wasn't inaccessible to them and would meet with them in an attempted discourse which would usually end up in some sort of finger-wagging lecture or one-liner meant to upstage his challengers. Chief of Staff, Ed Meese warned Reagan and advised him not to engage the troublemakers. Reagan, however, indulged their concerns on occasion…never once taking them seriously, but merely tolerating their points long enough only to meet them with the superiority complex of an all-encompassing angry parent who's seen it all and done it all. In one instance, a student reminded him that he grew up in a completely different world. It was a world without the complicated technology of things like television, jet planes, computers, space travel and nuclear energy. How could he possibly relate to them? Reagan acknowledged that the student was correct and then buried the student's argument, stressing that no, his generation indeed did not have those things…his generation *invented* them.

Reagan not only despised the counterculture from a political standpoint, but also as a frightened parent who was worried about the impact it was having on his teenage daughter, Patti, who was away at an Arizona boarding school. To be fair, protest and dissent, one of the bedrock elements of American civil society, faced hostility from conservatives in general, and not just Reagan. On campuses and streets, students exorcising their First Amendment rights faced teargas, arrest, beatings, and in some incidents, their own death. Miraculously, in the case of Berkley, when kids had bayonets and guns thrust into their faces as Governor Reagan declared a State of Emergency over a student protest, only one kid was killed. A year later, four students at Kent State University were shot and killed. This was the political and social climate amidst demonstrations, assassinations and an escalating death toll as the Vietnam War raged and the 1960s pushed on toward their ugly and tumultuous climax years.

Timothy Leary was arrested a shitload of times for possession of marijuana. He wouldn't see prison until 1970, but he'd soon escape anyway, having such leftist radical groups such as the Black Panthers and Weathermen coming to his aid. Until then, he continued various projects relating to his books and testified in favor of LSD before the drug was officially made illegal in 1968. On May 19, 1969, Leary received the good news that one of his prior convictions and a 30-year sentence was overturned when the "Marihuana" Act of 1937 was ruled unconstitutional. On the same day, he announced his candidacy to run against Ronald Reagan for governor of California. Just a few days earlier, Reagan's war on the student protesters of Berkley resulted in the one death. Of course, Leary's short-lived campaign never got off the ground, let alone was taken seriously. It was still in a time when the absurd remained the absurd and nothing more than a harmless headline for a few weeks, contrary to 47 years later when the absurd would become a destructive reality at the highest levels of government. The times did indeed change.

That spring, Leary joined John Lennon and Yoko Ono in Montreal for one of the couple's bed-ins for peace. Soon after, Lennon wrote a new song called "Come Together" that he was ready to give to Leary for his campaign against Reagan, which carried the slogan, "Come Together, Join the Party!" As the campaign evaporated into future trivia, Lennon reworked the song and quickly recorded it with the Beatles for the *Abbey Road* album, released later that summer. The group would release one more album of previously-recorded music, but *Abbey Road* was the last conscious studio effort of the Fab Four.

Lennon had the number five song during the week of the Kent State killings, just three weeks after the official breakup of the Beatles. "Instant Karma" was as much an invitation as it was a condemnation to the critics of Lennon's persistent call to unity, peace and love in an era of violence and upheaval. Another song, "Power to the People," had been successful as well, and it is difficult to imagine these songs in such high chart positions in twenty-first century America due to their topical nature relating to social justice. In direct response to Kent State, Neil Young penned a new song called "Ohio," and recorded it with David Crosby, Stephen Stills, and Graham Nash. Arguably an indictment of President Richard Nixon, the song climbed all the way to number 14 on the pop charts. As "Ohio" began its fall from the charts later in the summer, Edwin Starr's "War" became the number one song in the country. It was an era when artists reflected the turmoil of the times and it was not only accepted…it was popular. Such a song today would not only be invisible from the pop charts, but the artist would draw acerbic vitriol on social media for getting on a soapbox, and pundits paid by conservative media outlets would call for a boycott of the artist…just for voicing an opinion running contrary to their own. Ronald Reagan stood resolutely against the counterculture of the 1960s, and was just the kind of man conservatives wanted in the face of so much social change happening simultaneously. For the most part, they saw him as their future, and it would take a full decade to make that future begin to actually unfold. At the outset of this publication, it is important to acknowledge…nobody back then…not even in the Republican Party, could envision what would happen to America three decades following Reagan's presidency.

Ronald Wilson Reagan came screaming loudly into the world feet first after his mother Nelle Wilson Reagan endured 24 hours of painful labor. Born on February 6, 1911 on the second floor of his parents' apartment over a bakery in snow-covered Tampico, Illinois, Ronald was almost named Donald after a great grandfather on the Wilson side. Nelle's sister had already used the name, so the new baby became Ronald. It was his father Jack who gave him the nickname that stuck throughout the newborn's childhood. At Ronald's birth, Jack looked at him and suggested that he made a hell of a lot of noise for such a fat Dutchman. At least until he moved to California and onward to a career in Hollywood, everybody except Nelle called him "Dutch."

Those closest to Ronald Reagan have all shared the same thought about him in that no matter how friendly he was with you, or how often you interacted with him, he never let you get close in a way that would allow you to see behind the façade. People were fascinated by Reagan the man, and Reagan the politician, but could never quite get to the heart of his makeup. It is tempting to mistake the façade for the real thing, but it is almost unanimous among those who knew him that there was a distant side that not even his second wife Nancy could penetrate. It was in those quiet moments when he was completely lost in his own thoughts where he spent much of his time. It was evident that there were dimensions to Ronald Reagan that he just kept for himself. At the core was insecurity, stemming from the instability of a childhood marked by an alcoholic father. Upon returning home one night as a teen, Dutch stumbled upon his drunken father passed out on his back in the accumulating frozen white of a snowstorm. In what was possibly one of the more profound moments of his childhood, he stopped to ponder whether it would be better if he dragged his father to the warm safety of the house, or just go inside, go to bed and pretend he'd never seen him. Reagan recounted the incident subtly and matter-of-factly in his autobiography, but the implications are startling. It was an instance where he must have thought there might be a possibility that his life would be better if his father wasn't there.

Dutch was born during a time when the life expectancy was below 50. Diseases such as smallpox, tuberculosis and polio still took a vast percentage of the population, and antibiotics did not yet exist. Coming out of the first decade of the twentieth century when progressive measures had started to grab hold of politics, America was sowing the seeds for much of the modern world we often take for granted today. The early years saw the first regulations put in place for food safety. By the turn of the decade, women's suffrage marches drew enough attention to set the path to the Nineteenth Amendment to the Constitution. Following the tragic fire that killed 146 garment workers in the Triangle Shirtwaist sweatshop above Washington Street in New York's Greenwich Village just six weeks after Dutch's birth, conscious labor laws were put in place and unions became the bedrock of modern equity in the workplace, and Reagan would later come to know early in his adult life, the vital importance of unions. In the face of Old World conservative setback and obstruction, progressives and liberals jumpstarted the foundation that made possible virtually all the social progress of the twentieth century, steering America toward a more equitable civilization. Considering that the country was moving even closer toward fulfilling its promise during the 1960s, one might wonder what exactly happened to Ronald Reagan that would result in such hostility and change in political ideology. At what point, and for what reasons does he make that leap, abandon his principles and join the Republican Party? To understand such a radical metamorphosis is not guaranteed, and it has been speculated upon for decades. But we would have to at least go back to the early 1940s to seek out the origins, which this book makes an attempt at a little further ahead.

The trend in popular music during the 1960s and 1970s was to release at least one studio album per year, very often two, and sometimes three. If an artist went two years without a record, it not only seemed an eternity for fans, but the artist was largely forgotten about. In late 1979, Lennon was pushing five years since his last studio album, *Rock 'n' Roll*, which happened to be a covers record. If we want to talk original music, the interval was pushing six years. As a recording artist, the former Beatle had disappeared.

For the sake of recap, Lennon hadn't really worked that hard over the past decade. Instant stardom hit once the Beatles touched down at JFK Airport in February 1964. They were already popular for two years in England, but nothing could have prepared them for the mass hysteria of the United States. It is quite simple…here, there and everywhere, they became the biggest band that ever was, and ever will be. But the whirlwind of press conferences, interviews, concerts, living out of suitcases, hotel rooms, police escorts, strict security protocols and screaming rabid fans only lasted until they stopped touring in August 1966. Considering that the band only existed as a studio entity during their last three years, the members had a great deal of time to do as they pleased. George Harrison toured in 1974, while Paul McCartney took seven years before finally playing some dates in Europe with Wings and a full decade before touring the States again. Lennon had lived from his late twenties through his entire thirties as a legend, but only dealt with the rigorous demands of touring as a rock star for two and a half years of his life. It seems ironic then, that whatever happened with him between 1976 and 1980…call it a retirement, call it a hiatus…it wasn't much different from what he had been doing all along…living his life.

It was hardly uneventful though.

As the final year and a half of the Beatles progressed, Lennon had been greatly outspoken on the Vietnam War, supported protests and demonstrations and spoke of things like revolution in his songs. He saw his celebrity status as not only a vehicle to speak out, but considered it his responsibility. The immediate years after the Beatles was what scared the government though. President Richard Nixon in particular feared his influence and adhered to speculation that Lennon was mobilizing a surge of first-time young voters to support Democratic candidates, among other irreparable offenses such as instigating mass demonstrations. Nothing the paranoid Nixon anticipated ever surfaced or transpired, yet the FBI file he opened on the artist was as real as his attempt to have him deported and make his life miserable for the better part of the 1970s. In May 1973, Lennon told Dick Cavett, "I felt followed everywhere by government agents. Every time I picked up any phone, there was a lot of noise. I'd open the door and there'd be guys standing on the other side of the street. I'd get in the car and they'd be following me and not hiding. They wanted me to know I was being followed."[4]

The story and legend of The Beatles does not unfold nearly the same way without America in the equation, and Lennon loved America. Once the dust of the Beatles had settled, he chose to make it his home. He particularly loved New York City, and lived in several Manhattan locations. In 1971, lured by the rich history of urban bohemia, John and Yoko moved into an apartment at 105 Bank Street in Greenwich Village. John felt free for the first time in years and he felt completely at home in a community surrounded by artists, poets, writers and political activists. The Lennon home became a hub of sorts for radicals like Abbie Hoffman and Jerry Rubin, who John began hanging out with. The two who started YIPPIE (Youth International Movement) had sought out his support. Rubin believed the more visual and surreal the protest, the more attention they'd get. He'd be arrested while measuring the Pentagon, claiming he was trying to figure out how many witches he'd need to pull off a levitation of the building. It wasn't at all lost on the feds either that John had gone to Ann Arbor to perform in defense of John Sinclair who was serving ten years in prison for possession of two joints, or that he played a benefit for the victims of the Attica State Prison uprising. He had also demonstrated with the Onondaga Indians in Syracuse, New York, and went to the trial of the Harlem Six. For constantly standing up to social and political injustice, John Lennon was considered a danger to America by its own government.

Early in 1973, John visited assistant Beatles manager, Peter Brown at his apartment in the Langhorn on Manhattan's Upper West Side, and was so taken by the view that he decided then and there he wanted to spend his life looking out over Central Park West. The Lennon's inquired about the Langhorn but there was no space available. Unfettered and determined, they simply went to the place next door.

The architectural mixed vocabulary is difficult to define in any concrete terms. It is a mishmash of Chateau, Gothic Revival and German Renaissance. The Upper West Side was largely uninhabited and empty when Edward Clark, cofounder of the Singer Sewing Machine Company commissioned Henry Janeway Hardenbergh to design what would begin Central Park West's rise of the apartment buildings at the height of the Gilded Age. For its time, and only for a brief time, the Dakota stood alone and seemingly so far away from downtown and cut off from the rest of the city that it might have existed out west...even west of the Dakotas.

New York had become a city of rich and poor. The middle class was driven out by rising excessive rent, squeezing families who were barely surviving as it was. The breakdown of some one million people at the time consisted of half the population living in roughly 40,000 houses with five to fifty rooms. The other half lived in one room with an additional 24,000 immigrants stuffed into 8,500 basements that felt more like prison cells without light, heat or plumbing.[5]

The apartment building stigma of downtown, often containing the poor in large masses, earned its reputation on dingy tenements. A quarter of a century prior saw less than 20 millionaires in the entire country. By the 1880s, there were several hundred millionaires in New York alone. Technology and industry...the steel mills, steam engines, oil and mechanical inventions allowed for a new era of men's fortunes, and a need to cater to money. But money built mansions whereas apartments were for the poor huddled masses. Built in 1884, the Dakota was sympathetic to riches on several scales. Hardenbergh took into consideration that some millionaires only needed three rooms while some required 16. The unique layout accompanied multiple floor plans for a variety of buyers and preferences, the largest carrying all of the amenities of private mansions, and all contained in a co-op apartment building. Soon the Upper West Side would rise along Central Park for blocks and blocks in lines and rows of distinctive and elaborate apartment buildings. With all of the new money pouring in, New York City quickly became the most expensive place in the world to live.

Known as one of, if not the first apartment building on the Upper West Side, the Dakota didn't become nationally famous until it was featured in *Rosemary's Baby*, Roman Polanski's 1968 psychological horror film based on Ira Levin's novel. The grim blackened façade of the building's exterior is just downright sinister, and that is precisely why the location was chosen for Polanski's film. Decades of compounded dirt along with the fact that it was never cleaned, greatly contributed to the creepy allure that haunts the corner of Central Park West and Seventy-Second Street.

The Lennon's faced some resistance upon trying to move into the Dakota because of their reputation, not just as activists, but there was also that other little distraction that could conceivably draw lots of unwanted attention having been in a pretty popular band. They made the cut, however, and the notorious Board approved their residence. The rest of the tenants quickly found out after the Lennon's arrival, that all the anticipated loud and reckless rock and roll radicalism was much ado about nothing. The couple made it clear that they liked their privacy and remained a quiet mystery around the building. When they moved in, they learned that their new apartment was previously occupied by actor Robert Ryan. It was also known to them that Ryan's wife Jessie had died of cancer there. Soon after getting settled, the Lennon's decided to hold a séance out of curiosity. They brought in a medium that instantly made contact with Jessie Ryan. The ghost made it clear to John and Yoko that it was her home too, and she would be staying. She also told them not to be alarmed and that she would allow them to live undisturbed.

Moving into the Dakota coincides with a time when the cracks in the Ono Lennon marriage were plainly visible. Coming out of 1972, which had been a stressful year given John's involvement with radical politics, the One to One benefit concerts for children with mental disabilities of the Willowbrook School in New York City and an election season in which John was very much for George McGovern and was devastated at the news of Nixon's re-election, 1973 would be either a new beginning or a downward spiral, if not a random and bizarre sideways slide. Although John remained faithful for the first three years of his marriage to Yoko, his eye for other women was well-documented by those around him. At a party in Jerry Rubin's apartment on election night, John disappeared with a girl into the bedroom knowing full well Yoko was outside in the living room. Yoko later recounted that John was totally out of his head with drugs and alcohol because he was upset that George McGovern had lost the election. Perhaps on that note, we can blame Richard Nixon for John's infidelity. Whatever the case, Yoko was quietly bothered by the situation, but she claimed to have understood.

Well into the year, the Lennon's marriage had become a pressing issue, and Yoko began to entertain the idea of setting John free for a while to get his frustrations and yearning for other women out of his system. It was clear he loved Yoko, and neither of them doubted that. But marriage, his second, had had an effect on him, and they had gone so far as to discuss it openly with each other. Letting John loose to temporarily do as he pleased became an obsession for Yoko until she finally approached a 22-year old assistant named May Pang who had been working for the couple for three years. May was 19 when she walked into the building where the offices of Apple Records were situated. Feeling as though she had nothing to lose, she asked for a job. It was a simple matter of right place, right time when several doors opened at once and some executives simultaneously walked out of offices for their lunch hour. The secretary, possibly humoring May and going through the motions, mentioned that May was looking for work. One of the guys told her to meet him back after lunch, and suddenly she was working for John and Yoko.

The myth of Lennon's "Lost Weekend," named by John himself after the 1945 Ray Milland film, come from all directions, mostly containing the 18-month period he spent with May Pang, as some continuous binge of alcohol, drugs, decadence and debauchery. Much of the speculation focuses on areas that still remain as questions...mainly, how much influence over John did Yoko really have? Some suggest enough sway to actually select May to be with him, as if in some hierarchical culture where romantic pairings are pre-arranged...as if May were a subject of her employer and had no say in the situation. Yoko has denied such influence and maintains that she never insisted May hook up with John or forced the situation. According to Philip Norman's excellent publication, *John Lennon: The Life*, Yoko went to May and told her she had to accompany John to L.A. because she was busy with things to do and didn't consider herself a very good wife. Yoko insisted that she never said to hook up with John, although she knew it was a possibility because John was never without anyone.[6]

May Pang's account of the Lennon's separation is a little different. She had spent so much time around the couple that just the mere fact that it was obvious they had their problems did not phase her. There was too much going on and the work days were long enough to not want to think about anything whenever she did get to go home. She certainly didn't take the Lennon's marital issues home with her, nor was she thinking about hooking up with John. One day, Yoko went into May's office to discuss those issues with her. It caught her off guard, but what she wasn't expecting was when Yoko brought up the fact that May was single in connection with her ideas that John should see other women. May was startled, realizing where the conversation was going. She proceeded to quickly inform Yoko that she wasn't interested in John. Still, she insisted that May would be good for him. According to May, John never knew the conversation took place.[7] But he had his own version many months later when the subject came up with May. He told her that Yoko had come to him one morning while he was in the bathroom shaving...informing him that she had fixed him up with May. On an

15

upstroke, he nearly slit his throat and then nervously asked how she knew he liked May. She just knew, she told him.[8]

What became known as the Lost Weekend lasted from September 1973 to February 1975. It gets its reputation from two incidents at the Troubadour nightclub where John had a little too much to drink. On one occasion, he and Harry Nilsson had to be escorted out for heckling the Smothers Brothers along with word that John had assaulted a waitress.

"There was some girl who claimed that I hit her, but I didn't hit her at all, you know," he recounted. "She just wanted some money and I had to pay her off, because I thought it would harm my immigration. So I was drunk. When it's Errol Flynn, the showbiz writers say 'Those were the days when men were men.' When I do it, I'm a bum. So it was a mistake, but hell I'm human."[9]

On another occasion, John drew some unwanted attention that got blown out of proportion after he drunkenly placed a Kotex tampon on his forehead in front of a waitress.

The period with May Pang is also widely-associated with Los Angeles, again, thanks largely to the Troubadour incidents, although they only spent a few months out west and quickly went back to New York City where they had an apartment on East Fifty-Second Street. Despite May's initial reluctance to run off with John, the employer/employee nature of their relationship did in fact turn romantic after a while, and May was no longer on the Lennon's payroll. Once they returned to New York, they were living together as a couple. Of course hanging out with Harry Nilsson, someone he greatly admired but who had been a bad influence, had made for lots of partying, but contrary to legend, the 18-month Lost Weekend was actually the busiest and most-productive period of John's post-Beatles life. He recorded and released three studio albums...*Mind Games*, *Walls and Bridges* and *Rock 'n' Roll*, recorded hit songs with David Bowie and Elton John, reconnected with Paul McCartney and Ringo Starr, produced albums for Starr and Nilsson, jammed with McCartney and Stevie Wonder and had a number one song with his Elton John collaboration, "Whatever Gets You Through the Night." Elton predicted the song would reach number one, and when Lennon disagreed, they made a bet on it. If the song went to the top of the charts, Lennon would have to join Elton on stage at his Madison Square Garden gig later in the year. Perhaps Lennon's confidence was a little rusty, but Elton John was at his creative peak in 1974 and could do no wrong. The song did indeed hit number one just two weeks before Elton's scheduled Garden concert on Thanksgiving night. Lennon, of course, was a surprise for thousands of fans in the audience, but word had gotten out to some within his inner circle. May received a call from Yoko requesting a ticket…not too far from the stage, but not too close either. Near the end of Elton's triumphant show, he told the audience he was bringing on a friend. To the thunderous roar of the crowd, John walked onstage for the first time in over two years, and performed three songs…"Whatever Gets You Through the Night," "Lucy in the Sky With Diamonds" and "I Saw Her Standing There" with Elton.

Another myth surrounding the story of John and May is that it ended that night at the Garden. The commonly-accepted version is that Yoko collected John from backstage and told him he was allowed to come home, prompting him to leave May and return with Yoko to the Dakota that same night. While he and Yoko did talk that night at the Garden and reportedly went back to their home uptown for a day or two, John stayed with May for two more months and did not move back to the Dakota until February 1975. Nine months later, Sean Ono Lennon was born.

John Lennon never made any official announcement that he was giving up the game, going away, taking a hiatus or just simply disappearing for the next five years. It was just the way it happened, where the months turned to years, and he was too content to care or worry about where his career was going. Most of his time was spent taking care of Sean. He saw it as making up for the negligence of his own father and for not being there for his firstborn, Julian, from his first marriage. The next five years were centered around Sean. John remembered rather bitterly how his father had walked out, his mother had died when he was 16, and he was forced to live with his Aunt Mimi. He'd reflect with disgust how Mimi would go through his bedroom and throw things out she perceived to be garbage, much of which were drawings and remnants of childhood creativity, the spark of a budding artist carelessly discarded. John kept every little piece of paper Sean wrote or drew on. He'd often remark how he'd keep and treasure a napkin if Sean in his toddler years even put so much as a mark of paint on it, suggesting that it was part of his son. He was nuts about Sean and wanted to be present in his son's life and a constant in his upbringing.

Surrounding some dramatic circumstances, Sean Lennon was born October 9, 1975, John Lennon's thirty-fifth birthday. Yoko underwent a complicated C-Section that finally happened after a long and grueling wait for blood that matched hers in case a transfusion was needed. When both mother and newborn went into shaking spasms after the birth, Sean was rushed into Pediatric Intensive Care. A series of tests determined drugs in Yoko's urine to which John emphatically told the doctor neither of them had been on drugs, and had in fact been on a strict health food diet. Disgusted, John threatened to leave the hospital with the baby, to which the doctor warned him he'd get a court order declaring he and Yoko unfit parents. After some time hooked up to monitors and tubes, Sean and Yoko recovered enough to be out of danger. During their recovery, the doctor realized Yoko had tested positive from drugs they had given her for the C-Section. Relieved, John phoned Mimi to tell her about his new son.

After a few months, Yoko reversed the roles of baby duties. Her reasoning was that she carried Sean for nine months and now John should carry the responsibility for tending to him. To help, she hired a live-in nanny. Yoko then retreated to her first floor office where she spent her days and presided over business while John proudly told people that he was now a househusband. Still, there was Helen Seaman, who through her husband Norman, met the Lennon's in Montreal during the same bed-in attended by Timothy Leary, Tommy Smothers, and a random assortment of guests all huddled together in that seventeenth floor room in the Queen Elizabeth Hotel chanting "Give Peace a Chance." Norman Seaman had known Yoko through her first husband, Toshi Ichiyanagi, a radical composer to whom Seaman served as a booking agent for all of the major New York City venues that drew the attention of critics from *The New York Times*, *New York Herald Tribune* and other respected publications. Seaman took an apartment on the first floor of the Dakota when Helen moved in with the Lennon's to take on the role of fulltime nanny for Sean. John was indeed the househusband, and he was always within close proximity to Sean, often hanging around the upper floors while Helen spent most of the time with his son. By 1979, the Lennon's were occupying some 28 rooms, and there was a rumor going around the Dakota that they wanted to buy it.

With Helen taking the responsibility for Sean all day, John, left on his own to fart around, very often would spend much of his time in the bedroom. The bedroom consisted of a king-sized bed nestled between two wooden church pews. On the wall behind the bed hung a giant number nine, an electric guitar and a dagger, put there as a symbol of cutting away the past. John always had the latest hi-tech audio and video equipment including a Sony giant-screen TV, which he had sent to New York City from Japan, as it was the latest model, and not yet available in America. He also had boxes and boxes of expensive sound equipment that he didn't always know how to use or assemble. Ideas and fragments of ideas were always put down on tape, much to the contrary that he had nothing to do with music during these years. He may not have been out publically as a recording artist doing tours or promoting new music, but he always recorded new melodies that came to him, even if it was just in his bedroom. Rumors, and much later, myths, however, still persisted that John had gone "underground" and wasn't seen, didn't return calls, and again, just plainly disappeared, which could not be farther from the truth. John was out and about almost daily, taking Sean to the YMCA on West Sixty-Sixth several times a week so he could teach him to swim by the age of four. He was often seen on Columbus Avenue getting pizza for Sean, having breakfast in his favorite café, La Fortuna, or eating Chinese food at Mr. Chow. Quite a few family events were held at Tavern on the Green during John's hiatus. The little stowaway establishment sitting comfortably between the Sheep Meadow and Central Park West and just a few blocks from the Lennon home saw the celebrations of John's thirty-eighth and thirty-ninth birthdays, as well as Sean's third and fourth birthdays. Tavern owner Warner LeRoy lived in the Dakota downstairs from the Lennon's. John was also seen very frequently at the Plaza Hotel along Central Park South where he'd go for afternoon tea. The Plaza had an illustrious history of the wealthy and elite, musicians, actors, diplomats and politicians of all shapes and sizes. It was the place where, not too far from where John would sit in his growing adult years, Ronald Reagan made his speech to guests in June 1969 defending his action against the Berkley students just weeks after the violence and shooting. It was where he vowed to keep fighting campus protests with force.

He told guests in the New York City hotel that he found that it was necessary in California to bring whatever force was necessary to restore law and order.

In December 1974, Beatle Paul and Beatle George returned to the Plaza to put their signatures on the papers that officially dissolved the group from anything that may have still connected them together. In other words, if they announced their breakup in the spring of 1970, it was now official with the signing of their divorce papers four years later. And now adult John spent his afternoons there sipping his tea.

There was also Japan. After finally winning his legal battle on July 27, 1976, John Lennon was given residency in the United States, and was finally free to leave the country without fear of not getting back in. And so, they all packed up in June 1977 and spent four months in Japan. In the spring of 1980, at the insistence of Yoko, something we'll explore a little further on, he also sails to Bermuda. Bermuda marks a line where Lennon, in a period of both reflection and rebirth, faces a summation of the entire experience...who he was...where he'd been...and although he wasn't quite sure where the hell he was going, he'd find inspiration again to be John Lennon...and not just John, as "God," his restless farewell to the fame game states. It was as far away as he could get from the madness of everything he left behind all those years ago...those years of Beatlemania, Hairpeace, the arrested development of his early thirties...

The FBI.

Those years when the Nixon Administration put him through hell because of who he was and what he was supposedly capable of, and the reputation of being a radical that stretched back almost a decade, at least to the appearance of Yoko in his life. But it was a drug bust in England that the conservatives used in their attempt to deport John out of America.

Of all fucking things.

U.S. immigration law had automatic provisions punishing the most minor of offenses involving narcotics or marijuana, and allowed for non-admittance into the country and even deportation. Lennon's 1968 conviction in England was the basis for which the United States tried to keep him out, despite the fact that it amounted to a setup with the cop later locked up behind bars. In mid 1974, John had just begun promotion for his upcoming *Walls and Bridges* album and started doing a lot of interviews in what would initiate the last round of attention he'd give to the press for a very long period of time. One of his earlier interviews occurred live on the radio in June when he went on the air with Howard Cosell, but instead of talking about *Walls and Bridges*, most of the time was spent discussing his immigration case. Over the course of the next ten months, he made an effort to get his story out to as much of the country as possible, going on live television with his lawyer, Leon Wildes. In the case of *John Lennon vs. the USA,* Lennon was clearly the victim of a conspiring aggressor in Richard Nixon who had J. Edgar Hoover's FBI do his dirty work in what became one of the most political and influential deportation cases in U.S. history. Even supposing Lennon was convicted in the 1968 case, it was the most minor offense that could be committed, even in England where the statute under which he was convicted had been overturned and wiped off the books, as Wildes often made the point of mentioning.

In early 1975 during one of his TV appearances with Wildes, Lennon recounted the night in Britain seven years earlier when he and Yoko were staying in an old house that Ringo Starr had left for friends to crash or live in. It was a house that Jimi Hendrix had recently moved out of, and it was a night that America was making him pay dearly for.

"I was planted by Sgt. Pilcher who became very big and is now in prison along with a lot of his colleagues including his boss," he told *Tomorrow Show* host Tom Snyder. "But I was lying in bed with Yoko, not married to her…living together…and getting some weird press because she was Japanese and I wasn't living with my Anglo-Saxon wife. And two weeks before I was bust, a friend called me and said 'The cops are coming for you. They got Mick and everybody. They're coming for you next 'cause you're the loud mouth.' So not only that, but I wasn't even smoking pot at that time. But I knew that many other rockers had lived in the place before me. One morning we're just lying there asleep, and suddenly there's a banging on the front door. And Yoko goes to the door and presses the button…says 'who is it?' and they say 'It's a message from Apple,' our office. Eight o'clock in the morning, a message from Apple? It was a woman's voice. She (Yoko) opened the door and there was a woman and about five guys there and they started to push the door. They didn't say 'we're the police' or anything. Meanwhile there's another one at the bedroom window. They'd come over a roof, I mean this is very well-organized. And they were banging and banging. I mean we were terrified. And naked! Then they kept saying 'police police!' and they had plain clothes on. I thought *Cops? Mafia? What is it?* So I said 'I'm just gonna put my trousers on.'

And they said 'No, if you don't open it, we gonna bust the window and the door down.' So I was really terrified. I finally let them in. He says 'Alright, I've got you for obstruction of the law anyway!' And the comedy was, they only had two dogs in London that could smell marijuana at the time, and the dogs were late. They were on another case, so they had to stall for about an hour. And they were running all over the house, all over the place. They separated us. They broke their own rules, which is, you're supposed to be there while they're searching. They were all over the place. They wouldn't let me call the office to say I couldn't come to a press conference that I was supposed to be doing. And finally the dogs arrived, and they'd already searched the place. And there was a room full of junk that I'd brought from a previous home that was like cameras, equipment, and on the mantelpiece is a binocular case. Pilcher calls me over and says 'Is that your binocular case?' 'Yeah, it's my binocular case.' 'Will you look inside?' I looked inside and there's a little piece of hash, which is compressed marijuana. He says 'Do you recognize that substance?' I said, 'Yes, it's hash and I don't know anything about it.' And subsequently because I wasn't married to Yoko, I was terrified that they were gonna throw her out of the country because the press was really weird at the time. And I made a deal that if they left Yoko alone, I would plead guilty and pay a hundred pound fine and that would be the end of it. I made a deal with the cop and he dropped the obstruction charge and they took me to court, and...'be a good boy, people in your position...' I didn't even suspect I'd been planted. I thought maybe the chauffeur had brought it in the case with the stuff."[10]

Pilcher, as Lennon correctly stated, was later convicted of perjury on a drug smuggling case and trial, and jailed for four years.

Looking back on the entire experience as he hit that crossroads late in the spring of 1980, he knew he'd be much more prepared to handle picking up stardom should he decide to. And then there'd be the media. But John always had open access to the media. All he had to do was say the word and he'd be on some talk show. The media for the most part, was largely sympathetic to his situation which until his five year break, had publicly been about his immigration case. Dick Cavett's show had always been a hospitable forum for him. He had also become friendly with Howard Cosell, whose voice was revered on television and radio, mostly in the world of sports. He'd go see Cosell once more during that period of insanity, five months past their first interview. It was December 1974, but this time, their encounter would only be to talk about football. It was a rather strange but synchronistic period, late '74. John Lennon walked into a waiting area outside the broadcast booth of Los Angeles Coliseum where Cosell and Frank Gifford were trying to figure out how to accompany two guests during *Monday Night Football*. Both guests had been invited, but neither was expected to show up. Both did. Lennon was one. The other was the governor. ABC quickly decided on one segment each, after which Cosell approached Gifford.

"You take the governor, and I'll take the Beatle," he told him.[11]

During those initial years after the Beatles when John Lennon had been active in social justice causes and stirring up as much vitriol as he could from the political right wing, Ronald Reagan was leaving his imprint on California government with much larger ambitions in Washington. By the end of 1974, both men were embarking on new chapters in their lives. John was on the verge of getting back together with Yoko. Much has been made of the role she had played in his life straight from the outset, and all of the blame cast upon her regarding the breakup of The Beatles…the manner in which most people who were close to the Lennon's and witnessed firsthand, her manipulative spell over John. Some speculation actually suggested she brainwashed him after his return to the Dakota in 1975, and that despite her account of how the May Pang period began, the consensus seems to be that Yoko literally handpicked May and sent them off together so she could pursue a fling with another musician. While the whole thing was in fact rather forced and insisted upon by Yoko, there has to exist some truth to both sides, although it is quite clear that there were some deep-seated issues going on psychologically for John in how he related to her. The same can be said of Ronald Reagan who had a similar relationship to Nancy. In terms of being the strongest opposing embodiments of the 1960s, Lennon and Reagan shared the unique characteristic of holding their spouses in a rather maternal light. The hovering shadow of an overprotective parent pervaded over their relationships with their wives...so much so, that Lennon referred to and addressed Yoko as "Mother," while Reagan referred to and addressed Nancy as "Mommie." Both wives had a say in whether or not their husbands were able to perform a certain action on any particular day...more so Yoko in this case...although both women were caught up in the conveniently vague world of astrology, kept personal tarot card readers, and let it all inform the most mundane actions to the most crucial decisions. In this respect, whether inadvertently or intentional, it became a means of controlling their husbands who were already co-dependent, stemming perhaps from the insecurity and inconsistency of their childhoods. Certain passages of Reagan's White House diary which he'd later keep were clear indicators of how he would despair over Nancy's absence whenever she was away. In one entry he'd write, "Saw Mommie off for London and the Royal Wedding. I worry when she's out of sight for six minutes. How am I going to hold out for six days? The lights just don't seem as warm and bright without her."[12] Documentation from inside the Dakota just as in the White House, highlight the same sort of vulnerability. The famous Annie Leibovitz photo of a naked John curling up to Yoko in a fetal position is perhaps the most telling image, detailing the underlying maternal foundation of their relationship.

Six years almost to the date before the Leibovitz photo was taken, John was in transition and wanted to lead a clean life, have a kid and drop out of the music scene, opting to be a fulltime parent in the Dakota. Reagan, like Lennon, was about to go home too. After two terms as governor, he and Nancy would go back to private life. He'd do a weekly radio show and plan for the future. His next moves would be big. In the meantime, both men found themselves easing in to these transitional periods when the stars aligned one night in such a way as to make strange things happen, much like a sick joke.

AUTUMN AND EVERYTHING AFTER

In the hallways outside the broadcast booth where *Monday Night Football* was residing for a Rams vs. Redskins game, Frank Gifford walked outside to see Ronald Reagan with his arm around John Lennon talking about football. It was on December 9, 1974 when the two opposing embodiments of the cultural divide unexpectedly came together and met for the first and only time.

2

JUST A PRISONER

A few hours west of Holmdel, New Jersey and well into Pennsylvania, is the state capitol of Harrisburg. Approximately ten miles downstream from Harrisburg along the Susquehanna River sits a sandbar known as Three Mile Island, which is dominated by an ominous horizon-obscuring nuclear power plant. With the oil shortages of the 1970s, and oil having gone from three dollars a barrel to thirty dollars a barrel between 1973 and 1979, utility companies all over America began to press for nuclear power plants. Residents in the surrounding communities near Three Mile Island had grown accustomed to the three monstrous steam towers that loomed hauntingly in the distance. Although nuclear power plants were looked upon suspiciously by opponents of nuclear energy, nearby towns were generally convinced of their supposed safety. This was, in essence, the same naïve overconfidence that was sprawled out boldly by negligent, ignorant men in claiming the safety of the Titanic back in 1912. In the early morning hours of Wednesday,

March 28, 1979, Three Mile Island played host to events that would amount to the worst nuclear accident in U.S. history.

Three Mile Island's Unit 2 reactor had been generating electricity for just under a year when suddenly that morning, a small plumbing breakdown occurred. A plant operator opened up a valve to relieve pressure in the reactor. Little did they know that the valve malfunctioned and did not close. When cooling water began to drain from the open valve, the nuclear core began to overheat. With conflicting readings in front of them and a decision by the operators to shut off the emergency water system that would have cooled the core, technical failure and human error proved to be catastrophic. The core had reached 4300 degrees. At 5200 degrees, meltdown could occur, a situation too dreadful to imagine…a situation known as the China Syndrome. The haunting coincidence of this event was that a film called *The China Syndrome* had been released just twelve days earlier. That film, a reaction against nuclear power, imagined the same exact scenario. Years later, screenwriter Mike Gray in an interview for PBS, described the possible immediate effects, had a meltdown occurred. "The core could have turned into a molten white hot mass. It could have gone through the concrete base of the plant and into ground water, which is immediately below the foundations of the plant. It would have fractured the earth instantly in all directions, and geysers of radioactive steam would have spouted into the air through the parking lot, and a cloud of death would have wafted north into the city of Harrisburg."[13]

Contaminated water leaked throughout the plant while radiation was detected in the control room. As Governor Dick Thornburg declared a state of emergency, Three Mile Island's parent company Metropolitan Edison stated to the public that no radiation had been detected off plant grounds when in fact there was. It was also found later on, that the valve in question had failed eleven other times before at other nuclear power plants. Two days later as the seriousness of the situation became clearer, yet still with no definite understanding of what exactly had taken place, Thornburg ordered the evacuation of all pregnant women within a five mile radius of the plant. This led to panic and hysteria, as some 140,000 people fled their jobs and homes. President Jimmy Carter, a nuclear engineer himself, knew the potential for disaster as he visited the plant some thirty six hours later. Still, given the danger, Carter and those who championed nuclear energy cited the Washington Post by name as the ringleader in engaging in scare tactics designed to terrify the public with the idea of an impending explosion inside the reactor core, as well as the possibility of a mass evacuation. The evacuation obviously ended up happening anyway. With the President coming into town and the entire population struggling to get out, the scene unfolded like some bad science fiction movie. Only it was real.

The prospects of what could have happened at Three Mile Island were enough to frighten anyone into questioning or perhaps even rethinking nuclear energy. Harrisburg mayor, Robert Reid was livid.

"I didn't buy it, and quite a few other people didn't buy it," he said in an interview for PBS's 1999 documentary, *Meltdown at Three Mile Island*.

"I'm still angry. I was upset with the way things were handled, and that we were lied to."[14]

It is not definitively clear what the consequences of Three Mile Island have been, though many cancer cases have been linked to radiation exposure. The Unit 2 reactor was closed, but everything else went on, business as usual. The populations of surrounding towns that fled were convinced that it was safe to return. And despite increasing vocal uproar and protest throughout the country, life went on. Of course, the anti-nuclear side of the issue was and has been vindicated time and time again in the decades since, given the disasters at Chernobyl and Fukushima, along with the advent of nuclear plants as possible targets for terrorism.

Three Mile Island happened while an oil crisis, the second of the decade, was sweeping across the United States in the form of a gas shortage that sent prices soaring by 55 percent in just the first three months of 1979. Talk of the nation's supplies running out were part of the everyday dialogue. It became a driver's season in hell from spring to summer…a trying period of gas lines stretched for miles, with days reserved for even-numbered license plates only, and days for odd-numbered plates. Limits of five dollars worth of gasoline were imposed in some states. Amidst the American madness of traveler's turmoil, an energy crisis and an off-the-rails economy, Three Mile Island happened when things were only about to get progressively worse through a disastrous last 22 months of Carter's presidency, which this publication explores a little further along.

In Holmdel, New Jersey, a 29-year old Bruce Springsteen sat in his house taking in the news events of the past few days. He had been home for almost three months since his tour ended on New Years' Day. Home was not really home though. Springsteen was renting a house in what was supposed to be a short period of time between tours. Recording for his next record would begin in a matter of weeks, and given the long ordeal he experienced putting his last record, *Darkness on the Edge of Town* together, his next one would go smoothly. In reality, Springsteen had been without a solid and consistent place to call home since his parents went out to California a decade earlier. He'd been all around Freehold and Asbury Park, bouncing off different jobs, musicians, and places to crash amongst friends and acquaintances. Once he got somewhat established as a recording artist, though by no means financially secure, he rented houses in Holmdel and Colts Neck, New Jersey. Then he lived for a while in New York City's Navarro Hotel as he was recording *Darkness*.

But that chapter was over, thank God.

All of the unrest and disarray throughout getting that album recorded and released. The three years it took. And when you took that long between records in the mid-Seventies, you simply disappeared, as did John Lennon. Fans and critics expected yearly releases. Some acts put new records out every six months. Not Bruce Springsteen.

JUST A PRISONER

At this point, Springsteen was six years into his career as a recording artist for Columbia. He had been a musician since his early teens when he convinced his mother, Adele, to buy him the electric guitar he saw hanging in a storefront window near his hometown of Freehold, New Jersey. He played in bands since the age of 15, names now well-known in the Springsteen story... The Castiles, Child, Steel Mill and the Bruce Springsteen Band. In May of 1972, he was signed to Columbia by the legendary John Hammond and immediately went to work on his first album *Greetings from Asbury Park, N.J.*, released in January 1973. He received some favorable reviews, although there were many comparisons to Bob Dylan at the outset, which wasn't a bad thing if you were a songwriter. The thing is, Dylan was still in his reclusive years of not touring or giving interviews, and just not wanting to be much a part of anything having to do with the revered artist he was a decade before, while critics were always searching for someone to be what Dylan had been. It was tough to answer the much larger question of what exactly that entailed.

The New Dylan.

The Next Dylan.

Lester Bangs started off his review of Springsteen's first album reminiscing about a character named PF Sloan, just one of a dime-a-dozen folk rockers with a harmonica stuffing a shit ton of syllables into every couplet.[15] PF Sloan apparently had been the *next Dylan* as well. You can see where this is going, I'm sure. New Dylans didn't last long. New Dylans were in need at the time though, and so was a rock and roll savior, whatever *that* was. There was David Bowie and his temporary alter ego, Ziggy Stardust. But temporary is temporary, and Bowie was already flirting with the next phase of his ever-changing evolution, and as with Dylan, fans were beginning to realize that Bowie too, was turning out to be one of those artists you couldn't trust or depend on. Ironically, one year before the emergence of Ziggy, Bowie had written a song for Dylan, calling him out on his bullshit. One of Springsteen's early demos, a song called "Song to Orphans," talked about saviors never lasting long, so it wasn't as if he were searching out some new role within the music world that needed filling. He was just trying to get his music out there to be heard.

Primarily, the Springsteen experience was a live one. His first two albums, although hailed for their poetry, did not translate the effective quality and boundless energy of the live performances very well. He played everywhere, and when he was done, he went back and played there again. Before MTV and the Internet, there was only radio, magazines, and word-of-mouth. Today's type of recognition that self-marketing and promotion on the web along with the right song can get an artist within days, could often take years during the 1970s. The only way to get some recognition when your album wasn't a hit was to tour relentlessly. As Springsteen and his E Street Band crisscrossed the United States playing bars and clubs, pockets of word-of-mouth broke out in several areas of the country…Ohio, Virginia, California, and of course New York and New Jersey. It took California an extra year to catch on to him, but that was mostly due to his concentration on the Northeastern part of the country during 1973 and 1974. Up in Boston, journalist Jon Landau saw "rock and roll future" in him, and wrote his prophetic concert review accordingly.[16] Springsteen and Landau had taken a quick liking to each other, but the future of rock and roll's manager, Mike Appel, wasn't too thrilled about the instant and obvious chemistry between the artist and the writer. All three were involved in the making of *Born to Run*, the album that took Springsteen into a brief national stardom in the autumn months of 1975 before his "disappearance" over the next two years. However, it was the influence of Landau's input that helped the artist realize and achieve his vision of making the greatest rock and roll record of all time. *Born to Run* was a blockbuster, more so critically than commercially. Springsteen had the status of a cult figure, and that's a respectable status to have when you've acquired an audience with virtually no commercial success and the critics love you. It was in many ways, as they say, the best of both worlds. 1976 and his follow-up record could only be bigger. What could possibly go wrong at this point?

Well, a lawsuit or two for starters.

JUST A PRISONER

A quick backtrack...

Springsteen was a 22-year old kid in 1972 desperate to record music and have it heard. Perhaps on the naïve side, negligent when it came to the details of the industry, and just downright lazy, he trusted Appel when he signed what amounted to a bad deal with Laurel Canyon Productions, which entailed three contracts...publishing, recording and management. At the time, he was just interested in playing, and saw it as an opportunity for his big break. That break came pretty early after signing with Appel's company, and he ended up putting out his first two albums to much critical acclaim, and a diehard small but growing fan base. The albums, however, didn't sell, and lacked the push of hit singles. Springsteen was clearly a live act. By 1975, threatened with being dropped by Columbia, he set out to accomplish two things. One, to record the greatest rock song ever made, and two, to record the greatest rock album ever made. That album and its title track as already stated, was *Born to Run*, notorious for its painstaking and daunting production that channeled the studio techniques of Phil Spector's Wall of Sound. Shortly before the album's release at the end of the summer of 1975, Springsteen played a series of ten shows at New York City's legendary Bottom Line club, which got him worldwide media attention, including a live radio broadcast that went down in concert history. The attention also got him on the covers of Time and Newsweek simultaneously...something never achieved before by a rock artist. Appel saw big things ahead and tried persuading Springsteen to take part in several cringe-inducing gigs that his artist didn't want anything to do with, such as the Super Bowl (another unprecedented offer for a rock artist at the time), and some silly tent tour. Springsteen also realized as he got into 1976, that his bank account didn't look like one of a successful rock star. He began to wonder and eventually ask questions. What he found to his horror was that the deal he'd signed was far more financially advantageous for Appel. What was even worse was that he had appeared to have signed away his rights to his publishing, or so he was being told. Laurel Canyon could use his music however they wanted, and there was nothing he could do about it. Springsteen saw himself as a serious artist who had worked hard to get where he was, and believed he should have creative freedom as well as a say in how his music was used or not used. Upon meeting Appel, all he wanted was to play music and have it effect people in a positive way. He wanted his songs to speak to people in ways they could relate to. He always said he wanted his audience to look up at him on the stage and be able to see themselves. He wasn't one of those larger-than-life figures like Mick Jagger and David Bowie...stars who were so unattainable to their fans that they were placed on otherworldly pedestals that no mortal human could ever aspire to. Maybe that's how some fans wanted their rock stars to be...but not all. And that's where Bruce Springsteen came in. He wasn't the first to wear a t-shirt, jeans and a leather jacket onstage, looking just as unassuming as the audience. But he strutted the stage with the cocksure charismatic equivalence of Jagger and Bowie. Until early to mid 1976, there was the perceived feeling of having control of where he was headed. But then he and Appel found themselves in a suit/counter-suit situation that prevented him from entering a studio to record *Born to Run*'s follow-up. Appel, feeling squashed and threatened by the sudden presence and influence of Landau in Springsteen's life and career, tried to prevent his artist from recording as well as having Landau on board as producer of the next record. Engaging in the artistic fight of his life, Springsteen was seeking not only royalties, but most importantly, control of all his publishing. Not only did he want total creative control, but he wanted reassurance that his music could not be used in ways that would compromise its artistic integrity, or in ways that he just simply did not agree to. The cautious and envious Appel saw his star slipping away from him as he helplessly watched Springsteen and Landau forge a creative relationship that would play a major part in the artist's future success. The lawsuit and counter-lawsuit that saw Springsteen literally barred from recording his next album for nearly a year as well as the artist fighting for creative freedom and the right to use a producer of his own choosing, amounted in short to a divorce. By May 1977, his ties to Appel were severed, and Springsteen walked away with full control of his music, a new manager, Jon Landau, and permission to record his next album. Appel would be paid several hundred thousand dollars to relinquish his interest in Springsteen.

Darkness on the Edge of Town, Springsteen's fourth album, was finally released in June 1978. It had been an almost unheard-of three years between records and still with a new album of ten songs to tour behind, Springsteen was still writing new ones. Having missed a few years, he was by no means caught up in his work. Whatever the muse was, it was in full effect. So on the road, he played the new songs from *Darkness*, but continued to write new material. From a public point of view, Springsteen, just prior to the release of *Darkness*, had become the perfect candidate for a *What Ever Happened To...* He had done sporadic touring in regional bursts during the time he was being prevented from recording, but unless you were in his audience, his name had fallen off the earth. This can be difficult to grasp from a twenty-first century perspective, given that the trajectory of one's career usually has to see a star vanish for at least a good decade before surveyors of pop culture begin to ask *what ever happened to*. In the mid-1970s, two or three years were all it took.

By 1978, that groovy cat with the wild wavy hair, scraggly beard and raspy voice that adorned his first few records with stream-of-conscious street poetry and adventurous forays into sophisticated jazz arrangements by way of his precocious and increasingly talented band had morphed into something much more streamlined. He'd shaved the beard and cut his long curls into a somewhat hip and intelligent yet *I-don't-give-a-shit* bed head haircut based on Al Pacino's *Dog Day Afternoon* look. The lengthy adventurous epics and romantic tragedies were replaced with structured four-minute guitar-driven fits of anger disguised as rock songs with a raw edge that couldn't quite crack the Billboard charts significantly enough to give him the hit song he always wanted. Yet, his audience grew in proportion to the vast amounts of endless love he received from critics and peers in the industry. If the *Born to Run* experience was about hype, the *Darkness on the Edge of Town* experience was about delivering on the promise that critics had laid out for him. Many artists shy away from the praise they initially receive. It puts them off fame, and they often run in the opposite direction and do the opposite thing. Springsteen instead became what they predicted he would be, and even more importantly, what they wanted him to be. In essence, he became what they needed and what rock and roll needed.

The songs on *Darkness* were all angry and defiant in nature. While Springsteen was off the road during the period of the lawsuit, he got a chance to see some of the people he had known before his fame. Many of them weren't doing very well in life and many were struggling against a world of dead ends and a life of work with no payoff. Songs like "Badlands" were an indictment of the scripted hierarchical structure of society and the rage and frustration of counting on things that never turn out as planned. "Adam Raised a Cain" imagines the well-documented rocky relationship between Bruce and his father through the biblical tale of Cain and Abel.

The album was a far cry from the carefree characters and carnival sounds that haunted the boardwalks and city streets of the Jersey Shore and New York City inhabiting his earlier work. The theme of escape maintaining the foundation of Springsteen's writing had given way to an existential dread hovering over most of the songs. Still, the strongest quality of his work was his unwavering commitment to the elements that keep people pressing on in the face of adversity, loss and heartache, particularly the ideas of hope and faith which became staple words in his catalog. Songs like "The Promised Land" also embody a scorn for the same adversity that often has the potential to break the human spirit.

A Springsteen concert was an uplifting occurrence, often compared long before the analogies became clichés, to something spiritual or religious. The 1978 *Darkness* shows were broken into two full sets and several encores stretching up to three hours. The concerts were the full rock and roll experience spanning the spectrum of Springsteen's influences over all 25 years of the music's history at the time. Springsteen as musician began when he first saw the Beatles in 1964, but the broad scope of his musical knowledge and showmanship spanned all three decades and back to the mid 1950s, which meant incorporating the founding fathers such as Elvis Presley, Chuck Berry, Little Richard, Jerry Lee Lewis and Buddy Holly into his sets where they remained as staples. He wore his roots proudly, yet he was still as fresh and current as a punk rocker, making nightly leaps into the crowd. Stage-diving may have turned into an activity associated with punks, but it wasn't something mainstream artists on big labels did. Granted, despite jumping into the audience through most of his career, he didn't incorporate actual crowd surfing until 2009 when he was pushing 60 years old, but that is neither here nor there. We are merely establishing where Springsteen stands in relation to the setting of this book. Key moments throughout 1979 are pivotal in the unfolding of our main focus, the autumn of 1980.

And so, going into this particular book, Bruce Springsteen is four albums and six years into his career as a recording artist. It is well before *Born in the U.S.A.*, his seventh album, and long before he was a household name, tabloid subject and worldwide star. He is nicknamed "the Boss" for his exceptional and unique qualities as a bandleader, and total command of the concert stage as well as over his audience.

In America, he had already established himself as one of the best (if not the best) live performers in rock and roll. Critics praised him, fans were devoted in their support, and other artists revered him. In terms of popularity, he had long been headlining theaters since 1975, and had recently started playing in large arenas, although some such as the Spectrum in Philadelphia had been a regular venue since 1976. He was a staple to album-oriented FM radio, and the title track of *Born to Run* had already become a cult classic. What he didn't have yet was a massive radio hit, a Billboard chart-topping album and worldwide stardom. To many who weren't really fans, he was known more as the guy who wrote songs that other people had big hits with. "Blinded by the Light" was recorded by Manfred Man in late 1976 and the band had a big hit with it. In the spring of 1978, punk poet, Patti Smith recorded "Because the Night," a song Springsteen threw away while recording the *Darkness* album. More recently, the Pointer Sisters had a smash hit with "Fire," a song that Springsteen originally penned for Elvis Presley. It is tempting to imagine Elvis being found on his bathroom floor alive and recovering to record "Fire" in 1977, which could have been his first big hit since 1972's "Burnin' Love." Even David Bowie recorded two of Springsteen's early songs "It's Hard to Be a Saint in the City" and "Growin' Up" very soon after Springsteen himself recorded them. To have a major artist record two songs off a new artist's first album is a remarkable form of flattery. But despite all the love from within the industry, his notoriety was not based on radio airplay. His success had been steadily built on his live shows and once again, word-of-mouth. And so here we are.

If *Born in the U.S.A.* would make him a worldwide star in 1984, his 1980 album *The River* would first solidify his status as the biggest rock artist in America. And we can't fully appreciate and understand all that is entailed in the *Born in the U.S.A.* period without first going through *The River* and his most crucial and transformative year of 1980-81.

Having been home since early January with no further touring plans in the near future, Springsteen had lots of time on his hands. The Darkness Tour wasn't a long one, only seven months. But it was seven straight months with very little time off. During the penultimate show of the tour, on New Years' Eve in Cleveland, he was hit in the head with a firecracker that exploded in his eye just at the stroke of midnight. He disappeared from the stage for a few minutes and then re-emerged with a bandage under his eye.

"Well, I almost lost an eye thanks to some asshole," he told the crowd just minutes into 1979. "But I'm not gonna let that ruin my New Year and you shouldn't let it ruin yours either."[17]

Now he was at home in front of the TV. At 29, he had no wife or kids, and lived alone, and so was able to drift in and out as he pleased. The only thing on his radar by way of responsibility would be the eventual next record. He had written a few new songs since the tour ended, but none that really stuck out, and none that were really that good.

"Roulette" was good.

The events at Three Mile Island during that last week of March stayed with him as he watched over the course of the next few days. By Friday of that week, the mass evacuation was in place, and it seeped into his creative conscience. He had been moved particularly by the idea of people fleeing in panic…people frightened by something so devastating about to take place, that they just pick up and leave everything behind… their jobs, homes, possessions…their lives. And part of what made that idea so unsettling is the thought that these people were unsure if they'd ever get to go back, and yet, not sure exactly what they were running from. Within days of the events at Three Mile Island, Springsteen penned "Roulette," a song that places himself in the role of a man forced to leave his life behind. Although he is able to leave with his wife and kids, their lives have been altered forever by something unseen and largely unknown.

As opposition to nuclear energy grew, especially in the wake of Three Mile Island, a group of artists banded together to form Musicians United for Safe Energy. M.U.S.E. was made up of Jackson Browne, James Taylor, Carly Simon, Bonnie Raitt, Jessie Colin Young, the Doobie Brothers, Tom Petty and several others. A series of concerts would take place later in the year, and Springsteen was asked to participate by headlining at Madison Square Garden. At first, he was hesitant out of reserve of attaching himself to anything political. He was also reportedly concerned about politicians being in attendance. He had recently gotten his career back on track after it seemed to be threatened during the lawsuit, and had obtained control to some degree. The decisions he was making during those years reflected an obvious self-conscious painstaking effort to direct every minute detail of how his career would evolve. Perhaps he was a little on the jittery side when faced with the thought of being outspoken on anything just yet. This is in sharp contrast to the reputation Springsteen would have during the first two decades of the twenty-first century when he would embrace Democratic candidates and his liberal views would be well-known. In 1979, it was clear that he wanted nothing to do with politics and seemed, if anything, indifferent to the entire subject.

Work for Springsteen's fifth album began at the Power Station in New York City on April 3, 1979, with the recording of "Roulette." The original plans were to keep recording time minimal and have an album out by the end of the year. What it amounted to however, was a sixteen-month struggle to find an album within the group of 90-plus songs that had been recorded. Songs left over from the previous album would have been a great head start for most other artists, but not for Springsteen. As an artist, he was by no means caught up in his work, at least not on record. Since the Darkness Tour ended, he had written approximately 20 new songs. Although songs like "Independence Day," "Point Blank," "Sherry Darling" and "Ramrod" were to be included in the new sessions, it was more likely that Springsteen was going to take a fresh approach to the next album. The band rehearsed the new material during the month of March in the living room of Springsteen's house in Holmdel. Immediately following the recording of "Roulette," the band recorded "The Ties that Bind," a song written the previous summer that was added to the shows near the end of the tour. In mid-April, a few weeks after recording begun, Bruce was outside his home riding around on his off-the-road three wheel scooter when he accidentally drove into a tree. That night in the hospital, doctors told him that he had a torn muscle in his right leg and that he needed to stay off his feet for three weeks. Recording was temporarily put on hold as quickly as it had gotten started.

One night during the spring, Springsteen attended a Ramones show at the Stone Pony in Asbury Park, where Joey Ramone asked him to write a song for them. Never at a loss for words or music, Bruce went home and penned "Hungry Heart." We know by now the song never made it into the Ramones catalog, and proved to be the much-needed boost he needed in his radio airplay. However, it is interesting to know that the song was never intended for a Springsteen album. But as with every other musical idea he had during this period, he'd record it as if it had a chance of being on the next album.

As spring moved into summer, the band was on a strict schedule of five nights a week in the studio. The sessions began early in the evening and usually didn't end until the early hours of the next morning. Remembering those sessions, drummer Max Weinberg would later tell of watching the sun come up every morning. During the summer months, much progress was made, at least in numbers, with most of Bruce's first batch of new songs being recorded. Long time Springsteen fanatics well-schooled and versed in the studio archives are no strangers to what was recorded, what was released, as well as what was left to be forgotten about for decades until given the proper treatment over a series of box collections from the 1990s onward. However, for this particular study of Springsteen's work process as well as his artistic development, we will track his studio recordings as best we can, while taking into consideration the readers to whom this tedious information might be new or uninteresting. What does this detailed pool of knowledge mean to readers who are not Springsteen fanatics? Absolutely nothing. That said, the intent of our focus regarding Springsteen being one of the three main subjects of this book, is to demonstrate and highlight the ever-prolific artist's work process during the most formative period of his career. With that, the most notable songs to come out of that first recording cycle are "Cindy," "I Wanna Be With You (also recorded for *Darkness*), "Stolen Car," "The Price You Pay," "You Can Look" (But You Better Not Touch), "I Wanna Marry You," "Bring on the Night," "Be True," "Rickie Wants a Man," "Dollhouse," "Loose Ends," Hungry Heart" and "The River."

The initial intent sound-wise was to capture the raw intensity of the band's live performances. *Born to Run* and *Darkness*, although masterpieces, were both recorded under a process of many multiple takes and exhaustive layers of overdubs. That is not to suggest that Springsteen didn't make the correct creative decisions in the end. If not for that particular recording method, his original intent may not have been realized to its fullest potential. Both albums stand as testaments to the artist's vision as he climbed toward the creative peak of his career. Now, as Springsteen approached his thirties, not only was his writing and vocal style about to evolve, but so was the sound of the E Street Band.

The time spent in the studio during the summer of 1979 gave the band members ample time to really feed and play off each other. According to several accounts, including Springsteen's, this is where everyone truly came together as a band. In fact, they became so tight that most of the new material was recorded live. This in turn, would capture on record for the first time, that exceptional quality that made the band so unique. The band heard on the Darkness Tour was the band that was able to be translated onto tape during the 1979 sessions. As the new material progressed, the rhythm section began to function as a single unit, providing a vast canvas for the other instruments to make their way through, finding their own space without much direction. In short, the band began to know itself. In the studio, engineer, Bob Clearmountain found the process of mixing the E Street Band as a rather simple task. Instead of hitting songs full force with everything they had, certain musicians such as Danny Federici (organ) and Roy Bittan (piano) would hold back, usually playing a few simple chords or single notes until they felt that there was a space to do something. If there was a hole, someone would fill it. Everybody seemed to find their own space. If there was no space, that particular musician laid low. Where Clearmountain's job would normally be to mix instruments up or pull them back, his work was already done by the band, as they had a natural way of mixing themselves. With the exception of the various vocal overdubs that Springsteen would continue to do, the band's takes were done very quickly. Perhaps this is the reason that so many songs were put down on tape in such a short period of time. April to September would have been close to record time for them to finish an album, but it was Springsteen's dissatisfaction with the new group of songs as a whole that would put the next of several delays on the project.

It was Jackson Browne who ultimately convinced Springsteen to perform at the M.U.S.E. concerts at Madison Square Garden. A run of five shows were scheduled for mid September, and Bruce signed on to headline the final two, the second of which, September 23, was his thirtieth birthday. Although the shows were successful in raising an awareness of the dangers involved with nuclear energy, there was an underlying distraction surrounding Springsteen's appearance. Not everyone in the crowd or among the performers, had seen him perform before, and many had wondered just what the fuss was all about. Still, the audience was clearly a Springsteen crowd that at times was relentlessly unforgiving of the fact that other artists besides Bruce were sharing the bill. The now infamous chants of "Bruuuuuce!" filled the Garden for two consecutive nights. Out of the mostly Los Angeles-based line-up, only Jackson Browne, who was a good friend of Springsteen's, was aware of the loyal and sometimes selfish adoration that came from his audience. While artists like Bonnie Raitt took it in stride, performers like Chaka Khan were visibly intimidated. Bonnie Raitt who also went back several years with Springsteen, had an idea of what to expect. While reacting to the "Bruce" chants backstage, she joked, "It's a good thing his name isn't Melvin or something."[18] Another artist who performed was Tom Petty. He and his band, the Heartbreakers, three years and three albums into their recording career were about to go onstage to perform their set, which was just before Springsteen's. Petty, just on the verge of his commercial breakthrough was still somewhat a newcomer to the music scene. Before he went on, Browne approached him with a warning and some friendly advice. He advised him that should he hear anything that sounded like booing from the crowd, not to get thrown because they were really screaming "Bruce." In a 1995 interview, Petty remembered thinking "well, what's the difference?"[19] John Rockwell's *New York Times* review accentuated these disturbances, where the crowd was clearly there to see Springsteen, leaving one with the impression that the nuclear issue and even the other artists "were barely being tolerated." The crowd's notoriety for cooing 'Bruce' seemed to throw off some of the performers who thought they were being booed, and in some cases, they really were.[20] Rockwell's headline ironically read "Springsteen Makes Biggest Impact at Antinuclear Benefit." This seemed a bit unfitting in view of the secondary role that the anti-nuclear theme took amidst the Springsteen hysteria. In fact, Springsteen was the only performer who did not make some sort of anti-nuclear/political statement during his set. One week before the shows, Rockwell wrote of a possible resurgence of musicians taking an active role in politics, calling the event a "return to political activism by many veteran radicals of the 1960s, and a newly awakened political interest by the performers themselves."[21] With the 1970s already long-known as the "me" decade, where social conscience and political activism took a backseat to self-absorption and excess superficiality, a new era of serious-minded artists, old and new, began to surface and assemble for various causes, drawing a newfound respectability in the eyes of politicians, especially on the left.

Springsteen's set ran 85 minutes, extremely short for him, but much longer than the other musicians had played during the entire five-night stand. Both of his set lists were almost identical, consisting mainly of "greatest hits" such as "Prove it all Night," "Badlands," "Born to Run" and "Rosalita." "Sherry Darling," an underdeveloped song that he premiered during the Darkness Tour was also included, but had undergone some structural changes with new lyrics and the addition of a bridge following the guitar solo. Bruce also premiered a brand new ballad called "The River," which seemed to be the most personal and heartfelt song he had written up to that point in time. Mary, possibly the same character he sings of in 1975's "Thunder Road," had reappeared in the new song, which dealt with an unexpected pregnancy and marriage that followed in front of a background of economic ruin, no work and a young couple's dying dreams. It had been four years since *Born to Run*, and Bruce was letting his audience check in on the people who had flowered the album with hope, dreams, love, hate, lost innocence and ultimately that last chance to make things "real." In between, his writing had turned bitter and angry on *Darkness*. On this one new song, however, he seemed to have collected his anger and replaced it with compassion. Yet, regret still laces almost every line, as the unanswered questions of his youth had only gotten more intense. In "The River," Springsteen talks about everything that once seemed important vanishing into the air, turning to mere memories that haunt him like a curse. Mary pretends not to care, while he acts like he doesn't even remember those things. Still, he wonders about the dreams they once had. What happens if a dream doesn't come true? Is it a lie? Is it something worse? What is it that keeps sending him down to the river? Why does he keep returning there?

Perhaps the river that Springsteen sings about symbolizes some sort of hope or freedom, a place of reflection or inspiration, or just a place to dream, reminiscent of *Born to Run's* highways. The river is a place where this young couple always went in more innocent times, and now that their world seems to be coming apart, one of them repeatedly continues to go there…maybe not deliberately intending to go to the river, but somehow always winding up there. Ultimately there is a message of hope offered in the song, if only for the constant theme of returning…the idea that in the face of every letdown is still the hope of survival.

Before introducing "The River," Bruce appeared to be deep in thought. It was a manner of conduct that his audience would come to be familiar with whenever he was weighing something on his mind, deciding what to say and how he should say it. During these rare brief personal moments, he'd almost seem to forget the audience was there. He'd pace the stage staring down, sometimes with his hands on his hips. He would often clutch the microphone in its stand, staring down at the stage for seconds at a time, thinking how to begin. On this particular occasion, he walked up to the mic and slightly adjusted it, his hands shuffling about nervously as he checked his harmonica, perhaps to see if it was the right key.

"This is a…this is a song…this is called 'The River.' This is…this is new…for my brother in-law and my sister."[22]

He stepped back, blew into the harmonica, testing it, and looked over at guitarist, Steve Van Zandt, who accompanied him on acoustic for the beginning. In the *No Nukes* film that documents the anti-nuclear demonstrations along with the M.U.S.E. concerts, it is clearly evident that Springsteen was undividedly self-conscious of playing the new song. It is arguable that out of everything he had recorded that summer, this was the song he was most proud of, and the one he wanted most to be heard. Lyrically, it encapsulated where he was at that stage in his writing, and although an entire new album was not yet in the picture, his on-going story needed to be told. That night, he sang "The River" as intentionally audible as he's ever sounded, pronouncing every syllable sharply and clearly, as if he were making sure the audience heard and understood every word. He gripped the mic tightly, sweat running down his face, causing him to blink his eyes nonstop. He stood on the darkened stage bathed only in a deep blue spotlight, which reflected off his blazer almost mystically. For decades, the footage from that show served as one of the very few pieces of visual documentation of Springsteen's rise from cult figure to superstar, which happened over those two nights at the Garden, while the *No Nukes* film captures the moment he made that transition. That night, captured in the film, Springsteen walked onstage a cult figure, and 85 minutes later, walked off the biggest rock star in the world. To close the show, Springsteen and the E Street Band played Gary U.S. Bond's 1962 hit, "Quarter to Three." Edited down to some three minutes for the film, it is among the most stunning and powerful rock and roll footage ever captured. Bruce Springsteen had become the undisputed king of rock and roll, and *No Nukes* was his coronation. Even in its edited format, the footage is devastating. He frantically swings his hips like Elvis. He screams like James Brown.

He casually strolls over to the piano, leans over, and pounds the keys with his head and then with his feet, extending a nod and a wink to Little Richard and Jerry Lee Lewis. While singing, he hops up and down to the beat, shirt buttons undone, sloppy but cool, and to the screaming girls, sexy. Before tonight, his audience was pre-dominantly male. He has now become both rock and roll monster and sex symbol. Near the end of the song, he grabs hold of the microphone as the band comes to an abrupt stop.

"That's all I can stand!" he roars.[23]

The band kicks back in and holds a chord. He looks baffled and confused as he gazes into the crowd, the band holding the dying chord. He stumbles back to the mic, barely able to stand. He raises his arms and the music stops.

"I can't stand no more!" he growls.[24]

He punches the air, signaling the snare drum, and the band kicks into one more prolonged chord. He stands in place, breathing fast and heavy, his guitar slung on his side like a rifle. He looks to his left and then desperately to his right out into the audience. The next look on his face is a blank stare as his eyes focus on nothing...perhaps the rafters in the back of the venue... and his body begins to fall backwards, collapsing onto the stage. As he hits the floor, the band simultaneously stops on impact. The crowd bursts into a thunderous applause while many just stand there looking toward the stage, bewildered in confusion. Those who have seen him before know that this is Bruce being Bruce, and that it's part of the Springsteen package. The exhaustion, however, is real, as he lay on his back, catching his breath. The shtick that follows is classic Springsteen, as Clarence Clemons (saxophone), Gary Tallent (bass), and Steve Van Zandt (guitar) gather around him. Gary motions Bruce to get up while Steve fans him off with a towel. Within a few seconds, Clarence and Gary help him to his feet and walk him over to the microphone. The core Springsteen crowd cheers while many remain silent, wondering if it is real. Bruce approaches the mic looking as if he just woke up from a long coma and his audience is the first thing he sees.

"I can't go on like this," he says with a confused slanted smile.

"I'm thirty years old! My heart's starting to go on me! I can't!"

They cheer.

"I can't," he says again, shaking his head.[25]

This would become routine at his concerts as he'd near the end of his final encore. He would have false ending after false ending, and then build up to some variation of one of his "I Can't Go On Any Longer" speeches, pleading for the crowd to let him stop while reworking their energy level back up to another climax until they screamed loud enough for more.

And then he'd give them more.

"Well dontcha know that I…"

The band kicks back in.

"I danced 'til quarter to three…" he sings, and they're off and running again.[26] He acknowledges the audience behind the stage by climbing the platform in back of the drums to get closer to them. Then he signals Clarence and Steve to join him. After rocking for the people in the back for about thirty seconds, he jumps down from his spot. He briefly loses his balance, but quickly regains it after literally stumbling back to the microphone. The music is halted again, leaving only a drum roll. Then the drums stop.

Silence.

He grabs the microphone.

"IIIIIIII'M JUST A PRISONERRRRR…"

The birthday boy wails and drops to his knees as the band kicks back in on a sustained chord. They beat the chord to death. Then Bruce Springsteen slowly rises to his feet to grab the mic one last time and complete his eternal battle cry…

"…OF ROCK AND RRRRROOOHHHLLLLLL!!"[27]

3

LADIES AND GENTLEMEN, RONALD REAGAN

On Sunday, November 4, 1979, the United States Embassy in Tehran was invaded by several hundred armed Iranian students taking what was at first said to be at least 100 hostages, 90 percent of which were American. In the city of Qom, a spokesperson for Ayatollah Ruhollah Khomeini who was leading a revolution in Iran, said the occupation of the U.S. Embassy had Khomeini's full support. In the streets outside the embassy, tens of thousands of people marched to mark the one-year anniversary of a shooting of students by the Shah of Iran's security forces at Tehran University. The shooting however, was merely the final straw in a long history that Iranian revolutionaries had against America's support for the shah, otherwise known as Mohammad Reza Pahlavi. The Shah's authoritarian rule went back to a 1953 coup, and over the next two and a half decades, the United States were allies that supported and funded his government. Over a period of time, opposition grew within Iran, culminating in demonstrations and riots by 1978. In mid-January 1979, Reza was forced to flee Iran, ending up in Egypt. By early

February, Khomeini returned to take over and establish command over Iran after 14 years of exile. Over the course of 1979, there were several attempts at seizing the American Embassy. When Reza fell ill and learned he had cancer, the question of him being admitted into the United States for treatment became an agonizing decision, as the Carter Administration wrestled with fear of retaliation verses America's long-standing friendship with the Shah…this coinciding with Khomeini's declaration that Reza be returned to Iran to face trial. Finally, on October 22, Reza was taken into the U.S. for medical treatment, and immediately, the Iranians took it as political refuge on the part of America. And so, as the climate heated up in Tehran amidst anti-American sentiment, everything feared in Washington came to pass just 13 days later.

On Tuesday, Election Day in the United States, students outside the embassy in Tehran gathered around an American flag taken out of the building in Sunday's takeover, and burned it as a symbol of victory. The footage reached TV news all over the world, and the image burned its way through the collective retina of America. Carter spent every spare moment he had during the initial 24 hours trying to figure out what to do. He'd make it known as often as necessary that the shah would not be sent back to Iran. At the outset, he decided to send former U.S. Attorney General Ramsey Clark and George William Miller, staff director of the Senate Select Committee on Intelligence, to a staging point in Ankara, Turkey, in an attempt at getting permission from the Revolutionary Council to negotiate with Khomeini. Miller would also be responsible for the freezing of 12 billion dollars in Iranian assets in the United States. Carter was also painfully aware of several hundred other Americans situated in Iran, and directed the companies that employed them to get them out of there. The President also asked Algeria, Syria, Turley, Pakistan, Libya, and the PLO to intercede on behalf of the release of the hostages. It was clear that they were dealing with a madman, and the prospect of the captured Americans being killed in the name of religion or some unmet terms was in the back of their minds very early in the ordeal, which was made all the more difficult by the distinction between the Iranian government and Khomeini, and the fact that there was no central authority for the United States to communicate with. Khomeini quickly refused to see Clark and Miller. In response, the PLO announced from the U.N. that they would send a delegation to Iran to help negotiate the release of the hostages.

On the political front, Election Day passed amidst the unsettling news coming out of Iran. To Carter's favor, the Democrats did very well all over the country, getting new governors elected in Kentucky and Mississippi despite some strong Republican challengers. Still, at this stage in his Presidential term, nearly three years since taking office, there was not much weighing in his favor. Carter had come into Washington as an outsider, and he proudly declared himself one. He had been involved in politics but wasn't a politician. He didn't do deals and he didn't pat politicians on the back. His own party found that out early in his first and only term. Coming into office, he promised a fresh approach to government and a distance from Washington insiders. His focus was going to be energy, welfare and health care. He cut back on what he saw as needless and reckless spending, and began with the office of President of the United States by walking through his own inauguration down Pennsylvania Avenue, his wife Rosalynn, three sons, Jack, Donnel and James, and daughter, Amy at his side, giving up the traditional motorcade escort.

Carter's critics claimed that as an outsider, he didn't understand the levers of national governance. His presidency became caricatured as a failure and he was historically marginalized even by those within his own party. A term coming on the heels of Vietnam and Watergate at a time when those two wounds on modern American history were still festering, the downward spiral still seemed in motion. The Carter years were marred by high inflation and an energy crisis that was sparked by the country's dependence on foreign oil and overconsumption, and when the President spelled it out for the American people, many seemed to not want to hear it. Carter didn't sugarcoat. He didn't tell Americans everything was alright and that they were going to live happily ever after. He called for unpopular measures of discipline and conservation, which ran contrary to the unapologetic American excess of the post-Watergate decades. If anything truly put him at odds with the American people, at least pre-Iran, it was his "Crisis of Confidence" speech on July 15, 1979, otherwise known as the "Malaise" speech where the President narrowed the nation's woes down to a collective crisis of confidence and a lack of respect for the country's institutions and leaders. Many Americans blamed Carter for the very issues he felt were problems. Nonetheless, his televised address backfired.

Politics aside, it was widely agreed upon by most people who came in contact with Jimmy Carter that he was a kind, decent and compassionate man. Presidential speechwriter, James Fallows described him as a patient, stable and confident person whose quirks were few, and perhaps as admirable a human being as has ever held the job. His worst critics maintained he was complacent, arrogant, lacking in sophistication and possessed a "blissful ignorance" about how to get things done.[28] What is probably neutral territory by those who both approved and disapproved of Carter, is that he did not care about political consequences. He went with his gut and did what he thought was the right thing to do. Carter was even initially embraced by the same evangelical Christians who would eventually lead an entire movement toward the election of Ronald Reagan just four years later.

The rise of the evangelicals in Washington stemmed at the very least from a growing intolerance for the separation of church and state. The leader of the evangelical movement, Reverend Billy Graham believed the government had not only disavowed America's Judeo-Christian roots, but abandoned religion altogether. When the United States Supreme Court ruled prayer in public schools as unconstitutional, it did so with respects to the First Amendment and every American citizen's right to freedom of religion and privacy. Graham's opposition to the ruling was veiled by his choice of words and the idea that America had turned its back on religion, when it was evident that when he said religion, he meant Christianity. When evangelicals used the word *God*, it was without respect to the fact that the world's three dominating Western religions all had a different name for the same biblical god, so it was quite clear which god they meant.

But compared to the proper and tame years of the 1950s when Graham began his crusade, the Seventies were an out-of-control kaleidoscope of decadence. Even through the free love of the late Sixties, the conservative mindset could not have imagined the shock of a decade of women's lib, gay pride, Donna Summer, Studio 54, Plato's Retreat, Ziggy Stardust, the Sex Pistols, Kiss, the Village People, *Rocky Horror*, or *Deep Throat*, nor could they foresee their president resigning in disgrace. While prison seemed a possibility, Richard M. Nixon was immediately pardoned by Gerald Ford, angering evangelical conservatives who still voted on principle and not ideology. Politics had not yet become their agenda. Ford was helpless in a hopeless time though. The country had its ass kicked time and time again through Vietnam, Watergate and an oil crisis. As well-meaning and down-to-earth as he might have been at times, Ford, as historian Thomas Hine so accurately compared him to, seemed like a lost substitute teacher who has no control over a chaotic classroom.[29]

Consequently, it is during this period where politics becomes the agenda of the evangelicals who were now calling themselves the "Moral Majority" under the leadership of Jerry Falwell, reverend of the Thomas Road Baptist Church in Lynchburg, Virginia. Falwell, fueled by the ultimate prize of seeing Roe V. Wade, the Supreme Court's 1973 ruling on abortion overturned, did not hide the fact that his Christian movement was indeed political. The reverend would later draw controversy to himself occasionally, becoming associated with some of the most reprehensible and unconscionable statements in modern American history, most notably attributing the 9/11 terrorist attacks to God's punishment on America for homosexuality and liberalism. Perhaps no other American in modern history had been so publically outraged and disgusted by the social change of the 1960s and 70s as Falwell had been, to the point where he launched the Moral Majority with the sole intention of getting conservatives elected.

Despite the fact that the religious right later came to hold such a profound influence over the Republican Party, we cannot overstate the idea that government and alliances with politicians were nothing welcome by evangelicals in the beginning. Falwell even criticized Graham's friendly endorsement of Nixon as a mistake. And even Nixon himself never whole-heartedly embraced the evangelicals, yet called them out for being a "silent majority" for not speaking out against America's anti-war sentiment. The evangelicals hardly constituted a majority. By 1976, however, they were beginning to unapologetically insert themselves into the American political and electoral process, although they hadn't yet completely aligned themselves with or co-opted the Republican Party. It was a Democrat they got behind initially in Jimmy Carter. During the 1976 campaign, Carter spoke often of his deep connection to Jesus Christ. Much of mainstream America had not been accustomed to the phrase "born again," so the media suspiciously made it a point to check out candidate Carter by doing some research into the evangelical movement he identified with. Reporters had no idea what Carter was talking about when he spoke of his faith. Some charged that it reeked of a backwoodsy southern tradition and was seen as suspect to the rest of the country. The use of words like *crusade* scared the shit out of people who knew their history and watched suspiciously as this new religious revival pecked at the seams of American freedom. It is not as if American presidents weren't God-fearing before Carter or that evangelical Christians weren't pushing their views on decency and moral decay for the past few centuries. Fundamentalists straight back to Jonathan Edwards can be traced through a Puritan lineage that threads its way through the American story. They were out there pointing their fingers the entire time, though nothing truly influenced Washington to any profound level of change. Perhaps the biggest accomplishment through religious fear and paranoia was the addition of the two words *under God* to the American Pledge of Allegiance and the words *In God We Trust* as the American tagline during the frightened 1950s, due largely to the Godless communists. Though Carter did not align himself ideologically with the evangelicals and their agenda, his relationship with Jesus Christ was genuine, unapologetic and apolitical. With Carter up for the presidency, the movement, still not completely disavowing the idea that it not endorse politicians, was clearly in the corner of the Democratic candidate. As Bailey Smith, keynote speaker at the 1976 Southern Baptist Convention told the congregation, "Newsweek said about that candidate, his allusions to his personal relationship to Jesus Christ are considered bad form. But if there is anything we need, whether it's bad form or good politics, is a man who is more proud of his faith in Christ than any political aspirations he might have. And it would certainly be improper for me to call that man's name, but his initials are the same as our lord's."[30] The evangelical opposition to Carter came later and throughout his presidency when they began to realize he was more liberal than they could ever have imagined.

When looking at his presidential campaign announcement from Tuesday, November 13, 1979, it is hard to forget that Ronald Reagan was an actor. While such announcements were often brief and in the form of live stump speeches in some symbolic and sentimental setting, Reagan, who knew all the angles, facial expressions, physical gestures and body language, played to the cameras in ways no politician had done before or since. His campaign team knew how to capitalize on his talents and training, and that is exactly what it did. Rather than standing in front of a crowd on the stairs of some civic building or before a cafeteria filled with assembly line workers, Reagan sat at a desk in a very presidential-looking office equip with a fancy leather chair and the American flag. It was the first visual that viewers had as the televised address began with the words, "Ladies and gentlemen, Ronald Reagan." As the camera pulled away, he stood in place or casually sat on the corner of the desk, all the while, never once breaking form or straying from his perfectly-delivered speech. In 1979, such an announcement from a presidential candidate would normally come in the form of a news headline with a brief clip on the six o'clock news. In the case of Reagan, it was a primetime event meant for the maximum possible television audience. It appeared on television as if it were an actual presidential address from the Oval Office, and that in itself seemed genius on the part of the candidate's team. In a sense, he was already acting the role of President of the United States.

Reagan cut right to the heart of what many Americans wanted to hear at a time when the country seemed to be skidding out of the 1970s and into an uncertain future. He got right to the point and spelled out his resume detail for detail within the first 60 seconds of the 23-minute address, quickly appealing to Middle America by recounting his childhood as a small town boy growing up in Iowa and Illinois. He'd lived in an America where the people who had too little to eat outnumbered those who had enough…an America ravaged by the financial ruin of the Great Depression. He'd lived through the strife of four wars and saw his country bounce back on the strength of the post-war years when America became the "dominant force" in the world.[31] He'd seen America from the production booth as a sportscaster, as officer of his labor union, as a soldier, as both Democrat and Republican and as public office holder. In other words, as Reagan was spelling out for the country, he had been around, put in the necessary time, service and mileage and was undoubtedly qualified for the position. Despite his failed attempt at the Republican nomination against President Ford in 1976, his vision and plans remained big, and his base would grow immensely over the course of Carter's presidency.

The timing of such a candidacy announcement is striking when observing past elections. Reagan entered the race less than one year before Election Day. Such a move is unfathomable in twenty-first century politics where campaigns and 24-hour television coverage start a full two years before a Presidential election takes place. His candidacy came with primary season on the horizon, and conservatives were immediately drawn to him. His public image was crafted straight out of his ability to act and his familiarity with the camera. He believed what he was doing, and so he believed what he was saying. He understood the theater of politics and found it the optimum environment for his abilities. As it turned out, his performances in public life were far more effective than in his film career.

It is often suggested that Reagan was not a very good actor in the sense that his abilities in his craft lent themselves to lead roles. They did not. For intriguing exploration of this idea, one needs to look no further than *Reagan: The Life*, the Reagan biography by HW Brands which serves as a voyage at times into the subject's psyche, and ascribes his lack of true emotion on screen to his inability to go deep inside himself and touch on feelings and personal experiences that actors often keep readily available when needed. Those feelings did not seem to be on the surface with Reagan, which if we consider his limited sex appeal along with an acting range that wasn't very wide we can begin to understand the sense of detachment. People could know Reagan for years but never get close to him. There were parts of him that not even his family could get near. Brands attributes this to the alcoholism of Reagan's father, and the instability and inconsistencies that such a childhood can bring. On one hand the most important and trusted male figure in your life is throwing a ball to you one day and beating you senseless the next. Seen through this lens, his rather one-dimensional acting roles, devoid of any real depth or conflict, can be seen as a reflection of the real person whose personality usually always remained on the surface of human emotion.[32] It's not that Reagan didn't have feelings. It's not that he didn't get angry or sad or overwhelmingly happy. He just didn't show it, and if he did, it wasn't very often. Even his own children, well into adulthood tried to make sense of him. There was Maureen and Michael, his first two, who went back to his marriage with actress Jane Wyman. Maureen, his first, liked to joke about becoming a Republican before her father, even though she disagreed with him on a number of issues including the Equal Rights Amendment and abortion. Although she spent a great deal of time away from her father in early childhood, she was proud of him and supported him enormously throughout his political career, getting involved to a great extent in politics herself. Michael was adopted, and struggled the most not only with feelings of inadequacy in relation to his father, but to his mother, whose approval he also sought after. He spent much of his life convinced he was chosen to feel the wrath of God and therefore believed he was going to hell. On top of being molested by a camp counselor at the age of seven, something he long kept a secret, his early childhood was marked with a feeling of guilt and of being unwanted, as he often feared that his birth mother gave him up because she didn't love him and that he was *bad*. Michael desperately craved his father's attention and approval. His lifelong issues developed upon learning of his adoption at the age of four. Michael was said to be plagued by thoughts of possibly being born out of wedlock and therefore worried he was illegitimate, which in his mind amounted to being worthless.

Reagan's marriage to Wyman lasted only nine years. Wyman attributed the breakup to her husband's inattentiveness due largely to being consumed with meetings and negotiations on a constant basis. Reagan was a top union man and served as President of the Screen Actors Guild. After Reagan married Nancy Davis, another actress he met working in motion pictures, Wyman sent Maureen and Michael to Chadwick, a boarding school in Palos Verdes. Michael was only five at the time and Nancy found it appalling that a child that young should be raised in such an environment away from both parents. Ronnie (as Nancy called her husband) thought about filing for custody, but did not want the public attention, nor was he prepared to try proving Wyman was an unfit parent, which would have been required in a court. Reagan's other two children, Patti and Ron, both from his marriage to Nancy, were more estranged by way of being products of their own time. He was constantly worried about the profound influence that the 1960s counterculture was having on Patti as she was away at boarding school. His son Ron Jr. had recently raised eyebrows when he told his parents he was leaving college to study ballet. While the media expected it to be an embarrassment for the family, the Reagan's, at least on the surface, made it clear that they were proud of their son and showed their support of his decision. While Nancy wasn't disappointed, she was surprised in that she figured given Ron's talents and interest in writing, he'd get into it as a profession. She had already been worried for her son for several years since he had gotten romantically involved with a much older woman who had a teenage daughter of her own. The relationship went on until Ron was a freshman at Yale. During the Thanksgiving break of that year, Ron sat his parents down to inform them of his decision to study ballet and leave Yale. The Reagan's friend, Gene Kelly, recommended the Stanley Holden Dance Center in Los Angeles where Ron enrolled for a while. At Holden, he met Doria Palmieri. Soon after meeting Doria he was accepted into the Joffrey Dance Company in New York where he joined the Joffrey II touring company. Nancy was proud of her son, but she worried about him living in Greenwich Village. Although she herself had also lived in New York, it was a much different New York than she remembered. Doria soon followed Ron to New York where they lived together. At first, Nancy and Doria didn't hit it off, but much of it was trepidation based on the fear of her son being hurt and her memories of his previous relationship ending disastrously. When much of her husband's focus was on running for president during the final years of the decade, Nancy never lost her motherly instincts and stayed attentive to and protective of her kids.

While Ronald Reagan lost his instinctive liberal sentiments to the Grand Old Party at some point during the 1950s, his two youngest seemed to identify more with their grandfather, Jack Reagan, on politics. The enigma-like characteristics of Reagan's personality indeed go back to his own childhood, but even they are wrapped in contradiction. His father, Jack, a shoe salesman, struggled for years with alcoholism. He wasn't a year-round alcoholic who couldn't function or perform the daily duties of life. If he was an alcoholic, and that has been the word used repeatedly to describe Jack, he was indeed a functioning alcoholic who remained responsible, maintained work and tried his best to provide for his family, which he always did. Where he fell short was in his binges. He'd go months at a time without a drink, and then suddenly, quite often around holidays, spiral into benders that lasted weeks at a time. He was able to put down the glass or the bottle for long stretches, and he didn't drink through the hard times. Instead, he drank when things were going good, doing it more out of celebration rather than escapist necessity. It was during these prolonged periods where there were enough ugly incidents and scarring memories to profoundly shape the distance of his son's persona. Still, Jack Reagan had what his wife Nelle called a sickness, and that is how Nelle addressed it to her boys Neil and Ronald, often appealing to them to always remember that their father was a good person when he wasn't drinking.

As pragmatic as Nelle was to her kids regarding their father's abuse of alcohol, she was far less forgiving toward her husband himself, and would often let him have it, scolding him...many nights, the kids subjected to hearing shouting and cursing coming out of the bedroom.

Jack Reagan was a liberal Democrat. He stood for social and economic equity and was strongly opposed to racism and segregation in an era in which his family was surrounded by it. The revival of the Ku Klux Klan was a reality during the childhoods of the Reagan boys and Jack was adamant in making sure his kids were aware of the deplorable nature of these types of racist groups. At one point when D.W. Griffith's *Birth of a Nation* was the film to see, Jack refused to let his boys watch it. They pleaded. It was a historical piece that reflected a different time in American history, they argued. But racism and segregation still persisted and was a very present entity, Jack reminded. He told his kids that the Klan was the Klan and a sheet was a sheet and anyone who would wear one over their head was a bum.[33]

Jack often traveled for work, which accounted for the family moving around a lot. One night he checked into a hotel where the racist manager behind the counter proudly assured him that he would like it there because they didn't allow Jews. Jack picked up his belongings, telling the manager that he was Catholic and that if the hotel practiced such discriminatory exclusion toward Jewish people, then it would one day get to a point where Catholics were excluded as well.[34]

Needless to say, Jack slept in his car that night.

What Dutch Reagan found at an early age was that he loved an audience and thrived on attention. Being the younger brother didn't help the situation because naturally, Neil received more of the attention being much more sociable and the better athlete of the two. Dutch's nearsightedness almost guaranteed a disastrous time playing baseball, while his fourth-string status as a football player at Eureka College didn't help boost his confidence or settle his awkward, anxious, out-of-place feeling around others. The place Dutch found that solace and sense of purpose was on a stage with an audience before him. It was in the laughter and applause he first received in a church production at a very young age. It was an innate sense of effect he could have on a crowd, and it would become as vital as breathing in his life as it grew more evident that he loved to talk and perform in front of people, knowing they were hanging on his every word. At Eureka, between 1928 and 1932, he also took part in swimming, track and drama, while serving as Student Body President. He loved the microphone and got a chance to use it for pay when at the age of 22 he took a job at WOC in Davenport, Iowa as a sports announcer for ten dollars per game. His pay skyrocketed when he moved to WHO in Des Moines for a whopping 75 dollars per week salary where he covered title fights, track meets and Big Ten football games live, while recreating Chicago Cubs baseball games in simulated broadcasts through a play-by-play telegraph wire. His short career in Hollywood that followed also filled his need for an audience for a period of time. Beginning in 1937, he made 28 movies in his first four years, and although he wasn't an A-list actor, his name was big enough to land him future roles in the years following World War 2.

The war happened at a time long before conservatives and the Republican Party made a habit of laying claim to military support along with having a self-professed monopoly on patriotism. Reagan entered the war a New Deal Democrat and he'd exit the war a New Deal Democrat who had voted for Franklin Delano Roosevelt four times.

As a reserve officer, he had never given thought to the possibility of active duty and was placed on limited service because of poor eyesight when not wearing glasses. In March 1942, he received a letter from the War Department that contained big red letters on the envelope reading "Immediate Action." He knew that meant active duty. Reagan was ordered to report to Fort Mason out of San Francisco within two weeks. When he arrived, he reported to Colonel Philip T. Booker, 34 years, regular army, and graduate of the Virginia Military Institute. He was to serve as a liaison officer loading convoys with troops bound for Australia. Their mission was to build up a force there to prevent Japan from pinning down its flank on Australia and then being able to turn and attack the West Coast of the United States. When the time came for his physical exam, everything looked great except for his eyesight. One doctor told him he'd probably shoot a general if he were sent overseas. Another doctor told him he would probably miss. The end result of that exam was a report that stating that he was confined to continental limits and that he was only eligible for corps area service command or War Department overhead.[35] After a few months, Reagan received an order transferring him to Army Air Force Intelligence, Los Angeles, California. The Intelligence unit was established by General Hap Arnold to make Air Force training films and documentaries, train camera crews and accompany planes on combat missions. The unit took over the Hal Roach Film Studio in Culver City along with a nearby school that had been closed down. The post became known as Fort Roach. One of the greater achievements Reagan was part of at Fort Roach was the development of a new method for briefing pilots and bombardiers before their bombing missions. The ancient method of briefing consisted of an officer standing with a pointer in front of a map of the target to be bombed. The new method, concocted on a studio soundstage with a moveable camera hovering over constructed replicas of Tokyo, gave pilots a more authentic feel of the experience, and more importantly, mimicked some sense of a visual that was much more realistic than some confusing map. It is tempting on that note to consider the Fort Roach films as a rather primitive stage of virtual reality.

One of the more indelible experiences for Reagan during his time at Fort Roach was being privy to the atrocities of Nazism before the news broke to the rest of the country as to what had been taking place. During the last months of the war, the unit began getting secret Signal Corps films showing the liberation of Hitler's concentration camps, and Reagan was among the very first Americans to view the horrific images.

After the war, Reagan found himself back in Hollywood where he gradually became involved with contract negotiations and other activities for the Screen Actors Guild. This period was something of a political transformation and personal journey of discovery for Reagan prompted by what he felt was subversion and deceit that would leave him with a growing dislike of "big government."[36] When the war ended, he was still a New Dealer. He believed government could solve all the post-war problems just as it had ended the Depression and won the war. He didn't trust big business. He believed government and not private companies should own the big public utilities. He believed government should build housing to shelter the homeless, and that socialized medicine was the answer to better medical care. Like many people from his generation, he came out of the Depression and war expecting a better and much more egalitarian world.

In the post-war years, Reagan began seeing what he believed to be a rise in fascism in America. He saw racism beginning to reappear after four or five years of blacks and whites fighting side by side and scores of veterans groups popping up around the country attempting to sell the same kind of bigotry that America had just fought against and defeated. As the Hollywood star observed, in Hollywood if you didn't sing or dance, you ended up as an after-dinner speaker at events. So he began speaking out against the rise of neo-fascism and joining organizations like the United World Federalists and American Veterans Committee.

One of the turning points came on a day when he was speaking to the men's club at the Hollywood Beverly Christian Church where he worshipped. The pastor walked up to him after the speech and said he agreed with everything he had spoken about regarding neo-fascism, but that he should also be speaking out against the rise of communism in America...something Reagan had never even thought about. Soon after, he was speaking in front of a local citizen's organization. He had given some thought about what the pastor said, and wanted to establish his realization that he'd oppose any rising threat to American values. His usual speech defending American values against neo-fascism received applause after nearly every paragraph. When he got to the end, he told the audience that although he had done a lot of talking about post-war fascism, he was beginning to become suspicious of another ism...communism, and that he would continue to speak out against it just as much as he had against fascism.[37]

The room was silent.

Ronald Reagan walked off the stage.

No applause.

Days later, he got a letter from a woman who had been in the audience. She was disturbed by everyone's reaction to the last paragraph of his speech when he mentioned communism. There was a significance in their response, she believed, and what it meant was that the group had become a front for communists. She wanted Reagan to know she saw through it and that she resigned from the organization the next day.[38]

The decades of Reagan as liberal are pockmarked with the Red Scare and the formation in Congress in 1938 of the House Un-American Activities Committee, which served as a vehicle to expose supposed communist treason and ruin as many American lives as possible. The perceived communist threats grew in the paranoid conservative mind partly in reaction to President Roosevelt's New Deal. The committee not only took aim at communism, but liberalism, which to some conservatives became synonymous with anything "un-American." Liberals were equated as communists, atheists, radical, unpatriotic and immoral with ties to Moscow. Within a decade, the target became Hollywood because as conservatives would have the world believe, Hollywood was made up of a bunch of degenerate liberal communists who put Karl Marx above Jesus Christ, and the future of Western Civilization was at stake. Liberals were investigated as HUAC conducted hearings on communism in the film industry resulting in a blacklist of actors. The Red Scare had conservatives so frightened, that their fear and personal hatred overtook any sense of logic and rational thought that they may have had…and consequently, any sense of moral and ethical decency…shortcomings embodied by their alcoholic babbling ringleader, Senator Joseph McCarthy.

It is often said that the solution to a problem could potentially become the next problem. Such was the case with the atomic bomb, along with the secret technology that wasn't very secret by any measure. The bomb may have gotten the United States out of a ground war where a million lives could have been lost, but it simultaneously announced a cross-generational paranoia that America hasn't gotten over and probably never will. Whether postwar Russian aggression in Eastern Europe was the result of fear going back to Peter the Great or in the ideological imperatives of Marx or Engels, the U.S. interpreted it as a Soviet Communist agenda for world conquest. Some attributed McCarthyism to a bitter Republican-fueled conspiracy stemming from their bitterness over not being in power for 20 years. Others saw it as just another symptom of a kind of nationalism that always singled out threats to the status quo as something radical, foreign or un-American. Episodes like the Haymarket Riot, trial of Sacco and Vanzetti, Palmer Raids and the persecution of the International Workers of the World union were just a few examples of precursors that ultimately resulted in HUAC.[39] Wherever the origin lay for the political right in America, Reagan began an obsession with communism that would last well into his presidency over 40 years later.

As Reagan was getting into bed one night, there was a knock at the front door. He opened the door to find two FBI agents. He invited them in but questioned what he could possibly know that they didn't know already. One of the agents reminded Reagan that anyone who the communists hated as much as they hated him would probably know things that could help the FBI. They then informed him that he had come up in conversation during the meeting of the American Communist Party in downtown Los Angeles where somebody wondered out loud what the hell they were going to do about Reagan amidst some expletive adjectives preceding his name.[40] FBI investigations concluded that communists wanted to take control of Hollywood and influence the content of films by way of actors and writers who were members of the party.[41]

With FBI infiltration into the party, they asked Reagan to periodically meet to discuss the goings-on in Hollywood, to which he complied. Yet, in the long run, as a representative of the Screen Actors Guild, he opposed the blacklisting that merely amounted to a witch hunt. Speculation that he had been an informant has continued over the decades, citing his FBI file that went all the way back to the age of 32 when he reported almost having punched a man at a Hollywood party for making racist remarks toward Jewish people. The FBI, at the time, was on the heels of domestic Nazis, so it is ironic that their contact with Reagan was initially over the opposite side of the political spectrum. If Reagan did cooperate with the FBI regarding communists in Hollywood, there is no solid evidence that he threw friends or confidants under the bus, and it is more likely that he didn't say much more than what he was already saying in public. Ironically, the manner in which Reagan became close with Nancy Davis is almost farcical with respect to this part of history. Davis, the actress was mistaken for another Nancy Davis who was indeed a communist. When the actress found herself on the blacklist, she appealed to Reagan to help her out and clear up the misunderstanding. The two fell in love in the process.

Ultimately, Reagan did not believe that communists had any impact, influence or even infiltration in Hollywood. Testifying as SAG President in front of HUAC, he made it clear that their propaganda had already been exposed and they had been prevented from establishing any real presence. He believed they should be recognized as a political party, but regarding outlawing communists based on political ideology, he stressed that such a decision should be determined by the government. As a citizen however, he would hesitate to see any party outlawed because of its ideology.[42]

McCarthyism violated the core values and principles of American life and undermined the verticality of our national character. It used unethical and unconstitutional means to destroy careers and entire lives. In short, the biggest and possibly only contributing entity toward un-American activity was the House Un-American Activities Committee itself. And much in the atrocious fashion of the despicable parts of America's past, such as the slaughter of Native Americans and the institution of slavery, Joseph McCarthy became an embarrassing stain on American history.

4

STOP SCARING THE HELL OUT OF PEOPLE

When renowned maverick neurosurgeon Dr. Loyal Davis died of congestive heart failure in Scottsdale Memorial Hospital on August 19, 1982, his step-daughter, Nancy Reagan, who had been the First Lady of the United States for just over a year and a half, was at his bedside. President Ronald Reagan flew out to nearby Phoenix, Arizona for the funeral of a man who was not only his father-in-law, but probably the person who most influenced his political shift. Davis married Nancy's mother, Edith Luckett, in 1929. It was Edith's second marriage, the first being to Kenneth Robbins of Pittsfield, Massachusetts, ending in divorce. Loyal Davis adopted Nancy Robbins when she was 17, shortly after the marriage and moved the family from New York to Chicago with Nancy changing her name to Davis. Her new stepfather served as Chairman of the Department of Surgery at Northwestern University Medical School where he retired in 1963. He was a staunch conservative and was just as outspoken on politics as he was on his profession, and by all accounts was the greatest firsthand influence in steering both Nancy and her husband toward the Republican Party.

Ronald Reagan and Loyal Davis had a mutual admiration and respect for each other, though Davis was obviously the elder statesmen in a relationship that saw years of dialogue and debate between the two. Davis, an atheist, was not convinced of God in any conversation he might have had with Ronald Reagan, so while he may have helped convert the former liberal to conservatism, they still disagreed on the spiritual.

Let us be clear.

Loyal Davis did not solely turn Ronald Reagan to the opposite party. It was not some big *Darth Vader imploring Luke Skywalker to the Dark Side* moment as some might imagine. The many conversations between the two, however, accompanied a gradual gravitation to the right provoked by the reasons laid out in these chapters, and were indeed a turning point.

Another turning point came in 1960 when Reagan found himself supporting Richard Nixon against John F. Kennedy and he became self-conscious of the fact that he was still a Democrat even though he had not identified with the platform in several years. The more he found government to be the problem instead of the solution, the more his party affiliation bothered him, although Nixon advised him to show his support as a Democrat because it would demonstrate just how opposed to the platform he had become, and it would underscore the idea that Nixon was the better candidate. The full transition to the Republican Party came officially if not more symbolically through what became known simply as "the speech" in 1964 when he was asked to be co-chairman of the Goldwater campaign in California. Reagan had met Barry Goldwater a few years earlier at the home of Nancy's parents who were then living in Phoenix. Reagan spoke at many fundraisers throughout the summer and fall of 1964, but "the speech" happened at the Coconut Grove, a nightclub in the Ambassador Hotel in Los Angeles in front of around 800 Republicans. He gave the same talk he had been giving for years, recounting the expansion of the federal government and bureaucracy taking control of American business. He took aim at liberal Democrats who he felt were taking the country toward socialism, citing examples of his idea of government waste and what it was costing taxpayers. America was at a crossroads, he believed. People had a choice to reclaim their country or continue down the road to their liberties being taken from them. It was the same speech he had given in different variations in the past, and would continue to for a very long time, as would conservatives who to this day loosely throw around words like *liberty* and *freedom*. But in 1964, he was on to something new.

As the Coconut Grove cleared out following Reagan's speech, he was met by a small group of California's biggest campaign contributors who asked him to repeat the speech on national television if they could raise the money for the airtime. Reagan agreed, and the money was raised within a few days to buy a half hour on NBC one week before the election. The Goldwater camp catching wind of this became concerned with some of the content in Reagan's speech and wanted the purchased airtime to be used instead for a video of a meeting between their candidate and Dwight Eisenhower at Gettysburg. Some advisors to Goldwater were afraid Reagan's speech would backfire on their effort because of references to problems with the Social Security system. While Reagan had become notorious for criticizing communism and socialism, it was precisely socialist programs implemented by FDR such as Social Security that older voters had come to be dependent on, and it was an issue near and dear to their hearts. In short, Reagan scared them. In an era of America when across-the-board modernization had already been etched in stone and a thriving middle class owed its very existence to the socialist programs of the New Deal, Reagan seemed to want to move backwards in the face of progress. This was the same sentiment Democrats had spent a year claiming for Goldwater...that he wanted to do away with Social Security, while Goldwater spent the entire time denying it. Reagan could reopen the festering fears of retirement angst among the living and that alone scared them. But Goldwater couldn't disagree more with his advisors and gave his blessing for NBC to run the speech. There was something much larger happening. In that respect, Goldwater inadvertently became a somewhat pioneering figure in that he helped attract a new generation of conservative activists that assured the inevitable stamping out of the moderate wing of the Republican Party.

And so, on the night of October 27, 1964, the speech that changed Ronald Reagan's life, and for better or worse, the history of the United States… and to some degree, the world, began with an ideological change of heart and mind, and a simple twist of fate. A lifelong liberal who voted for FDR four times stood in front of a room full of conservatives who vaguely remembered his name as an actor, and if anything, were more familiar with him as the General Electric Theater guy.

"I have spent most of my life as a Democrat," he told them. "I recently have seen fit to follow another course…"[43]

In the year following "the speech," Reagan was coming under a lot of pressure to run for Governor of California. Most men he knew were already approaching retirement and the last thing he wanted in his mid-fifties was to begin a new career. Loyal Davis told him he'd be crazy to run for office. Davis had seen the dark and shady side of politics in Chicago. He told his son-in-law there was no way someone could go into politics without sacrificing those vital traits that accented conviction and dignity…honesty and honor. Political life entailed compromise and going into areas that no matter how well-intended you were, you ended up in anyway.[44] Inevitably, it happened. Political consultant, Stuart Spencer knew Reagan was serious about running for office when he decided to make multiple stops across the state by airplane despite his dislike of airplanes. The California gubernatorial race of 1966 did indeed see Reagan running against Governor Pat Brown. Entering the campaign, it was no secret that he disliked government and did not want to be called a politician, and instead referred to himself as a citizen politician. His lack of experience in public office was seen as a weakness to his opponents who made an issue out of it. Brown taunted him as a *citizen pilot* who told passengers they should trust him in the pilot seat even though he's never flown an airplane before and that his desire to fly the plane would make up for his inexperience. With regard to his opposition on the left, it didn't take very long for Reagan to be demonized as an extremist who could potentially do damage to the basic institutions of California government. It didn't help that he had the endorsement of the John Birch Society.

Reagan shared the common belief with the Birch Society that communism was the greatest threat to American freedom. Comparable to the short-lived Tea Party that arose in knee-jerk hostile response to the election of Barack Obama, America's first black President, in 2008, the Birchers were considered the lunatic fringe of the right, but much like the Tea Party, also got representatives elected in Washington…the only real difference between the two being communism and socialism as the root of their respective paranoia. Although Reagan identified with the core sentiments of the Birchers, he did not share their exaggerated belief that communism had penetrated American government as well as democracy itself, and was spreading like a dangerous bacteria. Even Reagan knew the communist threat had been greatly exaggerated going straight back to the witch hunts. Still, communism remained in his vocabulary throughout his entire public life.

When Reagan won the 1966 election, he celebrated with Nancy and three of their four children, Maureen, Michael and Ron. When the new governor phoned Patti in Arizona to tell her that he won, she began to cry. At 14, Patti was an anti-establishment child of the sixties and didn't like having a member of that establishment in the family.[45] The anti-establishment rhetoric, as Reagan referred to it, wasn't exclusive to just Patti in the Reagan family. Ron, whose becoming a ballet dancer prompted the media to wrongly assume the family's disappointment and embarrassment, was one whose childhood was marked with frequent roughhousing, playful boxing with his father, playing football, climbing trees, building tree houses, pelting his father with snowballs in front of a swarm of media cameras and shooting toy rifles. Seeming more like his stepbrother, Michael in this respect, it was probably more surprising a few years later when Ron at 12, began his own era of rebellion by imposing on his parents his newfound heresy. After years of suiting up in his Sunday clothes for church, he told his father he wasn't going anymore. Ron had concluded that the deity they worshipped was nothing more than fiction and a figment of their imaginations…a school of opposing lessons teaching the contradictions between the Old and New Testaments that never seemed to be questioned but were accepted as truth. Reagan let his son know in a subtle glance that he wasn't happy about his decision, but did not force him to go to church.[46]

Reagan's discomfort and distress over the negative views of his loved ones on Jesus Christ was no secret, nor did he ever attempt to hide it. In fact, Ron who later stressed that physical violence toward the kids was not in the Reagan DNA and that his father never hit him or his siblings, only witnessed him react semi-violently once, as he recalled an argument in the car between his father and a teenage Patti, who suddenly reacted with "Jesus Christ, Dad," prompting Ronald Reagan to lightly strike Patti, slapping the side of her face, almost sweeping her left cheek with his fingertips, telling her sternly not to take the Lord's name in vain. It was the one and only time he had ever witnessed his father do anything remotely like it, and it was a gentle brush of the cheek in order to defend Jesus.[47] One wonders had Reagan's brief encounter with John Lennon in the bowels of L.A. Coliseum gone on a little longer, if the former governor would have gotten around to chastising the former Beatle for claiming his band was bigger than Jesus.

In 1968, Governor Reagan went to bat for another California politician who couldn't seem to get a break. Not only had Richard Nixon lost the Presidential election to John F. Kennedy in 1960, he lost the California gubernatorial race to Pat Brown. As Reagan campaigned for Nixon on the candidate's second run for the presidency, it became clear through the applause and response of the crowd that conservatives really wanted him instead. Nixon didn't draw half the enthusiasm that he did. Reagan fed off this knowledge, and it would make him bolder in his future endeavors. He had clearly become California's favorite Republican, and he began to view himself as his party's chosen one…the one who was going to take the country where they felt it needed to go. Although Nixon was the Republican candidate for President in 1968, Reagan gave speeches as if he himself were running. He took aim at the left, bitterly denouncing their right to protest the now-unpopular war, scorning their agenda of social progress while dismissing the idea of Democratic candidate Robert F. Kennedy as a symbol of hope along with past figures John F. Kennedy and Martin Luther King, whose possibilities for future progress were cut short by assassinations. He spoke about civilization not being able to afford prophets shouting about the road to the Promised Land amidst burned out looted cities destroyed in riots. He spoke bitterly about politicians who wanted Social Security to be tripled without any plans of how to pay for it. *How are you going to pay for it* became one of several hypocritical mantras of the right which only could seem to muster up money for the war machine and feeding the rich. He ridiculed those in Washington as if to say *how dare they propose to divert money away from the war in order to pay for work programs in city slums*. Civilization could not afford these things…youth not honoring the draft or black people not obeying the law. All of these things pointed toward the Apocalypse.[48]

    Reagan, actor that he was, had little problem addressing social spending, the funding of which became some taboo subject and elusive mystery for the hawks on the right. Yet, he could say with a straight face that the war machine needed to grow even bigger. When Robert F. Kennedy became the next assassination, the prospect of ending the war, along with welcoming in a more equitable era was no longer a threat to the conservative agenda. America instead got Richard Nixon.

Justifiably understandable on some issues and enigmatically hypocritical on others, the about-face in Reagan's politics, just as with the ability to fully understand the core of his personality, still can elude us. The fully-formed Reagan that most of America came to know as a president was measured, poetic, soft-spoken, told jokes and he smiled quite often. Reagan in his formative years following his departure from the compassion of liberal values often seemed an angry, scowling, finger-pointing aggressor that resented youth and the inevitable social changes taking place. This to a large degree did in fact work against him during the 1976 presidential election when he was considered too extreme by many within his own party. The case may have been the same in 1980 had it not been for the dire set of circumstances presided over by the Carter Administration along with the inevitable shift further to the right among Reagan's constituencies…among them, the influence of economists and the so-called Moral Majority. Still, it was the left that was most afraid of him. Yet, among all of the fear and criticism, the left also underestimated him, constantly making him out to be a sinister figure, when most who dealt with him found a pleasant and personable character…human dimensions that the left failed to notice or else just attributed to acting.

What was it though that made him so compelling?

May it not be for the direction of some insiders, he may not have put on a friendly face and displayed that natural charm to the American public. At the outset of the 1980 campaign, he was told to soften his rhetoric in order to appeal to voters outside the conservative realm of thought. John Sears who had a great deal of influence over the early part of the campaign insisted on Reagan becoming the candidate to bring party unity. Richard Allen, hardliner that he was, told Reagan he had to stop "scaring the hell out of people."[49]

Several components are without question key to his allure…first and foremost, as is always mentioned, his undeniable charismatic personality as a communicator. His delivery and timing was everything, and it made all the difference. He honed this perfection through his years as a sports announcer, and of course as an actor. He once disclosed a secret so central to his career that it may be as close as we come to truly understanding how he operates, and although it appears simple and unassuming on the surface, it was nonetheless profound and telling when he revealed that the secret of announcing is to make reading sound like talking.[50] But then there were the words. The words he spoke reached deep-seated places within that angry populist sentiment, but with eloquence, intelligence, poetry and humor. This obviously means he had great speechwriters. His speeches were loaded with the use of parables and quotations from the Bible as well as philosophers and poets. Through those speeches, Reagan changed the relationship between religion and politics in America. He frequently mentioned his trust in God and used the word God twice as much as every President before him. The writing was rich, the language magnetic and his delivery unparalleled.

Although on the surface he was an optimist, he also saw what he believed to be evil in some things and never hesitated to call it out. It could be communism or it could be American government. The latter spoke to his redefining of populism to fit his narrative that government was something bad. Traditional populism railed against big business, banks, railroads and anything that could fit under the greed of the rich screwing the little guy. With Reagan's brand of populism, the government and the tax system were the problem. *Those who made the most and had the most should contribute the most* did not sit well with him and he interpreted it as punishment for success. Reagan would later say while addressing the nation for the first time as President, "Those who do work are denied a fair return for their labor by a tax system which penalizes successful achievement and keeps us from maintaining full productivity...For decades we have piled deficit upon deficit, mortgaging our future and our children's future for the temporary convenience of the present. We the people, this breed called Americans...special among the nations of the Earth...And as we renew ourselves here in our own land, we will be seen as having greater strength throughout the world. We will again be the exemplar of freedom and a beacon of hope for those who do not now have freedom."[51] It was that sentiment conservatives called a revolution. Reagan called it a restoration. He had a belief in American exceptionalism where the ideals on which America was founded were necessary for the protection of democracy and peace in the rest of the world. This kind of sentiment certainly had its opponents and would periodically get the United States into trouble.

Reagan's candidacy couldn't have come at a better time for Republicans, even if it ran contrary to the very foundation of his beliefs. But that is a common issue for conservatives who run for office and often get charged with a certain amount of hypocrisy when they enter any race. They exert enormous amounts of time and energy telling America that government is the problem, and then they ask voters to elect them so they can be part of the government. The question of the size of government which inevitably became an obsession for Republicans well into the next century began with Reagan. He'd remark on how since the beginning of the century, America's gross national product increased by 33 times with the cost of federal government increasing 234 times. With the workforce only one and a half times larger, federal employees were numbering nine times as many.[52] With Reagan asking to become part of something he saw as the problem, it recalls that same saying as earlier about the solution to a problem becoming the next problem. Regardless, the timing of Reagan's announcement on that November night in 1979 was impeccable. He was four years older than he was when he ran for the nomination against Ford, and even then, he was considered too old to be president. He refused to make age a factor publicly, but even Reagan knew he was getting up there in age in 1976, and with a sense of personal urgency decided it was time to run, even if it was against a sitting president of his own party. For Reagan, it may have been the right campaign in the sense of having a significant percentage of the country that supported his brand of conservatism. It just wasn't a big enough percentage, nor was it the right time. It wasn't unlike his explanation of what happened with

Goldwater in 1964, even after he had wowed the Goldwater crowd. The only difference with the voters between 1964 and 1976, Reagan believed, was that they were still in somewhat of a New Deal mode where they thought federal programs solved problems and were actually free.[53] Again, these issues were always a matter of interpretation on both sides of the aisle, but from the right side, *How are we going to pay for it?* never applied to the war machine or Wall Street. In addition, 1976 also saw the setbacks that come along with running a same-party race against someone who is already in the White House. A president gets round-the-clock media attention and takes top priority without having to pay for airtime. They also retain the loyalty of the majority of their party. Interestingly enough, the Ford campaign also succeeded in portraying Reagan as too conservative and too far to the right. The deceptive brand of traditionalism that would be painted and welcomed as "Morning in America" nearly a decade later was not as appealing. Reagan did appeal to the extreme nature of the fringes on the right, but it was not enough to take the entire Republican Party. Needless to say, many in the GOP didn't look at Reagan very fondly in 1976, finding his campaign against Ford to be insurrectionary. But nonetheless, the real story in Bicentennial America was that the nation was still much too close to the stink of the entire Nixonian experience, and even Ford was part of that stink.

Although it is often suggested that Reagan had many acquaintances but no friends, a few choice people are characterized as close friends with him. "Close" of course being open to interpretation in relation to his distant personality. Paul Laxalt, a Nevada senator was considered a friend though, who would serve as national chairman of Reagan's presidential campaigns in 1976, 1980 and 1984. Their relationship had its roots in the late Sixties and early Seventies, as the two corresponded and worked together on Lake

Tahoe and western issues as governors of their respective states of Nevada and California.

Laxalt had his finger on the pulse of the GOP. He knew Reagan's prospects for 1980 as early as 1976 when he'd receive letters from constituents saying they wouldn't vote for Ford under any circumstances if he got the Republican nod, and would write in Reagan's name instead. By 1978 though, Laxalt was also getting letters from other senators who sought his support, perhaps trying to secure him before Reagan announced his candidacy. That announcement was still a year away, but Reagan still led in the hypothetical polls. One of the notes he received was from Bob Dole of Kansas who informed him of his plans to run. Dole was aware of Laxalt's commitment to Reagan's candidacy, but was requesting to meet with him anyway to discuss his own campaign. Laxalt told him he wouldn't mind keeping in touch, but also re-established his commitment to Reagan.

"Good luck, but not too much," he wrote to Dole.[54]

Among all of the friends, acquaintances, colleagues, staff and supporters that surrounded Reagan during his political life, the one person who was perhaps closest to him in any capacity, aside from Nancy, was Michael Deaver. When it comes down to it, Deaver held the most influence and sway over Ronald Reagan than anybody during his years in political office. Not only did he have Reagan's trust, respect and admiration, but he became a friend of the family and was adored by Nancy who held him close as a confidant of sorts on matters concerning her husband's political career. In short, in a world of politics where facades, mistrust and deception are common, Nancy Reagan and Michael Deaver established a genuine friendship.

Deaver was a California native who graduated from San Jose State College with a Bachelor's in political science. After spending some time working for IBM, he began working in Santa Clara County as the executive director of the Republican Party. Naturally, he supported Goldwater in 1964, but learned a hard lesson upon the candidate's loss, as he recounted in 2002. "Always being a pragmatist, when I woke up the morning of the Goldwater election and realized that we carried five, six states, or whatever it was, I decided I was never going to do that again. I wanted to win elections. We had four or five Goldwater organizations that wouldn't speak to each other in California. It was just terrible, and the whole Goldwater organization, you talk about right wing. These were scary people, when I look back on it now. It was the John Birch Society, and it was get us out of the U.N., and don't let them fluoridate our water, and all that kind of stuff. Those were the people who were involved in it. So I just didn't want to have anything more to do with that."[55]

Deaver continued running assembly races trying to get back control of the lower house in California. He briefly supported George Christopher in the 1966 race for governor. Christopher had been the mayor of San Francisco, and quite possibly the last Republican to hold such a position in the city for the rest of eternity. Upon Reagan's victory, Deaver was called by Reagan's campaign manager, Stu Spencer to go up to Sacramento and work on the transition. At the outset, he spent some time as assistant cabinet secretary under William Clark, but through the upheaval of a staff shakeup, Clark found himself much closer to dealing firsthand with the first couple of California. "Clark really was a novice when it came to politics," Deaver said in 2002. "He didn't want to have anything to do with that, and I think he was a little uncomfortable around Nancy Reagan and didn't want to have anything to do with *that*. So he told me that he wanted me to take care of the political liaison as well as what I had to do in the Governor's office, which was the administration of the office. I did the administration and also ended up supervising the Governor's schedule and his personal staff. That then would put me in touch with Nancy Reagan."[56]

Deaver and his wife Carolyn lived just four blocks from the Reagan's in East Sacramento. The two couples developed a personal as well as a professional relationship during the governor's first term. Reagan became a much sought-after figure within the Republican Party, and was always traveling around the country to speak on behalf of congressional candidates at fundraisers. This required Deaver to travel with the Reagan's. "It was a very small organization, five of us, maybe, traveling, and many times it was two of us. It would be me and Governor Reagan. You know, when you travel that way with somebody, over and over and over again, you sit next to each other in an airplane, you talk about yourself, you talk about your family, you get to know each other. That's pretty much the way it was, and the same was true with Nancy."[57] Deaver was one of the few people whose view really mattered to Reagan, and possibly the only person aside from Nancy who he trusted enough to allow persuade him one way or the other on any given matter.

By January 1979, Reagan was far ahead of the crowded horde of GOP contenders. Some 40 percent favored him over Ford who followed behind with 24 percent. Senate Minority Leader, Howard Baker of Tennessee held nine percent, and former Texas governor, John Connelly, four percent. In the spring, Senator Robert Dole and former CIA Director, George H.W. Bush were two more names that entered the mix. Still, Reagan remained the frontrunner by far. In March, he announced the formation of an exploratory committee with him and John Sears as chairman and executive vice chairman. Sears, who would be Reagan's chief strategist, hinted that he would work for Senator Howard Baker unless he was put in charge. Jim Lake would be press secretary and Charlie Black in charge of field operations. Lake was one of three men who rose to prominence out of Bakersfield, Virginia who all had close ties to Reagan and ended up around the candidate in 1980. Lake along with Deaver and Lyn Nofziger's journeys took them all from Bakersfield to Sacramento and ultimately to Washington. Nofziger and Lake respectively served as press secretary to Reagan…Nofziger in 1966 and Lake in 1976. Black, a lobbyist and consultant who played a role in just about every Republican presidential campaign going back to Nixon would become a rich and influential figure during the Reagan Eighties with the 1980 foundation of his lobbying firm and ad placement agency with two young operatives whose names would later become synonymous with corruption, Roger Stone and Paul Manafort. Economist, Martin Anderson was taken on as chief policy advisor. The Reagan team also courted James Baker, but his commitment to George Bush was already in stone.

The only person the Reagan team was worried about was Jack Kemp, who at 44 was the champion of the "supply side" movement and former Buffalo Bills player. While Reagan may have made far too much of the supposed communist threat, it has been suggested in the face of all the alarmism that the United States will never be a communist country for the simple reason that Americans love football too much. And where the National Football League exists, capitalism will always prevail. If anyone could possibly steal the spotlight away from Reagan in terms of popularity among Americans as well as conservative credibility within the GOP establishment, it was thought to be Kemp. But Sears cut a deal with Kemp, promising to make him Reagan's campaign chairman if he didn't run in 1980. Paul Laxalt, who was already campaign chairman protested, went to Reagan, and Reagan backed the idea of Kemp.

It is questionable whether or not Jack Kemp would have run for president in 1980, and it is believed in many circles that his real goal was to be Reagan's running mate, neither of which ever happened.

On November 17, 1979, the revolutionaries in Iran announced that 16 Americans would be released. One day later, Khomeini made a statement suggesting that the remainder of the hostages would be put on trial. Carter responded making sure Khomeini received word that any trial, injury or death of a single American hostage would be met with direct retaliation against Iran. On Thanksgiving, just nine days after the announcement, the first in a series of little dramas that would turn the Reagan campaign into a soap opera occurred in the candidate's house. Mike Deaver arrived where he saw

Reagan, Lake and Black talking in the living room. Before he could enter to join them, Nancy stopped him and asked if he could wait in the bedroom. Deaver had been privy to everything for the past 12 years, so although it made no sense why he had to wait in the bedroom, he complied. After he felt he waited long enough, he walked out and into the living room where he asked what was going on. Reagan informed him what Lake and Black had just been telling him. The campaign was losing suspicious amounts of money. Where the total cost of operations including everything from secretaries to limousines should have run between five to ten thousand dollars a month, Reagan's office space alone was costing $30,000. The gist of what the presidential candidate was told by Lake and Black was that Deaver had been ripping him off. Deaver was knocked for a loop and almost speechless upon hearing the accusations, especially coming out of Reagan's mouth. Reagan insisted that's not what he was saying, although it was tough to get that point across to Deaver as he abruptly walked out of the room and left the house. His resignation came next as did Anderson's who seemed to know what was really going on. Nancy appeared to know something as well, or at least she had a hunch. She was furious over what they did to her friend and she directly blamed John Sears, who was described at the time as the Machiavelli of Republican politics. As the decade turned over, there would be a sense of starting from scratch within the Reagan team...more than once.

On a chilly Thursday evening in mid-December, President Carter stood on the White House Ellipse next to First Lady, Rosalynn Carter and their daughter for the annual National Christmas Pageant of Peace and Tree Lighting, which had in anticipation carried a bittersweet sentiment in a holiday season marked more by somberness than celebration. Breaking with tradition, the Carters turned lights on for fifty tiny trees, each representing one of the American hostages. In another break with tradition, 1979's tree would be completely dark except for the star of hope at the top. One star, one light… and in a powerful gesture, the rest of the nation's tree would remain unlit until the hostages came home. This was the president's message in solidarity with the American people at home and certainly those in captivity. In daylight, the silver garland and white balls gave the tree a festive unsuspecting appearance, which made the audience all the more surprised when 12-year old Amy Carter threw the switch onto one shining star engulfed in darkness.

5

STARTING OVER

Just before the holidays at the end of 1979, John Lennon stopped shaving and grew the last beard he'd ever grow. He'd keep the beard until the end of March when he'd shave it after a ten-day vow of silence. The vow of silence came at Yoko's insistence and was John testing himself as he continued on an ever-present quest for something seemingly unattainable...the discipline and willpower he yearned for. It was a struggle as he bounced on and off his spiritual path across the span of his adult life...at least since sitting in a lotus position next to the Maharishi 12 years earlier. In the face of it all, he never denied his humanity. If anything, he wore it on his sleeve perhaps more so than any of the Beatles. He was human, fragile, susceptible and vulnerable...a walking spectacle of comedic wit on some days, while on other days an exposed and festering raw nerve. Yoko wasn't any less impulsive and reckless, but she maintained an exterior of somebody who was extremely busy, disappearing for the majority of the day and often most of the night. If John was at all suspicious, he didn't make an issue out of it. It just became understood that Yoko was downstairs in the first floor office, known as Studio One, where she tended to the business of the Lennon name.

Yoko had come from Japanese royalty in an indirect vague historical sort of way, having a great grandfather, Atsushi Saisho, who was a descendant of a ninth century emperor and also served in the Imperial Household Council under Emperor Meiji. She had been rich twice in her life. First, coming from money, and then after her college years stubbornly not taking money from her parents while living the life of a struggling artist when she fell into the fortune of a Beatle. While her parents were more than well-to-do, they were not very supportive. Her father was a concert pianist who gave up his career to be a banker. Two profound memories of childhood had stuck with her... one of being sick in bed at the age of nine while a visiting doctor planted his mouth on hers and kissed her. When Yoko told her mother, the reaction she received was one of scorn as her mother suggested Yoko must have invited the doctor's advances. The other memory is of being alone in a public park with dozens of people around while she sat on a bench and dismantled a grapefruit one segment at a time, completely obliterating it.

The harshest critics of the Lennon's have insisted that at the very core, they were two empty miserable souls endlessly searching for material and superficial comforts to fill voids that had their roots in childhood, and were permanent because they were never properly dealt with, if at all. So while John went through LSD, meditation, Primal Scream therapy and a "lost weekend," nothing prevented him from being an unsatisfied mind with unlimited monetary resources, wandering aimlessly through the mazes of the Dakota on a daily basis with not a goddamn thing to do except wallow in his despair. It is true, his father walked out on him while he was a baby and his mother was killed in the street when he was just 16. Fame had come early, and he wasn't that far removed from the pain of his teen years when Beatlemania was happening. It's easy to be reminded of one of the more recent clichés, "life happens," thus making it difficult to stay in touch with once-important ideas, plans and concerns before we realize that the core of what really made an impact on our life ended up filling much of what turned out to indeed be a void. In the case of John, the Beatles happened. And it happened fast. It happened so fast that by the time he actually got a chance to exhale from the entire experience and survey with any real clarity what had taken place, a full decade had almost passed. In addition to his own state of mental health, he became more and more preoccupied with death, first with Yoko's due to the simple fact that she was older. Then to a greater extent his own, as he worried about what would happen to her and Sean. One time, she heard him muttering about dying and the bastards who were going to throw her and Sean out on the street and how he didn't know what to do about it.[58] So in November 1979, John made up a will, appointing Sam Green as Sean's guardian in the event Yoko died first. Green, a known figure in the art world went back a few decades with the couple, initially with Yoko who was far more active back then as an artist in her days before John.

The music world had changed immeasurably since John walked away. Still, the rumors of a Beatles reunion were always a constant. At the tail end of 1979, Paul McCartney organized a series of four benefit shows under the name Concerts for Kampuchea to be held in London in late December. This coincided with a relief program announced by the United Nations for victims of Pol Pot's regime in Cambodia which began in 1975. The bill at the Hammersmith Odeon included Wings, The Who, Queen, The Clash, Elvis Costello and a brand new band called The Pretenders. And yet, media focus was not on the tragic and unspeakable genocide in Cambodia, nor was it on the impeccable concert lineup. Instead, speculation was on whether or not other ex-Beatles would show up to join Paul onstage. It certainly wouldn't be John.

John wasn't the only one struggling. Yoko was battling heroin addiction in the early months of 1980. Both she and John dealt with the addiction earlier in their relationship. John had kicked it. Yoko had been back and forth, once actually going through a period of relapse and then quitting again cold turkey without John ever knowing. This time, she was attempting to get him out of the Dakota as much as possible, sending him and Sean out on little excursions here and there. Occasionally, John spent time with Sean out on Long Island while Yoko frequently cut out to Sam Green's house on Fire Island in the hopes of getting clean. At one point, she sent John and Sean away for a few days until she recovered from the "flu" that she was suffering from. John's journals testify to these outings as Yoko was getting over sickness. Accounts of this period of 1980 highlight that Yoko believed John had no idea she had relapsed and simply didn't want him or Sean to see her in such condition. The speculation with regard to Green over the decades has been that he and Yoko were having an affair that John was well aware of, but it was obviously nothing that she wanted to put out in front of John, so she sent him away. However much truth there is to that, the trajectory of this book is not concerned with Yoko's relationship to Sam Green, as it bears no consequence to the connections being examined, but let us simply acknowledge it to get it out of the way.

In the fifth year of John Lennon's hiatus, the artist had seriously taken to sailing and was spending a lot of time in his boat, the Isis, out on Cold Spring Harbor. A year earlier, he bought a Tudor-style house named Cannon Hill on Long Island's North Shore where he occasionally spent time. The warming months of early 1980 was a period of reading books on sailing and taking lessons from Tyler Coneys. Coneys owned the boat dealership where John got the Isis. Eventually, John took Sean out on the water as he became more relaxed with being in control of the boat. His interest in sailing went back to 1975 when Yoko was in the final months of pregnancy. During that period, he found a way to relax and de-stress by going on boat trips to Martha's Vineyard with friends like Richard Ross. On the flipside of that five-year period was John now initiating his own trips on Long Island Sound where he wasn't always alone in his celebrity.

STARTING OVER

"Where are you Billy Joel? I love your album!" John called out one day from his boat, referring to *Glass Houses*, Billy Joel's newest record.[59] Joel, like Bruce Springsteen, was 30, grew up on Lennon's music, and was of that one generation in the rock lineage that could boast of having seen The Beatles on the Ed Sullivan Show as part of their musical DNA. As it turned out, the Long Island resident had known one of his idols bought the house across the water. Yet, as much as he would have loved to have met him, he wanted more to respect John's privacy. Years later at an event, Joel met Yoko who told him how John had wanted to meet him too, but hesitated to go over and say hello for the very same reasons…*It's Billy Joel, we shouldn't bother him!*

As someone who grew up to the influences of Beatles records, Joel had done pretty well for himself, and at the time was sharing the pop charts with one of his other heroes, who just happened to be John's former partner. Paul McCartney's "Comin' Up" was also hot on the charts in the summer of 1980 when Joel's "It's Still Rock and Roll to Me" was the number one song. It was a stab at a dance track. Everyone had done one…the Stones, Rod Stewart, Heart, Kiss, Pink Floyd…And so "Comin' Up" became the closest example of a former Beatle's attempt at some sort of modern dance music, save for Paul's other disco-tinged "Goodnight Tonight" from two years earlier. The new decade was straddling both some stale remnant of the late Seventies as well as a push into melodic pop by way of synth-driven new wave, but not entirely avant-garde enough to keep it off the radio. So songs like "Cars" by Gary Numan could co-exist peacefully alongside Lipps' "Funky Town," Blondie's "Call Me," and Olivia Newton John's "Magic."

Pop culture entered a new dimension in television that summer with the advent of the cliffhanger as a vital and lucrative measure of attaining viewership. The concept was by no means anything new to TV. Shows like *Batman* often depended on them to get viewers back the next day for the second part of an episode, and primetime serials commonly held multi-part episodes that ended with the words "To Be Continued" flashing on the screen. The shock value of a cliffhanger's potential became fully realized when a CBS primetime show called *Dallas* ended its third season in March by having the main character shot in the final seconds. JR Ewing, an oil barren with a growing list of enemies could have been shot by any number of people, which made the initial shock of the shooting itself all the more compelling. It was the type of edge-of-your-seat anticipation that would usually leave the typical viewer waiting through the commercial break or returning the following day or week to see what happens next, but in this case, audiences would have to wait months until the next season began. The question "Who shot JR?" became part of the American lexicon in the summer of 1980. Shopping malls, beaches, boardwalks and any summer vacation spot with a souvenir shop sold iron-on t-shirts reading "I Shot JR" alongside the profiting of the Iranian hostage crisis in t-shirts that read "Bomb Iran" and "Ayatollah Assahola."

Hanging off cliffs wasn't just exclusive to the nighttime though. In the world of daytime television, *General Hospital* exploded deep into cliffhanger territory in the daily continuous saga of Luke and Laura. It was a budding and inevitable romance that had its seeds planted a year earlier, but it wasn't until the afternoon of Friday, July 11, 1980 when Kin Shriner punched Tony Geary off a yacht when the story escalated on a mathematical scale to the point of national phenomenon. Problems on yachts didn't only happen on television though.

Long Island Sound created the urge to go bigger and broader in John Lennon's sailing aspirations. After considerable discussion with Tyler Coneys, and Yoko's blessing, a yacht trip to Bermuda was arranged for early June. The expedition would consist of John and a small crew put together by Coneys. The plan was to fly Sean out to meet him once they got settled. Yoko wanted her psychics to select the yacht, but Coney's knowledge and experience far outweighed the usual influence of Mother. Coneys came up with a modern 43-foot vessel called the Megan Jaye. On board would be John, Tyler and his two cousins Kevin and Ellen, and the skipper, Hank Halstead, known as "Cap'n Hank."

The crew sailed out on June 4 from Newport, Rhode Island. Seas were calm and weather flawlessly sunny and clear for the first few days. It was a smooth and pleasant trip for the tiny group of five. John became the voyage cook, preparing healthy dishes of brown rice and vegetables. Much of his time was spent talking to Hank who himself had been in and around the music business during the 1960s working as a concert promoter. Over the radio, Paul McCartney's new song "Comin' Up" was heard by the crew numerous times, prompting John to seemingly awaken to thoughts of bewilderment toward his musical inactivity, wondering aloud what the hell he was doing sitting around when he should be writing songs. It wasn't that hard, after all.[60]

Then the weather changed.

The Bermuda Triangle is known for its mindfucks when it comes to its unpredictably changing atmosphere, like the violent storm that broke out rendering all three Coneys cousins seasick and useless to the safety of the crew. Hank, not having slept in sometime was also temporarily checked out, leaving John, 700 miles from home, to navigate through 25-foot waves and 65-mile per hour winds. It is quite easy to imagine the story of John Lennon ending there…his early death still part of the narrative, but only in the middle of the Atlantic rather than Manhattan. Hank woke up several hours later to find John steering the Megan Jaye through violent waters, screaming and cursing at the waves as they hit and washed up on the deck.

New assistant Fred Seaman, who Yoko hired in 1979, had also gone to Bermuda. Seaman, the nephew of Sean's nanny, Helen, spent a great deal of time around John doing odd jobs, running errands, fetching coffee, lunch, taking pictures and video and whatever John wanted or needed at any given moment throughout the day. In Bermuda, he gave John some mixed cassettes intended to turn him on to bands and artists like the Pretenders, Madness, the B-52s and Lena Lovich. Having been away from music meant he was *completely* away from music...not only checked-out as an artist, but as a listener. Of course, he heard the radio occasionally, but had stopped paying attention to what was new and hot at the time. In the B-52's, he immediately heard what he believed to be the influence of Yoko. The yelping vocal shrieks of "Rock Lobster" was exactly in his estimation what she had been doing in the Plastic Ono years...a vocal style she was ridiculed for. John called Yoko in New York. He asked if she had heard any of "this new wave stuff." He told her that she had been doing it for years.[61]

In retrospect, the period of Lennon's absence from music coincided with the beginnings of rock and roll having a legitimate and respected status amidst the establishment it once railed against. *Rolling Stone*, rock's universally-accepted gospel and collective voice of the counterculture, moved its headquarters out of its modest hippie-decorated location in San Francisco to the corporate world of New York City. Once a reflection of the revolution, the publication was now catering to and mixing with Hollywood and Washington D.C. elites. George Harrison had been to the White House on invitation to visit with Gerald Ford. Jimmy Carter quoted a Bob Dylan song in his inaugural speech. Dylan himself had discovered Jesus, and was literally preaching his way through concerts while wagging his finger at all the non-believers around him through condescending lyrics and between-song rants. They shouted for rock and roll. If they wanted rock and roll, they could go see Queen, he told them.[62] A few years earlier, critic, Dave Marsh ran an open letter to Lennon in *Rolling Stone*. With Elvis gone, the Sex Pistols making their mark, anarchists on the British charts and the White House having rock stars as visitors rather than trying to deport them, there was a gaping void that begged the presence or at least the commentary of Lennon. Marsh openly reminded him of these things. Critics and writers who prophesized with their pens tried the same shit with Dylan a decade earlier, not in the form of open letters, but similar questionable methods, and for their efforts they got albums like *Self Portrait* and songs like "Watching the River Flow." Now as the Seventies had turned into the Eighties, anyone who knew any better wasn't about to even attempt appealing to Dylan, as he was now the property of Jesus, preaching the Gospel. Dylan too, in his own way, was gone and he wasn't coming back. Lennon, they felt, was probably needed more than ever. What the world didn't know was that John had begun to write songs again. And not just a few scattered songs here and there. He was writing big...within the context of a larger whole.

A body of work.

An album.

Whether it was some natural evolution that spilled into full fruition from his dabbling with some half-hearted writing back in the spring, or if he was inspired by finally listening to some current music, or possibly even if he had the living shit scared out of him on the boat, John suddenly felt and knew it was time to break his creative silence. Given the large number of songs that flowed out of him so quickly, the former is more likely. It was a legitimate artistic creative outburst unlike something that would have been forced under the pressures of contractual obligations. Where it was coming from was real, sincere, authentic, and his heart was in it. John wanted to do this. He was going to record a new record.

The transition that saw Bruce Springsteen into the summer of 1980 was one of an arduous and daunting collection of months in the recording studio. In the weeks immediately following the M.U.S.E. concerts, he continued working on his next album. During those same weeks, Springsteen fans got their hands on the very first major biography of their rock and roll hero. As if being on the cover of *Time* and *Newsweek* simultaneously at the age of 25 wasn't noteworthy enough, having a biography about your life, work and impact by the age of 30 was not uncommon, but having it done by a major rock journalist was a credit. Dave Marsh's *Born to Run: The Bruce Springsteen Story* made the *New York Times* Best Seller list, marking the first time since recent Elvis Presley memoir books, that a book dealing with rock and roll made the list. After additional studio time, an album appeared to take shape as Springsteen selected ten tracks and arranged a sequence for them. By the last months of 1979, two reels containing the possible album were presented to CBS. The artist then had a brief photo shoot with *Darkness* photographer Frank Stefanko. Cover mockups were then made for the album, which would be called *The Ties That Bind*. For a brief few days, Bruce began to relax a little bit. Over a period of two consecutive nights, he joined the Beaver Brown Band onstage at the Fast Lane in Asbury Park. If he was ready to rest on it, the album would be finished. It was a major task, a follow-up to *Darkness* and its accompanying 1978 tour. Was he finished and ready to go public with his next artistic statement?

He didn't stay relaxed for very long.

Something was bothering him and it became clear.

He wasn't ready.

The reality of the new album coming out by late '79 dissipated when the entire project was suddenly scrapped.

Out the window.

So he too would start over.

Or perhaps keep going.

That was a year ago.

By the summer of 1980, he had accumulated and recorded four times the amount of music.

He later told Los Angeles Times journalist, Robert Hilburn that he felt the album wasn't personal enough. Later on, he would also complain in retrospect that it sounded too pop. It can be seen without a doubt where the album had an overall pop effect, sequencing "Cindy," "Hungry Heart" and "Be True" on the same side together. "You Can Look," although a fun little rocker that means well, did not work lodged between "The River" and "The

Price You Pay." The two surrounding songs are deeply personal and reflective, where "You Can Look" in its original rockabilly version sounds hollow, tinny and too light. And therein lies what the real problem may have been... the album was too light. It lacked intensity. The songs were indeed personal. But to have personal subject matter in the form of a single album of three and a half minute pop songs was not enough...especially with the music as up-tempo as it was. Songs with serious subject matter such as "Stolen Car," "I Wanna Marry You," "The Price You Pay," "The River" and "Loose Ends" seemed too sad and intense to share with "You Can Look, an almost comedic piece. Had the track listing been longer and broader in scope, some variety would have broken the album up a little more. However, the ten-song format chosen for the *Ties That Bind* album simply did not capture in full where Springsteen was at, and so the album was scrapped. As some point during this period, he came to the realization that life consisted of paradoxes, and that themes of happiness and sadness coexist, and so could coexist in his music. He could not accept this idea up to that point in time. He surely couldn't on the *Darkness* album. *Darkness* was raw anger, resentment and rage. Yet, he wrote "Sherry Darling" for *Darkness*, which he ultimately felt interrupted the album's consistency of miserable mood. He once called rock and roll the most beautiful thing in life, and to him, it had always been about happiness and escape. Except of course for those heartbreaking Roy Orbison songs he'd hear laying in his bed as a teenager. Once he saw the darkness, hardness, coldness, solitude and isolation trying to peer into the music, he couldn't make it coexist with the joy. He simply could not see songs like "Sherry Darling" and "Streets of Fire" on the same album together. During his search to find his fifth album, he learned to get over his fear of these coexistences, and accepted life's paradoxes in his music. There was no problem with the ten selected songs for *The Ties That Bind* coexisting together. But in a ten-song format, it just wasn't big enough in scope. It didn't cut to the heart of what he was saying. It merely scratched the surface and lacked the depth that *Darkness* and *Born to Run* plummeted into. He needed something bigger. Something enormous.

Recording resumed. The new decade had begun behind their backs as Springsteen and the E Street Band remained in the studio. During this period of time, Bruce mixed the live recordings of "Stay" and his Mitch Ryder "Devil With a Blue Dress" medley (aka "Detroit Medley") for the *No Nukes* soundtrack album. It would be the first live Springsteen recording to be officially released. Talk of any live album from the 1978 tour, however, seemed to disappear with the knowledge that he was working on his next studio effort. The "Detroit Medley" quickly became a staple to FM rock rotations for the next three decades.

Depending on who among the Springsteen camp or avid bootleg collectors is asked, it is said that 1979 and 1980 saw the biggest body of new material ever laid down for a new album in the artist's recording history. Though, some accounts of studio logs and vault contents suggest the *Born in the U.S.A.* sessions as the claimant to that distinction, and that could very well be true. When talking to Creem magazine's Dave Martino in 1981, Springsteen estimated 48 songs to the 1979-1980 sessions, and noted that they were all going to be on the record at one time or another. Thoughts must have harkened back to the lawsuit years between *Born to Run* and *Darkness* as 1980 progressed and there was no new album. The lawsuit was blamed for holding up the progression of the *Darkness* album and it was most likely viewed as a one-time freak instance where the interval between album releases was an unheard-of three years. His recording process, however, was about dedication. It was about being in it for life.

"If I thought I could've made a better record in half the time, that's exactly what I would've done," he told DiMartino. "Because I would've rather been out playing."[63]

Throughout his career, Springsteen has always acknowledged the remarkably lengthy amounts of time between albums and months spent in the studio. He has always insisted though, that the actual recording is done very quickly. It is the *album* that takes the time. While the music gets recorded in a matter of weeks, it takes him months to sift through 40 or 50 songs in search of an album. *Born to Run* had been narrowed to eight songs, *Darkness* to ten. With the upcoming fifth album, he had more material than both of his previous works with their outtakes included. In fact, he had recorded more songs than his entire catalog put together.

Studio work centered around a second and third cycle of songs that included "Restless Nights," "Take 'em as they Come," "Out in the Street," "Two Hearts," "Cadillac Ranch," "I'm a Rocker," "Held Up Without a Gun" and the voluminous landscape of tape goes on and on. By the summer of 1980, it had been decided that the new release, which would be titled *The River*, would be a double album. In retrospect, it was probably one of the better career decisions Springsteen made. After releasing only 18 recorded songs between 1975 and 1980, he needed once again to be up to date in his work. And yet, given all the hoopla and non-stop speculation and analysis surrounding the *River* sessions and the 80 or so songs that were recorded, he still had to narrow it down to 20 which seemed a lot by most other artist's studio releases. But even that would haunt him for years to come.

Although the double album decision was a critical one, the chosen songs have since been a subject for debate among fans, critics and Springsteen himself. In rock music, there are only a handful of artists, who without commercial or mainstream success, will always have the full undivided support of a loyal fan base that was there from the beginning. Among these fans, exist those who dissect every song lyric, concert performance, set list, bootlegged tape and outtake the artist may have to his or her name. Springsteen, like Bob Dylan and Neil Young, among others (Grateful Dead, Phish, Pearl Jam, Tori Amos) enjoys or suffers this category and level of analysis and adoration. Sometimes, however, with that type of adoration come the constant questions of why they put *this* song on the album and why they left that song *off*. Bruce Springsteen has been nailed to the cross for *The River*, not for the songs that made the final cut, but for the songs that were left off.

He has dealt with the same reaction to other albums as well, but not always with the same intense scrutiny.

There are exceptions.

We can't avoid the fact that he was whipped by fans for over 20 years for not releasing "The Promise" on *Darkness*, or "This Hard Land" and "Murder Inc." on *Born in the U.S.A.* Let's put the whole issue in perspective though, and ponder the following: At least six albums worth of songs were recorded for *The River*. Bruce Springsteen is the songwriter. Bruce Springsteen is the leader of the band. Most importantly to the finished product, Bruce Springsteen is the artist. The key to Springsteen's approach to the album has always been whether the track list and running order will work in accordance to the overall theme of his writing for that particular period in his life…the question of whether the parts will equal the whole in a cohesive structure. Springsteen was continuously searching for themes in his work. It was always necessary for his continuing narrative. Around the time of *The River*, it had become apparent to him that he had been telling a story all along, and needed to continue in the appropriate manner. Which songs he would choose for the final sequence would be agonizing at times. Critics would accuse him of being too conscious of himself. He'd always say that the release date was only one day of your life, but the album is forever. Once it's out, that's it. It's out there and it no longer belongs to you. One could argue up and down *The River* why songs like "Loose Ends" and "Where the Bands Are," two of his most beloved outtakes were left off, and why songs like "Crush on You" and "I Wanna Marry You" were left on. People's problems with *The River* come out of so many directions, that it was argued seemingly to no end until Springsteen finally addressed the issue formally by putting together the monumental 2015 release *The Ties That Bind*, a massive box collection consisting of the original double album, the aborted 1979 single album, and most of the known outtakes. The release, acknowledging the thirty- fifth anniversary of *The River*, was accompanied by a full promotional campaign, series of interviews and documentary where the artist spoke at length about the recording process throughout the 1979-1980 sessions and his ultimate selection of material. 2016 would see a full-scale world tour to celebrate *The River* as well as the existence of the entire box package and experience. The fact that Springsteen would later dedicate two years of his life to *The River* when he was in his mid sixties, 35 years after its initial release, is testament to the album's worthy status as a work of ongoing study and discussion. Yet, with all of this said, we must remember for the purposes of this book, that as we move forward with this chapter, we are now in the late summer of 1980, and Bruce Springsteen is about two months away from the release of his widely-anticipated new album. He is 30 years old. It is his fifth album. It is a double album, and it is called *The River*.

It wasn't a very well-kept secret. Once word quickly escaped that John Lennon was going into the studio, the phone began to ring with calls from anyone who had ever been involved with the Lennon's in some way. Yoko, as always, had strict influence and say over the project from the outset. The couple decided they didn't want to work with any musicians from past albums, but Yoko did suggest Jack Douglas as producer. Douglas had worked on past Lennon classics as chief engineer, and had since become one of the most in-demand producers with albums by Aerosmith and Cheap Trick to his credit. Upon John's return from Bermuda, work would begin immediately.

Within a week of returning to New York City, the Lennon's entered the Hit Factory where recording began on August 4. They turned it into an all-out event for everyone involved, adding to the facility their own custom décor bringing in carpets for the floor and rare orchids. Fresh sushi, sashimi and teriyaki chicken were brought in and served daily, and shiatsu massages were available to anybody who may have needed one. Upon first entering the studio, John hung a picture of Sean above the mixing console as a reminder that recording sessions had to end by a certain time because he needed to be home to say goodnight. Douglas wanted a modern edge to the sound and knew exactly who he wanted to recruit. On the night of August 11, he called Rick Nielsen of Cheap Trick who was just getting off stage after a concert at the Forum in Montreal. Before taking that call, Nielsen was going home to Rockford, Illinois where his wife was about to give birth to his son Dakk. He would enjoy a brief few days off seeing his wife and newborn son before embarking on a tour of Japan that would begin less than a week later. The band was hot at the moment and scheduling was tight. Nielsen was tired and eager to get home. Douglas, who knew Nielsen well, explained that John Lennon was recording a new album and needed a guitarist and a drummer to help him sort through a few songs he was struggling with. In other words, Nielson would not be going straight home to Rockford.

Jack Douglas was involved in Lennon's solo career straight from 1971's *Imagine*. Lennon knew his work and had known him personally for ten years, and he trusted him. The producer was given the task of hiring musicians that John considered contemporaries…people who would be able to jam on oldies as a warm-up, and would understand it as the mood he was trying to set. Cheap Trick was riding a massive wave off their last two releases, *Dream Police*, and *At Budokan*, which followed three solid power pop albums, the backbone of their creative peak. When Lennon walked into the studio to see Nielsen and drummer Bun E. Carlos, he recognized them instantly. John was told the names of who he would be recording with, but he couldn't place them with faces. As soon as he saw them, he knew who they were.[64]

Douglas played them an acoustic demo of "I'm Losing You" and John asked them if they had any ideas about it. Having done songs such as "Cold Turkey" and "It's So Hard," Cheap Trick often contemplated the question: *How would Plastic Ono Band approach this?*

Interestingly enough, the guitar riff that Nielsen put down in "I'm Losing You" was reminiscent of "Cold Turkey." Even John noticed it.

While Nielsen was recording, John turned to Douglas and Carlos lamenting that he wished he had had the guitarist on "Cold Turkey," complaining that Clapton had choked up.[65] Douglas quite liked what Nielsen and Carlos brought to John's acoustic demos, and had them flown back to New York a few weeks later to put down additional tracks. The tracks they recorded, however, would not be used in the final product, not by the decision of Douglas or John, but Yoko. According to Douglas, Yoko wasn't familiar with Cheap Trick, wasn't aware of their popularity and didn't want to give Neilson and Carlos what she saw as a free ride on John's notoriety.[66] Decisions made around the creation and release of what would become *Double* Fantasy, were evident of the power and influence Yoko had over John. In the end, it was a smoother and more polished sound they went with as opposed to the rawness of past albums and what was heard in the Cheap Trick recordings. Regarding Yoko's influence, there was an underlying struggle going on under which John would always yield to Mother. It must have seemed a matter of picking his battles or possibly more so just keeping the peace. To illustrate this point, the song sequence tells us everything. When John requested that everybody put their running order into a hat, the one common opinion was that everyone had John's songs on side one and Yoko's songs on side two. Yoko, who wasn't present for the drawing freaked out and dictated the terms, suggesting that if one was going to hear John, then they were going to hear Yoko too, and the only way to accomplish that would be to thread the songs together, one after the other…John, Yoko, John, Yoko, etc…Debate was not an option.[67]

By late summer, word had gotten out in the press that the Lennon's were working on an album but still had no record deal. In September, Yoko met with David Geffen, who was putting together a new label, Geffen Records. The label had not released any albums or singles yet, but Elton John and Donna Summer had already signed with him. Geffen had built his name through Asylum Records, recording artists such as the Eagles, Jackson Browne, Linda Ronstadt, Tom Waits and Joni Mitchell. Yoko played a straight-faced no nonsense approach to him. More or less *what can you do for me?* She spelled out her demands and Geffen didn't seem to have any issues or objections. When she asked him if he wanted to hear some of the new songs, he told her he didn't need to. And that was what made all the difference. Every label Yoko had approached asked to hear the music first, perhaps wary of new material containing her infamous banshee wail vocal style, which could have been a commercial liability to John and all involved. Had Geffen demanded to hear music upfront before offering to sign the Lennon's, Yoko would have walked. When he finally did hear the songs, John grabbed him as he was leaving the studio. He insisted that they take care of Yoko. He and John had everything they set out to have in life and in their art. Yoko never got what she deserved, and Geffen had to help him achieve that for her.[68] Years later, Geffen acknowledged that until the *Double Fantasy* project, he always saw Yoko as an ambitious woman who was pushing her own musical agenda on John's coattails, but came to find that John always initiated the push to get some recognition of Yoko away from him. One of the constant themes of conversation with John was his desire to see Yoko as a successful artist on her own.[69]

Double Fantasy was recorded in a matter of weeks, and by September, was being mixed. In between sessions, the Lennon's spent lots of time at La Fortuna eating pastry, smoking cigarettes, drinking cappuccino and reading the *New York Times*. As the couple was putting the last finishing touches on the record, their intervals at La Fortuna were sprinkled with the tragic news of Led Zeppelin drummer, John Bonham's death, as well as Bob Marley collapsing onstage in Pittsburgh a few weeks later. Marley's show in Pittsburgh would be his last before dying seven months later. In his biography of Yoko Ono, Jerry Hopkins draws the fitting parallel to these events in the number one song at the time…Queen's "Another One Bites the Dust."

In late September, the first of a numerous string of interviews the Lennon's would do was with David Sheff for Playboy. Sheff had done interviews with Jimmy Carter, Martin Luther King Jr. and Bob Dylan. After some hesitation amidst Yoko's intense scrutiny of Sheff's astrological charts, the writer went to the Dakota where he returned everyday for three weeks, collecting 20 hours of taped conversation with the Lennon's. Yoko told Sheff that it was a very important time for him and that the interview would mean more than he could ever comprehend at the time.[70] Although *Playboy* was supposed to get the exclusive, *Newsweek* rushed out a two page interview on September 29, claiming it as John's first major interview in five years. Aside from the obvious expected illusory accounts of domestic bliss, the Lennon's spoke in detail about their role amongst a new generation of punk, new wave, nihilism and self destruction. Yoko apparently was sold on John's idea that she pioneered punk long before anything that had been going on for the past four years. John commented suggesting that if Yoko ever went back to her old singing style, critics would accuse her of copying the B-52s. On the newer bands and artists, John made his love for much of the punk and new wave of recent years known, but was firmly against the destructive nature of drugs and artists destroying themselves. Sheff pressed him on the subject, citing Neil Young's song "Hey Hey My My" with respect to *burning out* as opposed to *fading away*. John hated it. He'd rather fade away like an old solider than burn out. Worship of the dead wasn't anything glorious…turning people like Sid Vicious and Jim Morrison into heroes. Gloria Swanson…Greta Garbo…people who survived…they were worthy of worship…not the ones who died. What made Sid Vicious a fucking hero? Did he die to save rock and roll? If Neil Young really felt that way, why doesn't he just do it? John was for the living. He wasn't having any of the dead icon bullshit.[71]

On October 9, Yoko threw a private fortieth birthday bash for John in Tavern on the Green's Crystal Room where they also celebrated Sean's fifth. It was a proper and fitting summation of the past five years where a Beatle had gone in one end, not quite sure of the future…but knowing he needed to get off the wheel. But he hadn't. His karmic impression was much different than it had been going into those five years. He was coming out the other side much more intact and self-aware than he had ever been, and he could now address the world as John Lennon again...whatever side of John Lennon he'd allow the world to see. In private, he may have over-thought the worst-case scenarios and dwelled on the catastrophic...but if his talk with David Sheff were any indication, he cherished the living and healthy, and going into the autumn of 1980, that would be his message for the new decade.

6

STATE OF THE UNION

During the first week of 1980, United Nations Secretary General, Kurt Waldheim flew to Iran in an attempt at negotiating with Ayatollah Khomeini on the release of the American hostages. Khomeini however, would not see him. Upon reporting back to President Carter, Waldheim stressed his concerns and observations that there was no government there, Khomeini was unapproachable and completely inaccessible and that the terrorists were making the decisions. Waldheim also had no reservations in his meeting with Carter in disclosing that he was scared shitless while in Iran and feared for his life.

On January 23, Carter gave what became his last State of the Union Address to Congress and the American people. His demeanor was grim as he sternly remarked, "It has never been more clear that the state of our union depends on the state of the world...and freedom and peace in the world depends on the state of our union. The 1980s have been born in turmoil, strife and change. This is a time of challenge to our interests and our values."[72]

Speaking of course to the double whammy of the hostage situation in Iran followed by the Soviet invasion in Afghanistan just a few weeks later, American interests abroad were threatened by international terrorism, anarchy and military aggression. Carter cited a list of specific developments shaping the challenges that lay ahead for the United States, including the steady growth of Soviet power beyond its own borders, overwhelming dependence of the Western democracies on oil supplies in the Middle East and the press of social, religious, economic and political change in the many nations of the developing world exemplified by the revolution in Iran. Regarding Iran, he stressed, "Our nation has never been aroused and unified so greatly in peace time. Our position is clear. The United States will not yield to blackmail."[73] The specific goals of that position, as Carter listed them, were to protect the present and long range interests of the United States, preserve the lives of the American hostages and secure their safe return, enlist the help of other nations in condemning the acts of Iran and to convince and persuade the Iranian leaders that the real danger to their nation was in the Soviet Union and from the troops in Afghanistan.

"The unwarranted Iranian quarrel with the United States hampers their response to this far greater danger to them," he told Congress. "If the American hostages are harmed, a severe price will be paid. We will not rest until every one of the American hostages are released."[74]

The president made it clear that the broader and fundamental challenge was in the Soviet Union, and that relations with them were the most critical factor between peace and global conflict, and then ran through a recap of the previous 40 year history with the Soviets:

"Since the end of the Second World War, America has led other nations in meeting the challenge of mounting Soviet power. This has not been a simple or a static relationship. Between us there has been cooperation, there has been competition and at times there has been confrontation. In the 1940's we took the lead in creating the Atlantic Alliance in response to the Soviet Union's suppression and then consolidation of its East European empire and the resulting threat of the Warsaw Pact to Western Europe. In the 1950's we helped to contain further Soviet challenges in Korea and in the Middle East and we rearmed to assure the continuation of that containment. In the 1960's we met the Soviet challenges in Berlin, and we faced the Cuban Missile Crisis. And we sought to engage the Soviet Union in the important task of moving beyond the Cold War and away from confrontation. And in the 1970's three American presidents negotiated with the Soviet leaders in attempts to halt the growth of the nuclear arms race. We sought to establish rules of behavior that would reduce the risks of conflict, and we searched for areas of cooperation that could make our relations reciprocal and productive, not only for the sake of our two nations but for the security and peace of the entire world. In all these actions, we have maintained two commitments: to be ready to meet any challenge by Soviet military power, and to develop ways to resolve disputes and to keep the peace."[75]

The basics of Carter's message, was that the Persian Gulf was of vital interest to the United States, and any interference with American interests would be met with retaliation by "any means necessary, including military force."[76] The hawkish stance surprised some on the Democratic side, although he received applause from both sides of the aisle. Anything showcasing muscle-flexing and threats of military action usually scored points with the Republicans, so it was no surprise he was appealing to some of his harshest critics who felt he was weak in his approach to terrorism and military aggression.

Iran was not the only country under seemingly verbal threat from the president. Carter was not happy about the Soviets invading Afghanistan, and although the situation was not the first priority of his administration's agenda, he spoke out against it with a promise to "make Soviet involvement as costly as possible."[77] In the Gulf region, the concern has always remained the same no matter who America's president has been. And so, Carter's view was that the United States could not afford to let the Soviets move into Afghanistan and surrounding nations and control the vast amounts of the oil supply. On such sentiment, talk is always cheap to those who are always ready to use force and are always looking for reasons to do so, but for Carter, it was not in his nature, nor in his conscience. While the Iranian hostage issue caused him personal anguish and concern, the Soviet occupation in Afghanistan was a security threat to the United States and he would have been forced into military action had they consolidated their hold and moved into other countries.[78] What the Soviets probably thought would be a quick invasion and flawless occupation turned out to be met with an Afghan insurgency and rebellion that would prolong the situation into a decade-long war.

Earlier in the month, the Carter camp discussed sending aid to the Afghan rebels by way of Pakistan. Carter's preference was to send weapons that they would be able to use in the mountains against tanks and armored personnel carriers. He saw a necessity in getting other nations on board as well, so Pakistan wouldn't be seen as completely dependent on the United States. Weapons manufactured in the Soviet Union were strategically provided to the rebels in order to obscure where they were really coming from. Shortly after, the president addressed the nation on the Soviet invasion, but did not mention the weapon sales. Throughout the balance of his term, it remained an ongoing secret operation. Carter also spoke of a cut in grain sales to the U.S.S.R. as well the possibility of a boycott of the 1980 Summer Olympics which were to be held in Moscow.

Autumn 1979 through autumn 1980 turns out to be a pivotal year in which many decisions and actions made by the U.S. in relation to the Middle East serve as the initial source of what leads to turmoil for the next several decades and well into the next century. It became a time when U.S.-backed regimes were beginning to be ousted by radical Islamists with strong anti-American convictions. U.S. leaders had no true understanding of the history of Iran let alone any comprehension of the depth of which fanaticism could plummet. It was difficult to fathom from a Western perspective how an Islamic fundamentalist dressed in garb some 1000 years out of style could appeal to a country being pushed to modernize by a monarch with a lavish Western lifestyle. That was the appeal of the Ayatolla Khomeini to the people of Iran as the Shah slowly but surely lost his country. The historical perspective from the Iranian side gets lost when attempting to fully get a grasp of what took place over time, and solely from a Western perspective, full comprehension is not entirely possible. With the withdrawal of British military presence east of the Suez creating a power vacuum in Iran during the mid 1970s, the Shah's regime maintained stability in the Persian Gulf. But the same things that some in the West admired him for, he was also vilified for in his country. All of the modernization, foreign influence and social progress he'd achieved during his thirty years in power, far surpassed the totality of anything accomplished in the entire history of the Persian monarchy, and although he believed Iran would regard him in a favorable light for his accomplishments, there were those who saw him as an enemy corrupting their traditions and destroying their ancient culture with Western values. Carter reminded Mohammad Reza Pahlavi in no uncertain terms of his wanting record on Human Rights. It was a cause Carter would champion his entire life, but nonetheless, despite the shortcomings, the Shah was a friend to the U.S. In Iran, he stood somewhere in the center of a left that despised him and a religious right that he was an obstacle to.

Like America, Russia had no real thorough grounding in the mindset of the Middle East, nor could either have anticipated the magnitude of force and ferocity with which an Islamic revolution could wage a two-front war facing down both communist rule and American influence and hegemony. Secular regimes such as Syria and Iraq were Russia's only allies in the Middle East, and much like America, the Soviets had consumed the previous two decades in the affairs of Europe and Asia.

The Soviet invasion of Afghanistan helped Ronald Reagan's decades-long anti-communist agenda by allowing him to be unapologetically outspoken and critical of the Soviets after nearly a decade of détente, which had become American foreign policy in relation to the Soviet Union and China. Although the policy of détente and the Strategic Arms Limitation Treaty

(SALT) had been designed and negotiated by Henry Kissinger, Republicans disapproved of what they saw as such a peaceful passive approach. Nixon and Kissinger were far from likeable characters to the liberal left, but it was the conservative right, Reagan included, that was appalled at their diplomacy. Reagan was also amongst hardliners who voiced criticism surrounding a banquet that would honor Soviet dissident, Aleksandr Solzhenitsyn some ten months after Gerald Ford assumed the presidency. The Soviet novelist and Nobel laureate was to be the guest of honor at an event arranged by the AFL-CIO labor federation, and even enemies of organized labor such as Strom Thurmond and Jesse Helms, both hardcore conservatives, insisted that President Ford attend. The point, obviously, was to raise a collective middle finger to the Soviets. The act would symbolize hostility in the face of détente…something they saw as the illusion of peace. Dick Cheney, a young up and coming hardliner with a hawkish mindset who was just on the verge of being named Chief of Staff to Ford summed up the sentiment in a note to his predecessor and peer, Donald Rumsfeld. His concern was over the president's failure to attend the event for Solzhenitsyn, and insisted that it was rooted in a misreading of détente that made the U.S. appear as appeasers more than peacemakers. Ford was caught between angering the Soviets and angering conservatives who would otherwise never be caught dead celebrating a dissident in any capacity. Still, détente had long been under criticism as U.S. relations with the Soviets deteriorated over the course of the decade.

But it wasn't just conservatives who opposed the non-hostile peaceful approach to foreign policy. There still existed Cold War Democrats like Henry "Scoop" Jackson, a senator from Washington who was of Reagan's generation, and despite his socially liberal stances, carried the same fear that went back 40 years. It was a generation that still occupied much of Washington and continued to believe that communism was still a threat to the future of the United States, as if it were ever. The anti-communist wing of the Republican Party regarded the pragmatic approach of Nixon and Kissinger's détente as a sellout on the level of what they saw as Roosevelt's appeasement of Joseph Stalin at the Yalta Conference. At the most basic level, they believed it sold the false impression that Russia was no longer striving for global domination.[79]

Perhaps President Carter's worst opponent and antagonist during this period was not Reagan, nor anyone on the Republican side for that matter, but from his own party. Massachusetts senator Ted Kennedy had recently thrown his gloves in the ring to challenge an otherwise unopposed Carter in what became an ugly primary season. Kennedy made things difficult for himself at the outset by slamming the president's decision to admit the Shah into the country. Given the response in Tehran, his criticism seemed unpatriotic to many, and all Carter had to do was appear presidential and somewhat strong, and the country would rally behind him in a time of national crisis. If anything, Kennedy at the beginning of his candidacy merely appealed to the very liberal percentage of the Democrats.

The Massachusetts senator charged that Carter was a secret Republican acting more as a conservative than a liberal. The president, he felt, was making too much of the recent crises and using them to scare the American public into re-electing him. At the same time, Carter's opponents on the right criticized him for being weak and not doing enough regarding the same issues. Somewhere in between was an honest man caught between politics and his own conscience.

Michael Reagan was concerned about Iowa and the political climate surrounding the primaries considering the fact that his father had not gone there. He pleaded with the candidate to get out there and campaign. Ronald Reagan was not worried though. He trusted Charles Black and John Sears and their reports that he was doing fine in Iowa. Michael still insisted he get out there, reminding him that every Republican was in Iowa except for him, and that he stood a very good chance of losing. Ronald Reagan was not moved. He was paying these guys a lot of money for their advice and thought he should follow it. Michael was upfront. John Sears was on his mind. So was Iowa. If you polled the people in Iowa on who was running for president, many would answer John Sears, and John Sears was in it for John Sears. Reagan listened to his son's concerns and promised him that he would look into it.[80]

Bush won early and Bush won first, taking the Iowa primary. Reagan had skipped the Iowa debate, playing select portions of his campaign as if they were guaranteed little victories and therefore chose not to work so hard at the outset. Through his advisors, he was initially of the belief that it wasn't a good idea to spend so much time focusing on one state. Bush felt he had dealt a major blow to his opponent by edging him out in Iowa, and acted as if it were a landslide. He hoped Reagan would finally go away…after three attempts at the Republican nomination that he would just disappear into the footnotes of history. Nobody wanted a hardliner, let alone an actor, he thought.

The media was just as quick as Bush to declare the actor dead.

"We have just witnessed the political funeral of Ronald Reagan." Tom Petit of NBC said on network television that evening.[81]

The Reagan camp at an early stage had become a dysfunctional family, and anybody around them could see it. By many accounts, John Sears was trying to consolidate power and influence within the campaign team. After the attempted fracturing of a longtime relationship between Deaver and Reagan, Sears wasn't finished trying to manipulate the situation and wasn't about to stop at Deaver. He didn't like Edwin Meece either, and wanted him out as well. Raising his name to Reagan during a meeting was the wrong move, however, as Reagan who had quietly noted complaints about Sears all along, had had enough. He got in Sears's face.

Who the hell is running the show here anyway?

The dirty rotten bastards had already run Deaver out of the campaign and he was going to be goddamned if he saw them run Ed out too. He had been forced to the wall. Reagan who very rarely lost his temper in front of anybody, finally saw the situation for exactly what it was, as Nancy physically stepped in, thinking he was about to punch Sears.[82] She suggested they all call it a night, and that's exactly what they did. Reagan didn't fault Sears's abilities, but he realized he was trying to control everything and insert his will over every aspect of the campaign. At times he felt as if he himself were working as a spokesperson for John Sears.[83] Sears had to go.

On February 26, primary day in New Hampshire, Sears, Black and Lake were called to Reagan's hotel suite where the candidate personally handed Sears a letter of their firing. It was at Nancy's insistence that Reagan let Sears go after she grew tired of all the infighting and watching her husband campaign all day only to come back at night and have to deal with the drama of his own team. She didn't go on to harbor any ill feeling toward Sears, and she credited him with having a major role in those initial post-governor years of her husband realizing his presidential aspirations and very real possibilities of the White House. Yet, Sears had become a negative and unnecessary presence, and it was time to cut him loose. The toxic team would be replaced with William Casey as the new campaign director, Ed Meece as Chief of Staff, and Richard Wirthlin, Chief of Strategy and Planning. Longtime Reagan loyalist and ex-press secretary in California, Lynn Nofziger, would once again serve as Press Secretary. Martin Anderson returned to oversee policy, and most importantly, Deaver would return to the picture.

After New Hampshire, Reagan phoned Michael at 6:30 the next morning. His son, on West Coast time, wondered what it could be, almost fearing that he had done something wrong and was expecting a reprimanding tone out of his father. It was nothing of the sort. Reagan wanted to share a press release with Michael before it was aired publically, pending Michael's approval. He read it to him over the phone, breaking the somewhat pleasant news of William J. Casey being named campaign director after the "resignation" of John Sears.

Michael indeed approved the message, and in being asked for approval, he received Ronald Reagan's approval, something he'd often sought after since childhood. It was by no means the first and only moment of acknowledgement from his father, but he took the phone call exactly as it was intended…as a nod and a wink from a father to his son, and more importantly, a sign of respect and value in his son's input.[84]

During the hour and a half press conference following the firing, Sears insisted that he would continue to support Reagan, but had harsh criticisms for the campaign as well as the candidate. Reagan, according to Sears, was insulated and out of touch with the problems within his staff…the infighting, incompetence and internal rivalries. He blamed all of the campaign problems on everyone but the one person who was supposed to be in charge of it all…John Sears. As the person in charge, however, Sears felt that he had never been in control. He stated that he had warned Reagan about financial problems within the campaign (his Thanksgiving Day allegations toward Deaver), but he didn't listen. He believed Reagan should be much harder on his staff and that the candidate opted not to pay too much attention to those running the campaign, instead allowing himself to be more influenced by friends who had been among his inner circle for years…eventually accounting for a great deal of his staff anyway. Black maintained that their criticism was not an indictment of Reagan's ability to run a country. "You can examine any other presidential campaign and you'll find worse problems," he told reporters.[85] Sears insisted that his commitment to the candidate's nomination would not change. "Ronald Reagan is the kind of man whom people can believe in as a strong president," he said. "Whatever our relationship has been is not really relevant."[86]

The most crucial period of Reagan's campaign and possibly his entire political life was the time between Iowa and New Hampshire. He had long been the frontrunner, but the decision by Sears to keep him off the campaign trail and out of debates with the other candidates backfired. Not only had he lost Iowa, but he was down 21 points in New Hampshire according to his internal polling. If he lost New Hampshire, it was over. The story of Ronald Reagan ends there, had he lost. He remains nothing more than a controversial piece of California history and an inconsequential footnote to American history if Bush takes the state.

Needless to say, Reagan destroyed Bush in New Hampshire taking 50 percent to Bush's 23 percent. John Anderson held 10 percent, and John Connelly, Bob Dole, and Philip Crane all had less than three percent each. All would soon drop out and endorse Reagan, except for Anderson who would go the duration as an independent. It was also in New Hampshire where Reagan agreed to debate Bush but also invited the other candidates who the newspaper originally sponsoring the event excluded. The candidates showed up but were not allowed to take part or speak, which angered Reagan. The debate was the site of Reagan's infamous "I paid for this microphone" outburst when the moderator called for the candidate's microphone to be turned off. It was also where Bush first uttered his "voodoo economics" phrase criticizing his opponent's supply-side philosophy. Bush wasn't happy and neither was the Nashua Telegraph, which was clearly in his corner. After winning in Iowa and becoming the obvious only real contender to Reagan, Bush thought he had an even better chance if he faced Reagan alone in New Hampshire and media focused its attention solely on the two of them. Bob Dole, however, complained to the Federal Elections Commission that excluding the other candidates constituted an illegal corporate contribution to the Reagan and Bush campaigns, prompting the Telegraph to withdraw its funds. Both sides wanted the debate and Reagan's team offered to split the cost with the Bush team. Bush declined, and the Reagan team ended up paying the entire cost. On that note, it was more than his own microphone Ronald Reagan was paying for.

In New Hampshire, a snowstorm blew in and kept Reagan's plane grounded. He was unable to get to Chicago where Nancy filled in for him with a brief speech in front of supporters. Still, Reagan called in through a telephone hookup as his wife spoke to a large crowd. He told everybody that even though he couldn't get there in person, he wanted to say hello. It was a warm moment until he mentioned the view from his hotel window. He told Nancy, with his supporters listening to a loud speaker, that he was looking out at all the beautiful white snow in New Hampshire. Her response that she was looking out at all the beautiful white faces didn't go over very well.[87]

Nancy Reagan's quotes were thrown back at her in what the media called a racial comment. The words did not sit well with anyone with enough conscience to cringe, and she regretted them from the moment she said them. She quickly corrected herself at the microphone, but it was too late. The effects of a grueling campaign…the blank minds and numbness that tricks the spontaneous voice into believing the right words are going to come out every time you open your mouth…Nancy Reagan was feeling it. The whole thing, however, blew over within a few days and was never spoken about much afterward.

Following New Hampshire, a rejuvenated and united Reagan campaign focused more on Jimmy Carter than on each other. They attacked Carter for his lackluster response to the Soviet invasion in Afghanistan, lack of a clear plan to bring the hostages home from Iran and his position on the Panama Canal Treaty. They also went after the economy, citing inflation, interest rates and the drop in value of the dollar against gold. The main idea was to portray Carter as weak on every pressing issue they considered vital.

On the other side of the aisle, Carter easily defeated Kennedy in the early Democratic primaries, taking Iowa, New Hampshire, Florida and Illinois. Despite this, Kennedy did not back down. The more states Carter picked up, the more critical and vocal Kennedy became, attacking the president as someone who had betrayed the Democratic platform and sold out his liberal values. It was still too early in the hostage crisis, but during the first initial months after the embassy takeover in Tehran, Carter's popularity actually soared higher and faster than any other president in the history of the Gallop Poll. Not even Franklin D. Roosevelt after Pearl Harbor had a faster spike in approval.

In March, Reagan took Illinois, Georgia, Alabama, Florida, South Carolina, Vermont and most of New York. April primaries saw him dominating in Wisconsin and Kansas, while Bush unexpectedly took Pennsylvania and Maine.

Five months into the hostage situation, opinions on Carter began to change. Criticism from the right charged that he wasn't taking any action and appeared weak and helpless. Kennedy was hitting him from the left. With his approval rating suddenly plummeting by the spring of 1980, he was taking a beating from all possible sides. A short time following the Iranian takeover of the U.S. Embassy, the president discussed and planned a rescue mission that initially never got past the planning stages. Still fresh in the collective American imagination was Israel's daring 1976 raid on Entebbe, and heroic rescue of Israeli hostages held by Palestinians in Uganda. Carter's plan was kept secret and finally announced at a meeting on April 11. The two-day mission (April 24-25) known as Operation Eagle Claw had been talked about and practiced the entire time, but wasn't given the go-ahead until five months after the hostage crisis began. The plan was for military operations to converge on Iran under cover of darkness in a staging area on an abandoned airstrip in Tabas, some 200 miles from Tehran.

From the outset, the plan seemed far-fetched and dangerous, but once underway, it was equipment failure in the rescue helicopters that caused Carter to call off the rescue and abort the mission. While withdrawing from their remote location in the desert, two American aircraft collided during a refueling operation, causing the death of eight American servicemen. On the flipside of the incident was the terrorist's strengthening of their guard as the embassy gates remained locked with the hostages still inside. Carter immediately went on national television from the Oval Office and took full responsibility for his decision and for the American deaths caused in the accident, although the tragic event would assure his undoing as President of the United States.

Another surprising primary upset happened on May 3, when Reagan took Bush's home state of Texas. After sweeping North Carolina, Indiana, Tennessee, Maryland, Nebraska and Oregon, Reagan became untouchable, and Bush won only one more state, Michigan, before dropping out of the race on May 26. He then asked his 202 delegates to vote for Reagan at the convention in July. When asked about Bush's concession and endorsement, Reagan told a reporter that it hadn't quite sunk in yet and that he would probably go home and let out a loud scream.[88]

Then there was the question of Gerald Ford. The ex-president quickly congratulated Reagan and came out publically in support of him. On June 5, Reagan went to Ford's Palm Springs house for a 90-minute meeting, after which Ford made it known that he would not be on any vice presidential list. By July 1, Bill Casey put together a list of names for screening…Jack Kemp, Donald Rumsfeld, Bill Simon, Richard Lugar, and Anne Armstrong. Ford, who was not on the list still drew the highest numbers in the polls. For many, Reagan/Ford was a dream ticket and Reagan knew it. But the reality was that Reagan and Ford were now both residents of California, which would be in violation of the Twelfth Amendment of the Constitution, which prohibits electors from voting for presidential and vice presidential candidates who are both residents of the same state. Nobody was chosen over the course of the next six weeks, as an otherwise uneventful sleeper of an election year took on a new energy and immediacy going into the Republican National Convention in Detroit. Somebody was going to be chosen at the convention. Still, many clung to the idea of a surprise announcement of a Reagan/Ford ticket at the last minute. Would they risk a possible violation of the Constitution? Would it be challenged? Was there a loophole? Was someone in the position of Gerald Ford, an ex-president and ex-leader of the free world willing to take a step down and serve under a new president?

Next, the phrase "co-presidency" started being passed throughout media speculation, as the entire Republican Party made its way into Detroit for the start of the convention on July 14. The first few days were back and forth insanity amidst further speculation.

Who is it going to be?
Nobody left is strong enough to fit the position behind Reagan.
Bush was his only real competition and he's finished.
Could it possibly be Ford?
How would that work?

Deaver liked Bush as VP pick and he made it clear to Reagan. Deaver saw Bush as a class person who would bring the right assets to the Reagan campaign. The son of former senator, Prescott Bush of Connecticut was a moderate with ties to both the East (Yale) and the Texas oil fields, and he possessed the handsome, youthful, sharp charismatic persona that could perfectly balance the ticket.[89]

Nancy met privately with Betty Ford on the second day. The concerns of how a former president might handle a secondary role were indeed being felt by those closest to the candidates, and Mrs. Ford did concede to Mrs. Reagan that it would be awkward to be in such a position. On the third and final day, the uncomfortable phrase popped up again. Ford gave a live interview to CBS Evening News. On the air, he told Walter Cronkite, "If I go to Washington, and I'm not saying that I'm accepting, I have to go there with the belief that I would play a meaningful role across the board in the basic, crucial, tough decisions that have to be made in the four-year period."

"It's to be something like a co-presidency?" Cronkite asked.

"That's something that Governor Reagan really ought to consider," Ford replied. "The point you raise is a legitimate one."[90]

The Reagan team watched on TV in disbelief.

Co-presidency?

Nancy Reagan was fuming.

How dare they go to these lengths on live television.

No matter what her husband decided, there was no way in hell that she was going to let him pick another president as his running mate.

Nobody took kindly to what they saw on television, most all of the top Republicans having watched it in Reagan's suite. This explained Ford's insistence on having his core people back on board in the event he accepted Reagan's offer…namely Henry Kissinger. In what amounted to a deal being struck between Ford and Reagan, according to the media Ford demanded control of National Security as well as domestic staff, but the media focused specifically on the role of Kissinger being the most pressing concern that neither could come to an agreement on. As Cronkite would tell the country later that night, the deal fell through. Deaver immediately phoned Kissinger on the order of Reagan and issued a verbal reprimand. Moments later, Ford entered Reagan's suite with many key people still present, and gracefully withdrew.

Ronald Reagan picked up the phone. He was calling George Bush. He wanted this bullshit settled already. He asked if anyone had any objections. Nobody did.[91]

From the floor of the Republican Convention inside Joe Lewis Arena, a sea of people glanced up in the direction of the anchor booth where they knew Walter Cronkite was talking to Gerald Ford. Although they could not tell what Ford was saying, they knew he was up there and they took it as a sign of something significant such as the announcement of the Reagan/Ford ticket they had built a movement around in past weeks. The moment was the peak of a suspense that had escalated throughout the entire week of the convention, and now Reagan was only hours from revealing his running mate. The Republican Party, however, found out not through Reagan, but soon after the interview when CBS reporter Leslie Stall was told by a high lieutenant of the Reagan aids that the choice was Bush. In choosingBush as a running mate, Reagan afforded the GOP a much more balanced ticket. Those in favor of Bush during the primaries liked him because he was more moderate than Reagan who scared many who felt he was far too conservative. Not only was Bush the second most popular in GOP contention, but his credentials on foreign policy were impeccable. He had been Director of the CIA, served as Ambassador to the UN, as well as the unofficial ambassador to China during a time when there was no formal diplomatic relations with the PRC. The Reagan/Bush ticket paired the conservative with the moderate and balanced private sector and domestic experience with foreign and administrative experience. The news quickly spread throughout the floor and up into the rafters as the venue erupted in random pockets of Bush cheers. Stall made the announcement from the floor in conversation with Cronkite who remained up in the booth. There had already been quite a number of Reagan/Bush signs in the arena during the course of the week, so it was clear not everyone wanted to see Ford again. In retrospect, if anything in the history of American elections had possibly been made too much of by way of speculation, it was the proposed Reagan/Ford ticket that never went beyond the hypothetical. Ford had made it clear after the meeting in Palm Springs that there would be no pairing of him with Reagan. Yet it was Reagan's pollster, Dick Wirthlin who persisted in keeping the possibility in the national dialogue as Ford continued to lead everyone else who was actually campaigning for president. Ford never was. Regardless, the entire GOP including Reagan and Ford themselves, did in fact entertain the hypothetical right up until the last minute.

The Democratic Convention in New York City amounted to a forced and insincere sense of unity where Kennedy finally conceded to Carter and reluctantly issued a halfhearted endorsement. His speech echoed the uncertainty that he had experienced throughout the primary season, although no longer taking shots at Carter, Kennedy still maintained with a sense of self-congratulatory pride that he was the one who upheld the principles of the party and reflected the liberal platform, as if Carter did not. While the overall optimism in the future was infectious in Detroit, the spirit for the Democrats in New York's Madison Square Garden, while energetic, was tainted by a sense of the wind having gone out of the sails.

Stuart Spencer joined the Reagan campaign after a phone call from Deaver following the convention. Spencer had played a key role during Reagan's two gubernatorial campaigns, but joined up with Gerald Ford in 1976. His immediate response to Deaver in the summer of 1980 was to ask if Nancy wanted him around, still remembering that she had been angered and hurt by his jumping ship to campaign with Ford. Nancy was more than happy to have him back. Not only had he been an important figure for her husband, but he was extremely supportive for her during the early years of her public life. Knowing Reagan's presidential aspirations even while he was governor, Spencer knew it would be overwhelming for Nancy. She had often expressed how all the political talk and activity of public life scared her and that she wasn't sure she was ready for it. He assured her she could, but didn't lie…it would get a lot worse.[92] She admired his straight forward, tough talking penchant for reality, but also knew that he genuinely cared. He'd always give a straight answer, and never carried the self-importance of someone like John Sears who by all accounts seemed to be in it for himself.[93]

Spencer, upon returning, observed that Reagan was talking to the press far too much for comfort. There was nothing wrong with it when Reagan had been governor, he thought, but somebody running in a national race on such a massive scale would be taken apart and scrutinized for every word, so the more Reagan put himself out there, the more he stood a chance of embarrassing himself or getting into trouble. Two instances stick out: In September, Reagan mentioned Tuscumbia, Alabama where President Carter had begun his 1980 campaign for re-election, and referred to it as the birthplace of the Ku Klux Klan. Another time, Reagan claimed the president had led the United States into a depression. Carter joked about it. What did he know? They were in a recession, not a depression. Yet, the ever-witty Reagan was always quick with a comeback and told an audience that a recession was when your neighbor loses a job, a depression was when you lost yours. Reagan's punch line was recovery, and recovery would be when Jimmy Carter lost *his* job.[94]

It was usually within a presidential candidate's best interest not to embrace fringe groups that held controversial stances against federal law. When it was political motivation fronted as religious, it became suspicious and a matter of going deep into unethical territory, and therefore candidates wouldn't go near such an association. But imagine a religious group that unashamedly acknowledged its political intent as the very reason for its existence. That is precisely what happened in 1980.

The Moral Majority wanted a candidate that would support the overturning of Roe V. Wade. Reagan, on the campaign trail, was asked about abortion.

"I happen to believe from all the study that I have been able to do, all of the information I've been able to get, that when you interrupt a pregnancy, you are taking a human life. Now that puts that human life within the protection of the Constitution…the guarantee of life, liberty and the pursuit of happiness."[95]

He championed the evangelical cause.

"I was asked once what book I would choose if I were shipwrecked on an island and could only have one book for the rest of my life. I replied that I know of only one book that could be read and reread and continue to be a challenge. The Bible. All the complex and horrendous questions confronting us at home and worldwide have their answers in that single book."[96]

Mike Deaver highlighted what his boss knew about strategy and politics appealing to the spiritual segment of the human heart.

"Reagan knew when he'd strike chords in groups of people. He would talk about prayer in schools and the values of developing a welfare system which kept families together, and reminding people that this was one nation under God."[97]

Critics of the Republican Party challenged that the current brand of conservatism was not the same kind of conservatism in the tradition of John Locke or Burke or John Adams who were more about preserving the best ideas and traditions in government by way of philosophical, moral and ethical standards. The modern conservatives were social Darwinists. They rose above poverty and so expected everyone else to do the same, if they so chose to. The Lord helped those who helped themselves, they believed. The evangelicals, with their perceived monopoly on God, gathered around candidate Reagan in full approval and made no effort to so much as disguise their agenda. It was clear what they wanted, and it had nothing to do with modern America. Jerry Falwell did not mince words.

"The Moral Majority is not a religious organization…the fact is, it's political…and one's membership is based upon citizenship in this country and a commitment to a pro-life, pro-traditional family, pro-moral and pro-American position."[98]

Televangelist James Robison was just as unapologetic in his distorted interpretation of God's politics and God's removal of Jimmy Carter.

"We all made a commitment to God that for the first time in our lives we were going to get involved in the political process and do everything we could to wake up the Christians. So I stood there and I prayed this prayer. I said, 'Oh God, we have got to get this man out of the White House and get someone in here who will be aggressive about bringing back traditional moral values.'"[99]

In Dallas, Reagan was about to speak before a massive crowd of evangelicals in a venue usually reserved for rock concerts. The event amounted to what was being called the First National Affairs Briefing of the Religious Roundtable. In short, it was described as "the marriage between Southern Baptists and the Republican Party,"[100] and served symbolically as an entrance of the evangelicals into the world of politics.

Backstage, Robison told Reagan that since the Moral Majority was "bi-partisan," they could not and would not endorse him as a body, but that it would be in his interest with some 50-60 million potential votes if he endorsed them. When introduced, Reagan walked up to the podium in front of 15,000 evangelicals while Robison pulled the strings.

"I know this is a bi-partisan gathering," the Republican nominee for President of the United States began. "And I know you can't endorse me. And I only brought that up because I want you to know that I endorse *you*."[101]

PART TWO

THIS IS GOING TO SHAKE UP THE WHOLE WORLD

7

THE TIES THAT BIND

*T*he River, released on October 17, 1980, was a milestone in Bruce Springsteen's career, and by most rock and roll standards, a masterpiece, perhaps not for the artist, but for rock and roll itself. *Rolling Stone* reviewed it as the third album in a trilogy that began with *Born to Run*. This is an interesting concept. In 1980, it could have very well seemed the third part in what could have easily been perceived as a trilogy. However, Springsteen's summation for this story, at least this particular part of the story, doesn't come until 1984's *Born in the U.S.A.* To be fair, a trilogy can be formed of *Born to Run*, *Darkness on the Edge of Town* and *The River*, but was he thinking in terms of a trilogy? Even *Rolling Stone* asked this question. Whatever the case, the opening lines of "Thunder Road" to the closing lines of "Wreck on the Highway" do suggest a three-part story, and it is easy to think of this run of albums as a trilogy, just as his later releases *Tunnel of Love*, *Human Touch* and *Lucky Town* also form a trilogy. The story, however, has always continued. And since it is all one story that is linked on and off again throughout his entire career though all of his albums in some fashion, we will not put a label on it.

At this point, let us consider the story Springsteen is telling. The lives of his characters have crossed over into their thirties and have been through the mill. Where *Darkness* leaves off, many dreams have been crushed, and the mood is one of regret, anger and bitterness. Where *Darkness* ends, however, there is defiance and an in-your-face continuation forward, as exemplified in the final verse of the album's title track. Where *The River* picks up, the darkness still hovers. Lives seem to be etched in stone, but where *Darkness* was steeped in denial there is acceptance on *The River*. The paradoxes that Springsteen spoke of to Robert Hilburn are all over the album. This acceptance of the good and the bad keeps a double mood consistency throughout. But the mood is much more complex than that. Happiness and sadness are broad themes…too broad to even use in an overview. The album runs us through love, marriage, betrayal, breakup, longing, regret, fast cars, cockiness, arrogance, comedy, alienation, fear, death and numerous unanswerable questions, particularly that of the meaning of life, which seems to be encapsulated in the final track, "Wreck on the Highway." His growing as a writer is apparent upon comparison with *Darkness*. As mentioned earlier, there are two types of people on *Darkness*…those who lose their dreams and succumb to the dead end world of whatever their lives have unwillingly become. They have given up. They are alive in the sense that they are breathing, getting up, going to their jobs everyday and coming home, but inside they are dead. Then there are those who still have a dream, who still hold out for some kind of hope…the ones who come home from work psyched up for…something. Despite whether it is real, imagined or unknown, there is still the excitement of possibility, the idea that something is just around the corner…something life-changing. On *The River*, these people are still there. There are some who have been married and split up ("Stolen Car"). There are those who long for marriage, a relationship, some kind of connection… anything ("I Wanna Marry You," "Hungry Heart"). Some have become so defiled and disillusioned, that they alienate themselves beyond any recognition of a normal life ("Jackson Cage"). Yet, some still come home and look for their friends, go on dates and tear up the town on the weekends ("Sherry Darling," "Out in the Street"). Some have just plainly fucked up their lives ("Point Blank," "The Price You Pay"). And there are those who stand by the belief that despite life's up and downs, and the falling down and getting back up and dusting yourself off...despite it all...that "two hearts are better than one." This belief is the one central theme that threads its way through the album. In "The Ties That Bind," the opening song, Springsteen sings to a girl who has been hurt too many times and has closed herself off to any future possibilities, a typical defense mechanism after a breakup, although there seem to be two...the other, besides alienation, being the rebound. Here, he tries to convince her that he's the one. He makes no promises of a happily-ever-after. Just a promise that things will look up one day, and that they will endure it all together. "Jackson Cage" imagines a life of solitude and alienation, and of the toll and consequences such a life can bring. "Independence Day" is the third in a series of songs that would be written for, about or inspired by Springsteen's relationship with his father. Where "Adam Raised a Cain" was fueled by bitterness and raging anger, and "Factory" was a distant tribute, "Independence Day" was brutally honest, yet compassionate. It was almost as if he was beginning to see his father in himself, or at least trying to see through his eyes. He writes of a son leaving home, but leaving with a sincere understanding of who his father is, and why he said and did the things he did that often contributed to their tumultuous relationship as Springsteen was growing up. The last lines of the song are so steeped in regret and confession they just stop short of an apology.

"Hungry Heart" was the album's first single. A catchy pop hook with a Phil Spector-like chord progression, "Hungry Heart," penned for the Ramones almost didn't make the album. Landau, who saw hit potential, convinced Springsteen to keep it. With the release of the *No Nukes* film that summer, a wider audience got to catch a glimpse of Bruce for the first time. Word of mouth from viewers and critics alike was that Springsteen was electrifying and had to be seen to be believed. With the release of *The River*, a larger audience and another rise in popularity was therefore inevitable. Once again, he had the respect of most major critics as well as his peers in the industry, and was the most sought-after artist in the business. The new album, however, was crucial. The double release allowed him to spread out his concert sets. It showcased his wide range of abilities as well as the versatility of the E Street Band. It would become the centerpiece of his first world tour (although he would not make it to Japan and Australia until 1985). And when it was all over, he would finally be able to exhale and breathe easier for a while without feeling the weight of obligations or career decisions. In short, *The River* would be the album to secure his artistic freedom for the rest of his career. It would also propel him financially into the rank of millionaire. It all started with the single in the early autumn.

"Hungry Heart" was most noted for its melodic marriage of Roy Bittan's piano and Danny Federici's organ, but vocally was a much different-sounding Springsteen. It was later revealed that the tape was slightly sped up to enhance the vocal melody that soured over a chord progression reminiscent of the Four Seasons' "Dawn." The unreleased outtakes on the bootleg circuit revealed Springsteen's voice to be much deeper and raspier, harkening back to his *Darkness* voice. For its use as a single, the vocal alterations seemed to have worked out for the better. In the mix, a wall of background harmonies were placed behind the lead vocal, and as the new Springsteen single, it was unlike anything his fans had heard him do. Yet, it sounded very familiar, recalling the early sixties pop sound that Bruce grew up with. While musically catchy and joyous, the song cut right to the heart of what the album is about…fucking up royally, moving on in the face of it and hopefully finding some sense of community and belonging in other people.

It is essential to remember that *The River* was released in the days before compact discs and streaming. That said, the two vinyl records that it was originally issued on are essential to its artistic value (The CD version of *The*

River was always kept to a two-disc format as well). While exploring these personal relationships, Springsteen seems to have carefully sequenced the song order. The album is a mix. Two distinctive single albums can easily be made of it. There is a fast rocking party album in there, and there is a slow-moving adult-themed album of a more serious nature in there. Both types of songs are jumbled together throughout both discs, but the sequencing is careful and deliberate. The first disc speaks of friendships and community…of longing for some kind of connection. The people of the *Born to Run* album had stopped running. Not all of them, but many had found or were seeking some sort of structure to their lives…a job, marriage, house, kids, etc…perhaps what Springsteen would later refer to as the illusion of the American Dream. On disc one, these people still look forward to the weekend and to the possibility of the night. Friday night still matters. That right there is the essence of *The River*…life's ups and downs, and in the face of the working life, the willingness, desire and energy to still be able to play. Songs like "Sherry Darling," "You Can Look (But You Better Not Touch), and "Crush on You" reflect a lyrical adolescence that had not been heard since his very first album…some moments even bordering on comedy and farce.

But things quite frequently go to hell on the album. Especially on the second disc, which deals for the most part with the loss of connection to those things important on disc one. "Point Blank," "Fade Away," "Stolen Car," and "The Price You Pay" all deal with the consequences of the choices people make. In "Stolen Car," a marriage falls apart as the narrator makes his way through guilt, fear and doubt about the future. The vocals are drowned in reverb for a distant haunting effect, as are the few drum crashes near the ending. The incidental piano melody underneath this rather sparse arrangement makes it the most distinctive noir-sounding piece on the entire album. "The Price You Pay," one of Springsteen's most underrated gems, recalls Jackson Browne's "Before the Deluge," and seems to be the one that sums up the album and where the artist's characters have been, and where they are going…coming so far, waiting so long, only to end up in a nightmare where everything has gone wrong. Perhaps the song is what becomes of the people in "Thunder Road" or "Jungleland" five years later. But unlike the songs on *Born to Run* and even *Darkness* to a lesser extent, the themes of night, highways, rivers and deserts that were once symbols of possibility, become symbols of consequence and uncertainty on *The River*.

Among the women on *The River*, some are single mothers disillusioned with the unplanned circumstances of their lives. Springsteen plays the part of naïve observer, convinced he is the one who is going to make all the difference in their lives. In "I Wanna Marry You," a syrupy ballad containing what are perhaps the most cringe-worthy lyrics ever penned by a 29-year old Baby Boom rocker, Springsteen sings of two young people coming together to face up to their responsibilities...a house, a family...not quite believing in some fairytale life or dreams coming true, but doing it because they either a.) Truly want to believe that two hearts really are better than one...or b.) Are of a certain age and they reluctantly act according to how they feel they're supposed to.

Some might challenge such an assessment and remind us that these are Springsteen's working class roots protruding from his creative skin, and that would be a fairly accurate assumption. The maturity level Springsteen was working from by his late twenties and early thirties was remarkable in comparison with most of the rock world. With the exception of course of artists like Bob Dylan, John Lennon, Neil Young Tom Waits and a few others, the majority of rock stars his age had not matured with their art. Mick Jagger, for example, had his early thirties reflected on albums like *It's Only Rock and Roll*, *Black and Blue* and *Some Girls*...conglomerations of sex, drugs and the excess of rock and roll life. Keith Moon and John Bonham had both overdosed by 32. Springsteen had never taken part in that lifestyle. His worst addiction was probably McDonalds or Kentucky Fried Chicken. He had made some money that enabled him to have some choice in how he would live his life, and he chose to stay in modest rented houses in Monmouth County, New Jersey, close to where he grew up. The people in those towns...old friends...

acquaintances, had jobs. People his age had gotten married. He watched some of his own friends tie the knot. Yet, there was still a struggle within these people to maintain a sense of community. The kids of *Born to Run* were learning often through rude awakening to accept the realities of life. And at the same time, while caught up in the whirlwind, were fighting not to lose each other or the ideals they once clung tightly to.

Sonically, *The River* best represents Springsteen and the E Street Band's assorted musical influences. The spectrum of sounds and styles is broad. The ever-present sax, piano and organ sound of the band hit the listener full force, this time with the intensity of a live performance. The stripped-down live sound is effective right from the first snap of Max Weinberg's snare on "The Ties That Bind." Ironically, "Sherry Darling" contains an underlying fake audience track in its mix. Why Springsteen chose to release this as a fake live song is one of the many questions that surrounded the album for years. It is true, as some fans have suggested that he could have used one of the many live recordings from 1978. Perhaps as the song later evolved to feature the "let there be sunlight" bridge, the only live recording came from the M.U.S.E shows and was a little shaky. The song, as Springsteen introduced it in 1978, was a throwback and a tribute to what he called "fraternity rock"... songs such as "Louie Louie," "Farmer John," and "Double Shot of My Baby's Love." The audience track does not hurt the song. It becomes part of its character, serving almost as its own instrument.

While the use of the guitar is important in the overall mix of the album, one noticeable difference between *Darkness* and *The River* is the absence of the guitar solo. Of *The River's* 20 songs, only three contain guitar solos. Highlight moments are dominated by the sax, organ and harmonica. In the previous two releases, although full band efforts, one or two musicians usually stand out above the rest on each album. The *Born to Run* album seems to get its character from Roy's piano and Clarence's sax. On *Darkness*, it is that exceptional blend of both Roy and Danny's keys along with Bruce's poison arrow guitar solos. If there is one instrument on *The River* that truly ascends to the heavens, it is the organ. Danny Federici shines on *The River*. "Jackson Cage," "Independence Day," "I'm a Rocker" and "Fade Away" are all defined by his integral organ parts. "Restless Nights," one of the songs that did not make the final cut but was later released on box sets, is perhaps Danny's finest moment in a recording studio. The song also features one of Bruce's finest vocal performances as well as one of his best guitar solos…further testament as to why *The River* baffled the fans who had gotten hold of the outtakes very early on and couldn't understand the choices the artist made.

The subject of marriage comes up a lot in *The River*. The album, however, is much more about relationships than it is about marriage. Springsteen, at 30, did not have the sense of perspective or experience to delve that deeply in to the complexities of marriage. At least not the way Dylan had on *Blood on the Tracks*. He would not take on the subject again until 1987's *Tunnel of Love*, where the songs would be autobiographical and more multi-dimensional. Yet, *The River* came out at a time when people were still getting married at a very young age. Generations of kids straight out of high school often bought into that promise of the American Dream…the white picket fence life that many found didn't exist. Instead, what they found was a life of hard work and very little payoff…many, though not all. People still get married in their twenties. Perhaps they always will. But if the current divorce rate, which is down in 2020, having been on the decline after reaching 50 percent in recent decades, is any indication of just how sacred those vows were, then marriage was indeed a dying institution in the wake of the album.

The River appeals to emotions in all of us. It speaks to the human condition, so in that respect, it is universal and timeless. Yet, it comes from a much different time and a much different world where one person could work hard and be the hero. Amidst a wall of smokescreens and roadblocks, the 1980s brought the yuppie and AIDS. The 1990s brought a global market economy that dictated the restructuring of the American household, calling for both husband and wife to work. Springsteen was bringing rock and roll into territory that very few had attempted. No rock artist would even dare release an album like *The River* in the twenty-first century. If the record were released today, it would most likely come from a country artist in a genre that still believes in the muscle-flexing aspects of old-school tradition… those blue-collar working-class macho clichés that the guy is going to be the knight in shining armor, take care of his girl, make all her dreams come true and live happily ever after…at least until one of them gets caught cheating. Once again, those feelings and emotions are eternally valid, but the world was much different then. *The River* captures a period in time…the maturing of the Baby Boomers. It is a portrait of American life amidst the disillusion of the Nixon through Carter years and still has enough bravado, fun and cheer in its grooves to mark it as one of the grand celebratory rock and roll documents, and along with The Clash's *London Calling*, serves as a culmination and summation of rock's first 25 years.

Ann Arbor, October 3, 1980. The University of Michigan's Crisler Arena was the scene of opening night of a yearlong tour in support of *The River*. The three Michigan shows Springsteen had done in 1978 were indicative of his growing support in various markets. Going from clubs in 1975 to theaters and auditoriums by 1978 was a steady incremental climb, but by the end of the tour, Bruce packed Detroit's Cobo Hall in a significant leap forward compared to the crowd size he drew at the Masonic Hall Theater just three months earlier. With most shows on the Darkness Tour sold out, his concert at Wings Event Center in Kalamazoo only sold half of its 6000-seat capacity. Ann Arbor was hardly the case, where a sold out crowd of 14,000 came out to hear the still-to-be-released new album along with the wealth of showstoppers that were building his reputation as the greatest performer in all of rock music.

The greatest performer in all of rock music kicked off the first show of his tour with his biggest song and forgot the words. "Born to Run" and an arena filled with crazed fans who rise to their feet to scream at the top of their lungs to the FM rock staple that has become the national anthem of rock and roll…and the song's creator and artist approaches the microphone to sing…and nothing comes out of his mouth. At the instance he realizes that he doesn't know his own lyrics, he hears the overpowering wall of the crowd singing them back to him. It is a unique dynamic that has become one of the bedrock characteristics of a Springsteen concert, unmatched by any other artist or band's audience …the overwhelming intensity in which Springsteen fans as one unit of sheer force and energy literally scream every lyric to every song, very often drowning out Springsteen himself. While it is common for fans to sing at concerts and assume they've been part of a loud audience, there has never been much comparison to the volume of a Springsteen crowd…not the Grateful Dead, not Metallica, not even a football crowd. And so the Boss was in good hands as he forgot his own song in front of 14,000 people in Ann Arbor. Bob Seger in attendance visited Bruce backstage during the intermission. The two talked about doing a song together, and the Detroit rocker wanted to do "Thunder Road," which Bruce had just closed his first set with. Regardless, the Boss played the song twice and brought Seger out to share the vocals during the encore, much to the delight of the ecstatic crowd.

The tour began a few weeks before the new album was released so much of the material still had yet to be heard. The first few shows barely resemble the shows that came later in terms of set list. Many songs were being tried out for the first time in front of an audience, and Springsteen had not yet found a structure to the show, which could often take up to the first six weeks of a tour before the right sequence and flow was realized. Songs like "Wreck on the Highway" which soon found a permanent spot late in the second set was played early in the first set. For Springsteen, it was all about pacing. A three-hour show needed to consist of an arc that followed ups and downs throughout, and the band tried different songs in different slots during the first few weeks. Nonetheless, Bruce and the E Street Band still finding their way turned in nightly performances to phenomenal reviews. Still, with all of the communal participatory joy that audiences experienced at Springsteen shows, the early weeks of the tour were not without its drama. In Chicago, two shows at the 4300-seat Uptown Theater turned out to anger a lot of fans who were unable to get tickets due to the fact that someone as popular as Springsteen was playing such a small venue. There were indeed smaller markets where he had played in the past, but Chicago wasn't one of them. Onstage, Bruce addressed the situation.

"I wanna thank everybody for coming down to the show the past couple nights....thank you very much....and....alright... bulletin here...this is only the sixth show of our tour tonight and uh....and I got a lot of letters from a lot of folks, kids that couldn´t get tickets and waited on line a long time and couldn´t get in and uh....just wanna let you know we´re working on coming back real soon....this tour we´ll only do up until December, and I think we´re trying to come back sometime in November so tell all your friends and stuff that we´ll be back and we'll do a show for you, alright?"[102]

A show at the 18,000-seat Rosemont Horizon was then added for November. Chicago wasn't the only city where tickets were impossible for many fans. In Los Angeles and New York City, ticket scalpers found their way into vast quantities of the supply and were selling them through agencies at unheard-of amounts. Tickets with a face value price of $12.50 being scalped at enormous premiums were cause for Landau and Springsteen to contact California Congressman Mel Levine to work with them toward cracking down on ticket agencies.

Those who were lucky enough to score tickets to any one of the fall shows were treated to the full gamut of Springsteen in transition. Always known as quite the consummate rock star, he began to voice his concern for the audience. As if he weren't already giving his fans the greatest show on Earth, there was a human element to his onstage persona that wasn't even seen just two years before, and that counted for everything to some fans. In Chicago he met a fan who had just been on a bus for ten hours to see him. Backstage was crowded, and the guy only had a brief moment with him. It was his twenty-first birthday and he was crying because this one moment was the most important thing in the world to him. Bruce saw the emotion in his face and was struck by the sincerity. Within ten minutes, he'd know more about the kid than his own parents knew about him. It was sobering…the ability to reach people that way, and to know that his music made that kind of connection in people's lives. He knew it was a dynamic between artist and audience that had to be honored and not blown off the way some rock artists blew off their fans. It was something he took seriously.[103]

In St. Paul, Minnesota, he met a few random fans at the airport where he was told about a critically ill kid who wouldn't be able to go to his show the next night…a friend of whoever he was talking to for those few seconds. Bruce, being rushed off into a station wagon, told the kid to get him his friend's name through the record company.

But damn, what were the chances of that happening?

What were the chances of that kid even reaching the record company? A chance encounter with Bruce Springsteen ends with him speeding off in a car, and that was all it would be. Given the continuous flow of people approaching him on any given day, something as brief as that encounter could easily be forgotten about or be sidetracked by the overwhelming nature of constant distraction.

Bruce remembered though.

Onstage at the St. Paul Civic Center, he addressed the kids he met at the airport. He couldn't see them…didn't know where their seats were…probably didn't remember their names or what they looked like…but he spoke to them again from the stage.

"I met a bunch of guys at the airport yesterday coming in. One told me he had a friend who was sick. If that fella who told me his friend was sick will come to the side of the stage during the break, I got something for your friend backstage."[104]

Yet, the aging compassionate Bruce at 31 still maintained the ever-present sense of humor and lighthearted trips down Memory Lane.

"I used to live in this house that was on like the main street," he told the crowd during the intro to "I Wanna Marry You." "In town was a street called South Street...and every day I used to watch this one girl walk by...and I think...she'd been married, she'd been divorced and she had a couple of kids...every day I used to sit on my porch...and I was...I was about 18 or 19, I guess...I used to try and figure ways I was gonna go up and introduce myself to her...well, I never did and I moved away...and you usually think that sometime...usually figure that you're gonna forget about these things, you know, these people you only see for like ten minutes...or you only see walking by or something...as you get older, but for some reason you never do...and every time, I remember...I used to imagine that I was back in that house and she was walking by...and I was gonna stumble across the street and drop some of my albums on the sidewalk...oops, excuse me, my albums (laughs)...but you only get those chances once...and if you ain't got no albums, what are you gonna do ? (laughs) This is a new song, this is called 'I Wanna Marry You'...this is ladies' choice...Big Man...Here she comes..."[105]

With Springsteen, Clemons and Van Zandt vocally bouncing off each other, "I Wanna Marry You" then becomes one of the finest moments of the nightly set list, as the "Here She Comes" intro transforms the song into an emotionally glorious trip through some of the most soulful melodies Springsteen has used and often reused over the years...the ones evoking Sam Cooke and Curtis Mayfield that take the moment to heights that equal the hardest rocking showstoppers. We hear these same melodies in "Drive all Night" and years later they surface again in Springsteen's 1988 live intro to "All That Heaven Will Allow." They reappear again in "Roll of the Dice" and in a slightly transformed chorus of "Better Days" during the last shows of his 1993 tour, a year that often saw him using the phrase *rock and soul* during performances.

Writer Divina Infusino perfectly summed up the unique live dynamic while reviewing the Milwaukee show two days after St. Paul: "Fans stood or sat tight in their seats captivated by a performer who never let them doubt that he was on this stage for them. In his book, he implied, they counted for something, their lives counted for something. That's the original promise of rock n' roll, and these days, few musical events fulfill it like a Springsteen concert."[106]

Two weeks into the tour, the band was in St. Louis for two shows on October 17 and 18 when Springsteen needed to get out of his hotel for a while. He took a cab into town and got out at a local movie theater where Woody Allen's *Stardust Memories* was showing. He got a ticket, went inside and got on line to buy popcorn when he was spotted by two teenage fans, brother and sister, Steve and Lisa Satanovsky who approached him. It was the type of encounter most fans couldn't even imagine let alone dream of. After talking to Bruce for a few minutes out near the concession counter, they invited him to sit with them in the theater, to which Bruce agreed. Following the film, Steve and Lisa took a random once-in-a-lifetime shot at asking Bruce to come back home with them to meet their parents. Bruce obliged, getting into their car and heading back with them into the Missouri suburbs. Upon entering Steve and Lisa's house, Bruce saw their father sprawled out on the couch and their mother sitting at the kitchen table. At first, she didn't believe her kids that the young man in front of her was really Bruce Springsteen, even after her son pulled out the album covers. Finally, she told him to show her his driver's license…after which, Bruce spent the next few hours talking to the family and eating watermelon. At one point, they even phoned Bruce's mother in California. The family invited Bruce to dinner the next night, a Friday night, but he had a show to play. However, he arranged for ten free tickets to the Satanovsky's for the Saturday show. In telling the story to Dave Marsh a few weeks later, Springsteen incorrectly remembered the city as Denver, and the exact date was widely speculated upon for years among Springsteen enthusiasts. A local TV station looking back on the event in 1988 reported that it was January 1981, one day before Bruce's Checkerdome concert, but the evidence is contrary. First, Springsteen himself told Marsh, *the other day*, when referring to the date. Second, he mistook the city for Denver, which is easily understood considering the grueling pace under which he was touring, along with the fact that Denver happened to be the next city after St. Louis. The date was in fact Thursday, October 16, 1980, the night before his two-concert run at the Kiel Auditorium began. Finally, considering the fact that *Stardust Memories* was not a Midwest suburban box office blockbuster, it is highly unlikely that it would still be playing in January after opening in late September. Steve and Lisa's mother, Sophie became friends with Bruce's mother, Adele, corresponding in written cards and went on to attend many shows over the years, often receiving shout-outs and song dedications from Bruce.

Over the course of the controversial four-night stand in Los Angeles between October 30 and November 3, Bruce addressed the scalping situation.

"I don't want to go blather on all night," he said early in the show just before "Two Hearts." "There´s something that´s happening here in Los Angeles that I´d just like to take two seconds to talk about. The highest price that you were supposed to pay for a seat here tonight was 12 dollars and 50 cents. We've gotten a lot of letters. I've talked to a lot of kids that are telling me they're paying 100 dollars, 200 dollars, 150 dollars for seats…and…what I'm saying is, what you have here in Los Angeles is you have a situation where you have ticket agencies where you have legalized scalping going on, somebody (the crowd boos) they can take…they can buy your ticket in New York City when you buy a ticket…the most a ticket agency can sell it for is a dollar fifty more than the price that is on it. What´s happening here…what´s happening here is there's people taking advantage of your desire to come down and see a show and they´re not given another choice. Tickets should go to the fans. They should not go to scalpers. In 1977 there was a bill introduced that would make the process by which these outrageous ticket prices come about illegal. And what…what I would like to see happen in this town would be if we could get together somehow and put some public pressure on the fellows in Sacramento and other beings in the State Assembly. And if you came in here, and I´d give you this information, I know they'd talk about it. What I´m saying is, man, people are…they´re getting beat and I don´t like to see it. It hurts me when I hear about it. Some kid comes up and tells me they paid 80 dollars to sit in a certain seat, it´s just not right. And so all I´m saying is it´s got to be Sacramento and the State Assembly, and all I can say to people that are making all this money, I mean, they don´t deserve it, you guys deserve it a lot better so…"[107]

In the end once again, to those who attended, the shows were triumphant experiences in the aging but ongoing effort of rock and roll…something only 26 years into its existence. Bob Dylan, one of Bruce's greatest musical influences and heroes was in attendance for the first L.A. show and was so impressed he went back for the final night with Jim Keltner, his then drummer. A local USC reporter, Gary Karr, captured the essence of the L.A. shows: "Devoted to his fans until the end, Springsteen performed a marathon four and one quarter hours, an unheard of feat in the era of present day 90 minute shows…Springsteen's music is more than fun. It is a celebration of the glory of rock, the highs and lows of life and the struggle to obtain happiness against seemingly insurmountable odds. Springsteen and the E Street Band put on an unparalleled show…he rewarded his audience with the best show they will ever see."[108]

Indeed it was.
Until the next one.
And the next one.
And the next one after that.

8

CLEANUP TIME

Rocky's Pawn Shop in the Deep Ellum section of Dallas, Texas, was located on the same street where President John F. Kennedy was killed. On one of the windows of the yellow wooden doors in the front hung a sign that read "Guns don't cause crime any more than flies cause garbage." The store specialized in guns and advertised itself as a discount headquarters for police equipment. Deep Ellum had a rich cultural history of American roots music where people like Huddie "Lead Belly" Ledbetter and Blind Lemon Jefferson passed through. The place served as a center of entertainment with a number of theaters and music venues aside from the plethora of pawn shops that lined Elm Street. Isaac Goldstein owned Rocky's, which was just down the street from Honest Joe's, a much more well-known pawn shop owned by his younger brother Rubin, who simply became known as "Honest Joe." Joe's store dated back to the early 1930s and became a central hub of activity attracting customers from all walks of life including politicians and actors. Jack Ruby's Carousel Club for example had items purchased in Honest Joe's.

Joe, for that matter, was friendly with Ruby, said to have mob ties, and speculation has it among JFK conspiracy theorists that Joe's van was seen parked in the lot behind the grassy knoll just before the President's motorcade came through Dealy Plaza. When Joe died in 1972, his wife took over the business, but in recent years, Rocky's had also become a prominent and vital presence on the block.

On October 13, 1980 a mentally unstable man named John Hinckley Jr. walked into Rocky's on the same day he should have been in court in Nashville, Tennessee. Ten days earlier, Hinckley had gotten to within six feet of President Carter during a campaign stop at the Convention Center in Dayton, Ohio. He had checked in to a Sheraton where he signed his name and identified himself as a writer from Lubbock, Texas, requesting a room with a view of the Convention Center. He paid $35.52 for room 818 and used his time in Dayton to perhaps case the possibilities for access and proximity to the president. One week later, he was in Nashville where the president was campaigning. At Nashville International Airport, he was arrested in the south concourse for possessing concealed weapons, but quickly released after paying his own bail of $62.50. Three guns were confiscated, a .38 and two .22 caliper pistols. When Hinckley returned to Dallas, he purchased two .22-caliper RG-14 six-shot revolvers from Rocky's. The registration document he filled out listed his address as Lubbock, his age as 25, and he checked no to the question of whether or not he used narcotics, was a felon or if he had ever been committed to a mental institution. He had in fact been under psychiatric treatment. For identification, he showed an old Texas driver's license with an old address. With no regulative measures in place to verify his background, this information was quite sufficient enough for the gun dealer to allow Hinckley to walk out with two guns, and there was nothing in federal law to stop it or even delay it.

Jimmy Carter decided the best place to launch his fall campaign would be in Tuscumbria, Alabama. He had a strong loyalty in the South in 1976, and the fear in 1980 was that a growing conservatism among blue collar workers and farmers would swing their votes toward Reagan. Carter felt he needed to remind people of his Southern roots.

As the President rode into town from the airport to speak at a rally, there were groups of Klansmen wearing white sheets and waving signs reading "Reagan for President." It wasn't his first encounter with the Ku Klux Klan. When he was governor, they paraded around the State Capitol in Atlanta when he dedicated a portrait of Martin Luther King. This memory was not lost on him as he spoke to the crowd of some 25,000 supporters and made a very specific effort to denounce the Klan.

"There are still a few in the South…indeed around the country…some, I heard from today…who practice cowardice and who counsel fear and hatred. They marched around the State Capitol in Atlanta when I was governor. They said we ought to be afraid of each other, and white ought to hate and be afraid of blacks, and that blacks ought to hate and be afraid of whites. As a Southerner, it makes me angry when I see them with a Confederate battle flag. And sometimes I see the raising of a cross, and I remember that the one who was crucified taught us to have faith, to hope and not to hate but to love one another. As the first man from the Deep South in almost 140 years to be president of this nation, I say that these people in white sheets do not understand our region and what it's been through, they do not understand what our country stands for…they do not understand that the South and all of America must move forward."[109] Given the cultural zeitgeist since Civil Rights, it was not uncommon to remind those who needed to be reminded… racism and white supremacy was a disgusting vestige of the past that had no place in America in the dawning of the 1980s, nor would it be tolerated. With that in mind, it would have been unimaginable to fathom in 1980…the prospect of a U.S. president encouraging such marches while praising its racist participants as "good people" six presidents later. It's not that America would move that far backwards over the next 35-40 years...it would happen in just one or two following the 2016 election.

But let's stay in 1980 for now.

The Shah's death over the summer seemed to mark a turning point in Iran's attitude toward dealing with Carter. This period of time coincides with Carter's realization that U.S. diplomatic efforts and trade embargo were having an effect, and that worldwide pressure wasn't helping Iran either. In early September, shortly after beginning his fall campaigning, he received word through German Foreign Minister, Hans-Dietrich Genscher that Iran wanted to begin talks with a high American official to work out terms for the hostages' release. Genscher had been in communication with an emissary from Khomeini. Carter was wary, as no Iranian had ever been permitted by Khomeini to correspond with any U.S. officials. The administration knew some of Iran's revolutionary leaders had gone to school in Germany and had close ties and connections there. They were not expecting such news out of Bonn, however. Yet, the follow-up messages from Iran were intriguing, giving Carter reason to believe there was hope in pursuing the recent developments accordingly. In a speech, Khomeini confirmed that a proposal had been made and that the terms and demands for the hostages would only be a few...the return of Iranian assets, return of the Shah's assets and to comply with Khomeini's wishes that the U.S. no longer concern itself with Iran's affairs.

The President sent Deputy Secretary of State, Warren Christopher to Europe to meet with Sadegh Tabatabai, the emissary involved in the talks who happened to be the brother-in-law of the ayatollah's son, Ahmed Khomeini. To complicate matters, the focal point of Christopher's trip ended up becoming a Soviet military buildup along the Iranian border and how best to deal with it. The eventual meetings seemed favorable to both sides, and when Tabatabai was scheduled to fly home to report back to Khomeini, Iraq decided to attack Iran, bombing the airport in Tehran. Carter was blamed and accused of arranging the invasion. It took Tabatabai a full week to finally arrive back in Iran and when he did, all talks were stalled.

The Alfred E. Smith Dinner in New York City on October 7 was where both candidates finally appeared together for the first time in the campaign. The dinner at the Waldorf Astoria was an annual event that raised money for charities of the Roman Catholic Arch Diocese of New York. Carter skipped dinner and only showed up for his speech, disappointing a lot of people. Reagan made a short self-deprecating speech, while Carter spoke about foreign policy in a manner that Nancy thought was boastful and inaccurate. He also spoke about religious intolerance, aiming his words at Reagan's fundamentalist supporters. One minister had recently issued a statement suggesting that God only hears the prayers of "redeemed" Christians. Carter recalled a 12-year old Jewish boy at a town meeting in Pennsylvania who asked if God heard his prayers. The president remarked how such a question in the United States of 1980 should never have to be asked. "In our zeal to strengthen the moral character of this nation we must not set ourselves up as judges of whom God might hear, or who would turn away."[110]

The yearly dinners were usually filled with lighthearted humor and jokes, and although Carter set a serious moral tone, he still took the opportunity to playfully jab Reagan on the presidency, appealing to him that it was a "terrible burden" and a "terrible experience" that he did not want to take on. In reality, both candidates seemed clueless to the other side's intentions and motivations.[111] Carter just couldn't relate to or grasp Reagan's mentality, while Reagan simply detested and frowned upon Carter's, as did his critics. Carter, like Reagan believed the American people should not look to government to solve their problems. He was also a deeply religious man. But among profound differences, they viewed Carter as weak because in their estimation, he valued Human Rights over national security, and was more concerned about controlling arms than building more nuclear weapons. When Carter gave his speech at the University of Notre Dame and advised Americans to get over their fear of communism, Reagan emphasized his fear even more, and then projected it outward onto the psyche of the nation. As with many, Carter was frightened by the thought of someone with Reagan's reputation being behind anything having to do with nuclear weapons or the military in general. He'd offer this assessment to a crowd in Chicago:

"If you've got just a strong military and you are jingoist in spirit and just show the macho of the United States, that is an excellent way to lead our country toward war. The Oval Office is not a place for simplistic answers. It is not a place of shooting from the hip. It is not a place for snap judgments that might have serious consequences."[112]

This did not frighten conservatives in the same way, nor were some earlier critics of Reagan bothered, such as Leon Jaworski who once called the candidate an extremist who troubled open-minded voters.[113]

Jaworkski, a former Watergate special prosecutor became the honorary chairman of Democrats for Reagan saying that he would rather have a competent extremist than have an incompetent moderate.[114]

Reagan's public persona during the 1960s was often one of a bitter and angry man and many moderate conservatives remembered that person… the same man who said in 1965, "We should declare war on North Vietnam. We could pave the whole country and put parking stripes on it and still be home by Christmas."[115] It is telling that given how weak the economy was along with the situation in Iran, that the two major presidential candidates remained neck and neck in the polls right up until the very end. But Reagan gave the impression in his tone and rhetoric of a new Republican Party…one that was going to embrace the working man as it began to appear that Carter and the Democrats were out of touch with blue collar values, and plainly unaware of the growing resentment for affirmative action, the welfare state and the increased government spending of Keynesian economics. This is what ultimately appealed to the American people...even as the polls were indeed a clear indication of how wary of Reagan half the country really was. At least until the election.

Reagan's charming charisma wasn't the only element working against Carter, but it played on the fact that there were criticisms of the president on his own side, where faith in his presidency was never fully embraced. Ted Kennedy's earlier charges that Carter was a closet Republican, though slightly absurd, were not totally unfounded. Considering that Carter approached Washington as a populist outsider and often hinted at a strong military, and eventually spoke big about consequential action toward Iran and/or Russia, it wasn't uncommon to wonder if he had conservative tendencies or if it was merely muscle-flexing and macho posturing in an aim to impress the hawks on the right and redefine his presidency. Pollster and political consultant Pat Caddell urged Carter early in his presidency to pick some conservative issues to hijack in an attempt to steal them from the Republicans and make his own. Writing to the new president in early 1977, Caddell was also aware of the potential for political backlash from the left as he told Carter that it was an opportune time to co-opt many issue positions of the other side, thus eliminating parts of their next presidential platform. If the left actually implemented a right wing agenda, what would they have to oppose? But then again, Caddell was also very aware of the fact that they could ruffle some feathers on their own side.[116] All this considered, regardless of the usual explanations popular among negative assessments of Carter...an outsider who didn't understand the manner in which Washington worked or the bureaucracy that exceeded presidential grasp, other accounts are a little more profound in their observations. Stephen Hess of the Brookings Institution and a former advisor to Carter, for example, suggested Carter as a "process president," based on Jack Knott and Aaron Wildavsky's hypothesis that Carter placed "emphasis on methods, procedures and instruments for making policy than on the content of policy itself."[117] The critique was that Carter was far less concerned with setting goals than with the need for goals. His priority was not the content of policy, but how policy was concocted and implemented. In this estimation, Hess saw Carter as an activist with a passion not for what needed to be done, but for how it was done, and his downfall was his "failure to set consistent policy goals."[118]

The inability to set concrete and coherent policy whether public, foreign or domestic, still owed both to his difficult relationship to the people he needed in Washington, and his own often-condescending tone. Most people genuinely liked him. Even his worst critics still liked him as a person. But by many accounts, the nice guy could turn harsh, abrasive and antagonistic in an instant. Senators on Carter's own side were unable to connect with him. They would often walk out of White House meetings disgusted, feeling Carter had talked down to them. It's not that he burned bridges. Bridges, simply, were never built where they easily could have been. Speaker, Tip O'Neil believed that Carter never understood how the system worked in Washington politics, nor did he want to learn.[119] To Carter, senators amounted to little more than high-level lobbyists. Encapsulating the gist of his shortcomings as we move forward, Carter had very few friends in the federal government and therefore did not have the personal connections often necessary to achieve his presidential goals and purposes.

The obvious pressing issues going into the crucial months of autumn were the situations in Iran and Afghanistan. Carter maintained right up through the last presidential debate that military force was never off the table, although it was furthest from his first option, while t-shirts in shopping malls and bumper stickers on the streets read BOMB IRAN. Always a man of peace through diplomacy, he prided his presidency on his ability to work successfully for a peace treaty between Israel and Egypt, and tied the United States to both nations in a common defense capability which he believed to be a big step forward for the security of America. Yet, when met with critics on Iran or the Soviets, or faced with questions related to how he would deal with a shut off of Persian Gulf oil, or how to counter Russian expansion beyond Afghanistan, he re-established his State of the Union message that any threat to the stability of the Persian Gulf would be a threat to the stability of the United States, and then hint at military action. The questions arose because the consensus on the right was that the U.S. was "woefully unprepared for a sustained military presence in that part of the world," and Carter even acknowledged U.S. presence as inadequate.[120]

Reagan pointed out during the Cleveland debate on October 27 that America was in a war that was winding down during the eight years prior to Carter which would account for a change in military spending going from war to peace. BUT…Republican presidents during those years, contending with a Democratic majority in both houses of Congress, faced opposition when requests for defense budgets were cut. Ford left a five-year projected plan for a military buildup to restore U.S. defenses. Carter cut that plan by 38%, cut 60 proposed ships out of the Navy building program, stopped the B-1, delayed cruise missiles, stopped the production line for the minute man missile, delayed the Tridents submarine…. "and now he's planning a mobile military force that can be delivered to various spots in the world which does make me question his assaults on whether I am the one who is quick to look for use of force."[121]

The reality was that after Carter's botched rescue attempt, the use of force was highly unlikely before the election. William Casey and Reagan's team, however, remained wary of an "October Surprise" whereby Carter would work out a deal to have the hostages released. Casey put together a watch team, later dubbed by Ed Meese, "the October Surprise watch." Every possible scenario of an outcome was considered whereby a deal between the Carter administration and Iran could be reached, and then Reagan's team would devise a response for every scenario. Little did they know such a deal had been in the works during the weeks immediately before the start of the Iran/Iraq War. In one confidential memo from the team intended for Meese and dated October 19, they stated, "The Iranians know that the race is very close and that Carter will be susceptible to pressure in the next two weeks, perhaps more so than in the past month." The memo goes on to state Iranian objectives, those that were agreed upon by both Carter and Reagan and then goes on to say "The negotiations will conclude when the Iranian's feel they have reached the point at which the cost of further delay is greater than the benefits to be expected from additional concessions. This will depend on 1) the events in the Iran-Iraq War, as they relate to Iran's ability to continue fighting 2) the perceived firmness of Carter's negotiating posture, and 3) the prospect of Reagan's election. It is recommended that beginning now, up to the time the hostages are released, Governor Reagan's posture be to emphasize the following: 1) note that there are increasing signs that the hostages' release may be imminent. Greet this news cautiously, but favorably. Ronald Reagan should express his hopes and prayers that the hostages will be coming home soon, even if it is the day before the election. 2) Insist, though, that the U.S. not complete any deals or trades until all out people are at home, and the conditions are made public. Add that we must be mindful of the long-range consequences of any arrangement we make."[122]

The fact that Reagan's team, as Americans, wanted the hostages returned home safely with zero harm done is doubtless and without question. As political strategists, they just didn't want it to happen before the election. Casey wrote to Reagan and Meese regarding Carter's efforts, stating that it was probable that the president would be perceived as engaging in last-minute desperate attempts to work out a deal for his own political gain and once again, botch it up. Casey's advice to both was to sit back and watch the fireworks.[123] By the debate in Cleveland, the concern was less and less.

In Cleveland, Carter told the moderator and the audience that he had recently asked his 12-year old daughter, Amy what she thought the most important issue was, and she said, "Nuclear weaponry and the control of nuclear arms."[124] The comment drew laughter and the president took some heat from the media for bringing his daughter into the discussion, as if a 12-year old would truly be thinking about nuclear arms. In the final days of the campaign, Reagan supporters began showing up at rallies holding ASK AMY signs. The overall tone in response to Carter since the debate had been one of mockery...an at-long-last revealing and unfurling of revelations that he was clinging to negativity, much in the same way he began his presidency and needed to remain on the defensive, as he was not only running on the future, but on his record of the past four years. Regarding that four years, Reagan summed it up as plainly as any candidate had ever spoken words on the cusp of a turning point that history still hasn't been able to fully comprehend. Yet, it indeed marked a turning point:

"Are you better off than you were four years ago? Is it easier for you to go and buy things in the store than it was four years ago? Is there more or less employment in the country than there was four years ago? Is America respected throughout the world as it was? Do you feel that our security is safe, that we're as strong as we were four years ago? If your answer to all these questions is yes, why I think your choice is very obvious as to who you'll vote for. If you don't agree, if you think that this course that we've been on for the last four years is what you would like to see us follow for the next four, then I could suggest another that you have."[125]

Given the passage of time necessary for history to be an accurate judge of the events that take place, some situations seem to be well-understood in their own time period. Being in the thick of it...the energy crisis, gas shortage, inflation and unemployment spelling out one giant across-the-board domestic disaster on top of mounting pressure from a hostage crisis and instability in the Middle East with the Soviets breathing down its neck, there is no disputing the fact that an overwhelming majority of Americans had lost faith in Carter. If one needed a prior turning point that inevitably hurt the president, the debacle that was Operation Eagle Claw probably sealed his fate a lot sooner than Reagan's dominance in Cleveland.

When John Hinckley Jr. purchased his guns from Rocky's in Dallas, he was replacing the arsenal that was confiscated by the police in Nashville where he was stalking President Carter. Hinckley was half a decade into a slow and inevitable downward spiral that saw him dropping out of college and bouncing between Texas and California after his parents relocated to Colorado in the mid 1970s. He enrolled in Texas Tech in 1973 after his parents pressured him to get into college, but all he got out of the experience was learning that he was a racist after living with a black roommate. In a journal, he'd write that the differences between black and white were too great to overcome in order to be integrated in America. He'd soon fully identify as a white supremacist.[126] By that time, he had begun buying guns while voicing his thoughts in a diary after seeing and becoming obsessed with the movie *Taxi Driver* and its main character, Travis Bickle. Martin Scorsese's 1976 classic starred Robert De Niro as Bickle, a mentally unstable cab driver obsessed with a teenage prostitute named Iris, played by teenage actress, Jodie Foster. Bickle, a loner who is angry and sickened by the ills of society also begins stalking a presidential candidate who he plans on assassinating.

There were two areas of fascination for Hinckley within *Taxi Driver*, a film he watched some 15 times. The first was Bickel, whom he strongly identified with, from the character's alienation from society to his obsession with Iris. But where Bickle was hung up on Iris, Hinckley's pre-occupation was with Jodie Foster. At one point, he trekked up to New Haven when he found out she was attending Yale…planning, stalking but then retreating. That fall, Foster received word of a kidnapping threat against her that although amounted to nothing, was nonetheless cause for concern. October had faded into November, as the winds and wuthering of autumn 1980 now fully in place, announced its permanence as the backdrop for a season of mysterious unsettled nature…of some nondescript malevolence in the air and in the stars.

During the first weekend of November, the Iranian Parliament was rumored to be talking about the release of the hostages, going as far as setting Iran's conditions. President Carter suspended his campaign and returned to the White House to meet with advisers. In the news, Gerald Ford and Henry Kissinger began accusing Iran of trying to influence the outcome of the election. Still, neither Carter nor Reagan would comment on Iran or the hostage situation while on the campaign trail. On Monday the third, Reagan was in Illinois, Independent John Anderson in Minnesota, and Carter was in the middle of one last 36-hour trek around the country, hitting the Midwest before flying to the Pacific Northwest to hit Oregon and Washington at the eleventh hour.

In the eleventh hour of Bruce Springsteen's second set, his spontaneity was beginning to surface in the new songs as he and the band were firing on all cylinders and operating as one single mechanical unit. As he stretched out "You Can Look" (But You Better Not Touch), he began to ad lib vocals on top of an extended breakdown:

You can look…you can look…
you can look…you can look…
you better not…you better not…
you better not…you better not…
goin' downtown…gonna buy a gun…
gonna be a long…shiny one…
goin' downtown…gonna buy a gun…
goin' downtown…gonna buy a gun…
gonna buy a gun…gonna buy a gun
gonna buy a gun…

9

HEAD-ON COLLISION

The poll results were disturbing. On the eve of not only the election, but the one-year anniversary of the hostage crisis, people began to realize the hostages weren't coming home anytime soon. Americans had lost faith, and more significantly, they had lost trust. And they were speaking. Carter's numbers took a massive plunge as all the undecided voters moved toward Reagan. Even as they campaigned in Oregon and Washington, they knew they had no chance. When the president returned back to the White House in the early morning hours of the fourth, he talked to Rosalynn and then told his family the situation. Remarkably, they were at peace.

Tuesday, November 4 was what John Lennon referred to as *Erection Day*.[127] When Carter lost in a landslide, Lennon predicted Reagan would be assassinated and the U.S. would be overtaken by George H.W. Bush.[128] Two of the networks called the election for Ronald Reagan by 7:30 that night. At 8:30, Carter phoned Reagan to congratulate him. The grateful new president-elect took the call just as he was stepping out of the shower at his Pacific

Palisades home. He was ecstatic yet surprised by the margin of his victory. He promised Carter that he'd work with him to heal and unify the country. An hour after the phone call, Carter delivered his concession speech and went to bed. Soon after, Ronald and Nancy Reagan left for the Century Plaza Hotel where the president-elect would thank his supporters.

On the morning of November 5 after carrying only six states, Carter prepared for the interim, designating Chief of Staff, Jack Watson to head the transition team. He quickly met with the press as a sign of good sportsmanship and to show that his team was in good shape and was ready to be supportive of the in-coming president and aid in a smooth transition period. He stressed that he would back Reagan if in his presidency he made an effort for progress on inflation, unemployment, SALT and other issues that were important to him. From there, Carter flew to Camp David for some rest and to plan for the future. For having lost an election, he was in what he called remarkably good spirits. He'd come to deeply regret losing the 1980 election, but at the time, the final year of his presidency had been far more stressful than the first three combined, so some time away was much-needed.

Bruce Springsteen spent the day in his hotel room and did not come out until it was time to leave for his show at Arizona State University. During sound check, he walked the arena through all tiers of the rafters and across the floor seating as he often did, trying to get an accurate reading of the sound from an audience perspective. Several hours later deep into the first set, he stood center stage to address the crowd just before "Badlands." The song usually featured a keyboard intro of Ennio Morricone's "Once Upon a Time in the West. This time there was no intro as Bruce just strummed some chords while approaching the microphone.

"I don't know what you guys think about what happened last night, but I think it's pretty frightening."[129]

The crowd exploded in an approving applause.

He had gone into territory he had not gone anywhere near before, and it was clear what he was referring to. If there was any trepidation about voicing post-election concerns onstage, it went away instantly.

"You guys are young," he continued, "and there's gonna be a lot of people depending on you comin' up. So this is for you."[130]

What followed was a version of "Badlands" so blistering that it ended up on his *Live 1975-85* box set years later. Greil Marcus wrote about Springsteen's remarks soon after, boldly predicting that his future writing, whether directly or indirectly, would reflect the 1980 election, and its eventual inevitable consequences. Nothing in his personal life or in the news events of the day had ever motivated Springsteen to share his fears of a Reagan presidency. Or was it Republicans in general that frightened him? He hadn't voted since 1972, and it wasn't for Nixon. His early club tours coincided with Watergate. His initial fame came during the Ford years. And although a gas shortage and a hostage crisis marred the Carter years, damage to the country's economic stability as well as its morale had been a factor for the better part of a decade, long before Carter took office. The memory of Nixon, Watergate and the Vietnam War were still too close behind. Yet, Springsteen's work shut all of it out. None of his music reflected any of those things, although his last few albums did share a blue collar sentiment, championing the *little guy*, which seems to be a natural part of his progression in what ultimately resulted in concern with regard to the election. He had stayed away from politics his entire adult life up until that point, which is why his comments seemed to have come out of nowhere.

Ten days later, some other things would start to change onstage as well. Bruce started feeling a sort of monotony, even in his multiple versions of the set list. At the Summit in Houston, he told the band in the middle of the show not to look at the set list anymore, and to just wait for him to call and count off the next song. Very often, drummer, Max Weinberg would be able to pick up which song was coming next just by the way Bruce counted it off... the intro to everything becoming a Hail Mary pass...*One, two, three, four...*

John Lennon wasn't a fan of Ronald Reagan. Although he never spoke out against him publicly, he wasn't a supporter, as Fred Seamen would claim decades later. Lennon, whether or not always vocal about it, was involved with left wing politics right up until his death. One month after Reagan's election, the Lennon's took out a public ad to show their support of union workers in Los Angeles and San Francisco striking against the Japan Foods Corporation for higher wages. The company was a subsidiary of the multinational Kikkoman. They wrote that they were with the union workers in spirit and remarked how sad it was that in a country where democracy was the foundation of its constitution, citizens still had to fight for equal pay and equal rights.[131]

Despite Carter's quick acceptance of the election results, pundits and pollsters were scratching their heads over the landslide, which couldn't be farther from the "too close to call" outcome they predicted. The popular vote easily went to Reagan with 43, 903,230 votes, decimating Carter who received 35, 480, 115 votes. With Reagan scoring 489 electoral votes, and Carter only 49, Reagan Headquarters had been a scene of jubilant celebration. Also partying were 13 newly-elected Republican senators whose victories largely contributed to the new Big Picture: For the first time since 1954, the GOP held the senate majority. Among the losing Democrats were George McGovern, Birch Bayh, Warren Magnusen, Frank Church and Herman Talmadge. McGovern commented on how the amount of virulence and extremism taking over the political process was unprecedented. Out of an entire group of Democrats that were targeted by the National Conservative Political Action Committee, only two, Alan Cranston and Thomas Eagleton were re-elected. With respect to the popular vote, only 52.4% of the eligible voting population showed up to vote and it was the lowest turnout since 1948.

Across the Atlantic, Europe was coming to terms with the news. Conservatives like Margaret Thatcher, Prime Minister of Britain, felt Reagan would ultimately provide more leadership for the Western world, though some governments feared confrontation with the Soviet Union. Concerns aside, all of Europe was impressed with the size of the conservative victory. In Iran, where Tehran Radio referred to Reagan as a fascist cowboy, a delay in releasing the hostages seemed all but certain. Although both major candidates were greatly disliked, it was Reagan who the Iranians didn't want to see elected.

On Sunday, November 16, newspapers across the country ran feature stories on *Double Fantasy* and John Lennon's return. The album was finally coming out that week, and between his new single slowly climbing the charts and the media attention, John had to acclimate himself to something he hadn't had to deal with for some time. The phone rang at the Dakota. It was Julian, and John took the call. They talked for a bit and Julian told him he was broke and needed some money, which John wasn't happy about, apparently feeling used.[132] He knew their relationship wasn't much to speak of, but had talked about it extensively during the *Playboy* interview two months earlier. Although John's remarks about the nature of his relationship to Julian compared with his relationship to Sean were rather scathing, spelling out the vast difference between an unwanted child and a planned child, and that the "Saturday night special" isn't going to get all of the attention that the planned child is going to get, he still acknowledged that he was going to be in his first son's life very soon.[133] A trip to England would be discussed in the weeks ahead, and John would make an effort at being a better dad. They both hung up the phone that day, neither of them knowing that it would be the last time they'd ever talk to each other.

Double Fantasy was released the next day, and listening to the radio, John was amused by WPLJ's on-air listening party to preview the album. The Playboy interview hit the newsstand that day as well, an issue dated January 1981. John was feeling insecure about the reception *Double Fantasy* would get. He saw himself as no longer relevant compared to more current artists and bands like Bruce Springsteen or The Cars. Springsteen was on his mind that month, as he observed the 31-year old's rise from cult figure to superstar. John was 40 and had nine years on Bruce not only in age, but as a recording artist who had experienced the rollercoaster of stardom and how people could get eaten alive if they didn't know how to handle it. He was concerned about how Bruce would deal with it, and what it would do to him. In some ways, he felt sorry for him. Bruce Springsteen was the "it" guy in the autumn of 1980 and John Lennon knew it. Regarding The Cars, he liked their latest single, "Touch and Go," and was also digging The Pretenders and the B-52s. The kind of uncertainty about his role in current rock music was nothing uncommon and certainly not unique to his mindset. Pete Townshend just happened to be experiencing the same exact anxiety for several years, and because he never took an extended hiatus the way John did, his awareness of the newer bands and the place of The Who was probably far more excruciating.

That week, John only saw Yoko at around seven in the morning before she left to go to the studio for the day. She began working with David Geffen on a new song called "Walking on Thin Ice," which she eagerly wanted to have out by Christmas. Left to his own devices, John had breakfast while reflecting on death and contemplating the afterlife as he sat at the window looking out over Central Park. Life was going good now. His ties to Yoko, at least on the surface, seemed stronger than they had earlier in the year, and he had a close relationship with Sean. He also had a hit single climbing up the charts and a successful new album out. There was plenty to do and plenty to plan for. And all of that death stuff was so far off.

Double Fantasy itself ended up working cohesively as a John Lennon and Yoko Ono album as opposed to just another Lennon solo album. The deliberately-balanced approach worked not only in song sequence, but also in the perfect Kubrickian symmetry of the album cover, offering both John and Yoko's name, one on each side of a centered black and white photo of the Lennon's engaged in a kiss. Regardless of whether the sequencing was a mutual agreement between the couple or was dictated by Yoko, the songs served as a domestic dialogue between the two artists.

While the record was underscored by a theme of moving on together, or at the very least, hitting the reset button, the very first sounds heard, harkened back to the Plastic Ono Band album where the ringing of a bell opened "Starting Over" just as it had on "Mother" a decade earlier. It was a sense of coming full circle and renewal, and John made that clear in his lyrics. "Starting Over," the first single, was climbing the charts almost too quickly for John to notice with all of the press and promo going on simultaneously. The song was a throwback to Elvis Presley's "I Want You, I Need You, I Love You," where John channeled the same shivering voice and vocal style. Even as the Beatles progressed into their own, John's early rock and roll influences never left him. He'd play "Hound Dog" at the Garden in 1972 and jam with Chuck Berry on the Mike Douglas Show the same year. His *Rock 'N' Roll* album of 1975, the last thing he released until that point in time, was filled with chestnuts of rock's first decade. His very reasons for liking certain newer songs on the radio were precisely because of what he saw as 1950s influences, as he'd talk about during *Double Fantasy* promotional interviews. "Starting Over" mixed an obvious Elvis delivery with the ever-present familiar sense of melody that had come to characterize John's body of post-Beatles work.

In sequence, Yoko answers "Starting Over" with "Kiss, Kiss, Kiss," and anyone listening for the first time expecting a John Lennon album was not only in for a shock to hear Yoko's voice so suddenly on the vinyl, but it was Yoko being Yoko in typical Yoko avant-garde fashion. Sonically, it wasn't unlike what the B-52s, Lene Lovich or Hazel O'Connor had been doing in recent years and months, but if John saw Yoko as the precursor to any new wave movement, it was the originator now imitating the influenced. It wasn't uncommon though. Many artists had come back around to put their own stamp on sounds begun by the very artists they themselves first influenced. So while bands like The Who had an undeniable influence on bands like The Jam, it was clear Pete Townshend was in turn influenced by the work of Paul Weller in the late 70s and into the early 80s. John's ex-partner, Paul had certainly been soaking up the modern sounds of the last half decade and none of it had anything to do with the Beatles' stamp on pop music. John was different, and the notion that he wasn't paying attention to current trends until Fred Seamen turned him on to certain things in the spring of 1980 seems plausible. There is not much of any current influence to go by in what we hear in John's *Double Fantasy* songs. Musically, they are not very far removed from anything original that he put out prior to his hiatus, but do occasionally venture into the latest slick modern pop production trends of the day, and that is evident by the album's third track, "Cleanup Time." The remainder of the album is a conversation between John and Yoko and husband and wife in a relationship that was by no means perfect or even healthy, at least not by any orthodox standards. It does not paint a picture of a happy marriage, but one of weathering the storm and coming out the other side. Much has been made over that sentiment, however, and it is often suggested that John and Yoko's marriage at this point was virtually non-existent, and that *Double Fantasy* is a false display of a couple coming back together. In reality, the couple had come back together five years earlier, and perhaps the album is really part of the denial stage in something that had actually run its course.

On Thursday, November 20, Carter met alone with Reagan in the Oval Office. The discussion was cordial, friendly, detailed and unrestrained. The president-elect spent most of the meeting listening as Carter urged him to set aside time to be briefed on his responsibilities under the SIOP (Single Integrated Operation Plan, the procedure for deployment of nuclear weapons). The president spoke to him about agreements with Britain and France on the handling of nuclear materials and launching a nuclear attack, intelligence with China, support for Afghan freedom fighters and Pakistan, stealth airplanes, why the B-1 was not needed, Strategic Arms Litigation, the importance of announcing that the SALT II would be effective until a more acceptable treaty was negotiated and the significance of the nonproliferation policy. He had stressed SALT II was in the national security interest of the country and not an appeasement of the Soviet Union and made his feelings known unequivocally to Reagan. Carter also emphasized the need for the MX which had taken ten years to develop. He brought Reagan up to date on the hostage situation, and assured him that his team would be kept in the loop during the transition. He then urged Reagan to keep up the Camp David process and keep in touch with Israeli Prime Minister Menachem Begin and Egyptian president, Anwar Sadat, suggesting a summit meeting. The president also brought up the question of the F-15 sales to Saudi Arabia and insisted they were both in agreement before a policy was adopted, to which the president-elect responded favorably to.

Carter later remembered Reagan's comments during a brief discussion on the possible execution of Kim Dae Jung who had been arrested for sedition. Although the president-elect didn't say much throughout the meeting, Carter specifically recalled him saying he admired the South Koreans for the way they handled demonstrators, and how when President Park Chung-He was faced with students demonstrating on campus, he closed all the universities and drafted the demonstrators into the army. Reagan told Carter he was envious of how much authority the president of Korea had. The one thing that struck Carter the most about the meeting and its aftermath was the fact that the entire Reagan transition team refused briefing on any of a wide range of vital situations, namely the hostages in Iran, the following year's budget and the sale of the F-15 to Saudi Arabia. He wondered whether the decision to not be briefed during the transition period came from Reagan himself or whether his subordinates used it as a strategy to distance themselves from responsibility for any decisions or actions Carter might take as president until Inauguration Day.[134]

After the Reagan's left the White House, the Carter's did some photo ops, returned to the South Grounds, and took off for Camp David.

That night, some 700 miles northwest of Camp David where the president and First Lady were watching a screening of *The Blues Brothers*, Springsteen and the E Street Band played the Rosemont Horizon, their first ever arena show in the Chicago area. Early in the second set, a concert ritual was born during the instrumental opening of "Hungry Heart." As the band made its way through the beginning of the song, the audience spontaneously began to sing the first verse to the delight of Bruce. This meant one thing. Everyone knew the words. Hell, everyone knew the words to all of his songs for that matter, but this one was hot in everyone's heads just as it had cracked the Top 20 on the Billboard charts that week, and *The River* became the number one album in the country. He had finally gotten what he always wanted…an official hit song. Being at the top of the album charts didn't hurt either.

Between Chicago and Largo, Maryland, the weekend had begun. The band had two days off. Friday, November 21 saw the entirety of the country glued to their television sets for various reasons. In the afternoon, regularly scheduled soap operas and game shows were interrupted by special reports from Las Vegas where a massive fire had ripped through the MGM Grand Hotel, claiming 84 lives. This overrode most programming from mid-afternoon through the early evening hours. John Lennon and Yoko Ono were occupied with other things as the MGM tragedy unfolded on television. Floating about freely outside in the crisp autumn air as the Dakota hovered about and loomed against their horizon, the couple wandered Central Park in black leather jackets and newsboy caps. They were accompanied by photographer Allan Tannenbaum who took some promo pictures for the coming media blitz of *Double Fantasy*. With Tannenbaum, they'd also shoot a nude lovemaking video the following week in a SoHo gallery on a set that had been built into a white bedroom. That night, America tuned in to CBS to watch *Dallas* in order to find out who shot JR Ewing, as the shooter's identity was finally revealed in Season Three's third episode. It turned out to be the most-watched television event in history up to that point in time.

On Sunday, November 23, the E Street Band rolled into Largo to begin two nights at the Capitol Centre. With the start of the holiday season approaching, the tour itinerary seemed to be designed in such a way that would allow the band to be close to home during the final weeks of the year. The Northeast states would be their stomping ground from the end of November to the New Year. This would be the peak and pinnacle of Springsteen's concert history, at least until his career-capping and age-defying tour de force run in the summer of 2016. The shows over the next five weeks were the ones that would build the myth and legend of Springsteen, and seal his reputation as a live performer doing marathon concerts.

The next day, Nancy Reagan received a phone call from her son, Ron, who told her that he had just married Doria Palmieri. Considering it was not announced, no invitations, no formal ceremony nor reception, it was a potential hindrance to the president-elect in the form of tabloid gossip and a question of conservative values. When asked about it, the president-elect responded, "It was an elopement," to which his son quickly answered publicly, "How could it be an elopement? Doria and I have been living together for a year and a half."[135]

The couple was married that rainy Monday morning in New York City by acting New York Supreme Court Justice, Lester Evans, and it was probably the last thing Ronald Reagan needed during the transition period. The news, however, was inconsequential, and Nancy was even a little relieved since she had been worried about the sleeping arrangements between Ron and Doria when the entire family would be staying at Blair House for a few days before the inauguration. Now that the couple was married, they wouldn't bring sin to Blair House in the form of pre-inaugural scandal.

Just before Thanksgiving, John and Yoko met with Ringo Starr and fiancé, Barbara Bach in their suite at the Plaza Hotel. Bach's nude pictures were featured in the current Playboy, the same issue with John's interview. Bach not really taking part in the discussion, tended to her kids while John, Yoko and Ringo talked about projects they were working on. Ringo was in the beginning stages of his next album and needed new material. The two ex-Beatles agreed to work together as John offered to write some songs. That was how they left it.

Some 25 blocks south of the Plaza, the scene at Madison Square Garden was charged with the electricity of the first of four Springsteen shows. Due to sports scheduling at the Garden, the third and fourth shows had to be booked for December, and all four were instantly controversial as thousands of tickets went missing. With the demand high enough to sell out a month's worth of concerts, most ticket orders were not met, much like the case in Los Angeles a month earlier. It was surrounding these particular shows where ticket scalping was brought to the forefront as a problem for the concert industry. A full-scale investigation later revealed a scalping ring from inside the Garden itself where five ticket sellers employed by the venue sold large blocks of tickets to brokers for payments totaling $11,000. Some of the tickets with a face value of $12.50 and a $2.50 broker's commission were sold for $100. Springsteen was not the only artist whose shows were effected, as Rush and Van Halen's performances at the Garden that year were also part of the scalping ring, as was the Broadway show *42nd Street*.

Springsteen and the E Street Band hit New York City for the Thanksgiving holiday weekend in what became the venue's most-anticipated concerts since the band had last played there for the *No Nukes* shows 14 months earlier. "Hungry Heart" was hot at number 18 on the pop chart and still climbing, while *The River* was spending its third week at number one on the album chart. Bruce couldn't be any hotter at the moment. WNEW-FM, New York's rock station that championed Springsteen from day one was on hand to do the honors as DJ, Vin Scelsa stepped up to the microphone just after the house lights went down.

"Hello, I'm Vin Scelsa from WNEW-FM, and I want to say Happy Thanksgiving to you all! I want you to say hello and welcome home to New York…Bruce Springsteen and the E Street Band!"[136]

"One, two…" the Boss counted off, and they were into "Born To Run" with the adoring crowd in the palm of his hands, screaming back every word, at times drowning out Bruce himself. The next night, they did it again. Three and a half hours both nights…31 and 32 songs withthe concerts growing to marathon length. By December, he was averaging 35 songs per night, pushing the shows well past midnight. Much of the River Tour saw the exclusion of his first two albums, with the exception of "Rosalita," the second set closer. Most of the shows on the tour saw around 30 songs. It was during the holiday season between Thanksgiving and New Years when the length of the show noticeably grew. There was a special occasion feeling surrounding cities like Boston, Hartford, Philadelphia and New York…a feeling that warranted the inclusion of songs from *Greetings* and *The Wild, the Innocent and the E Street Shuffle*. He also brought out "Rendezvous," a *Darkness* outtake for a few weeks. One would think that he would trim the portion of *River* and *Darkness* songs to accompany these one-offs and rarities into the set, but he didn't. The set just got longer. Everything was played.

"Starting Over" cracked the Top Ten and hit number eight during the first week of December. With such good news, John Lennon was delighted to see the cover of the *Soho News* on Wednesday, December 3, which featured a photo of Yoko with the headline, "Yoko Only." *Finally*, he thought, she was getting attention on her own. With this, he became inspired again and accompanied her to the studio where he added a guitar track to "Walking on Thin Ice." After the session, he told Yoko, "You've got a hit, Mother!"[137]

At this juncture, John expressed to David Geffen that he too would like to see Yoko's single released by Christmas. Suddenly, he was bombarded with ideas. *What about a Yoko solo album? We could call it Discono!*

Hold on!

Slow down, John!

Geffen wanted to do things right and there was no rush as far as he was concerned. One thing at a time.[138]

Springsteen spent the early morning of December 3 riding in his rented Winnebago from Rochester to Buffalo, accompanied by *Rolling Stone* reporter Fred Schruers, who had been traveling on and off with the tour since the St. Paul show back in October. The snowy and icy conditions in the 22-degree cold of Buffalo didn't stop the artist and writer from walking around downtown where Bruce wanted to enjoy the "fresh air." The pair stopped in at a local record store where Bruce loaded up on cassettes from The Drifters and Gene Pitney. Toots and the Maytals' *Funky Kingston* was the current selection in his personal tape player according to Schruers. It wasn't long before the guys behind the counter recognized him and put on "Hungry Heart." A few girls also ran up to him in a bookstore asking for autographs. But not everyone in Buffalo knew who he was. They next stopped at a McDonalds where the normalcy of their settings completely set Bruce at ease. He was never comfortable with the restaurants that had the menus in the window. Places like McDonalds were occupied by real people and there was nothing phony or pretentious about ordering quarter pounders in a setting full of real people. In fact, for Schruers, listening to Bruce ramble on about how the entire situation was "nothing but real" must have seemed reminiscent of a line that would one day be mocked in the film, *Almost Famous*...a rock star lamenting his loss of connection to the real world. [139] That wasn't Springsteen though. Springsteen never lost his roots and stayed grounded as much as he could. He seemed to enjoy the fact that as he looked around, nobody recognized him. To come to a moment like that and realize how rare and precious it is was further testament to the level of fame Springsteen had achieved by the autumn of 1980. On Thursday, he gave Buffalo an unforgettable 34-song set at the Memorial Auditorium, and was again headed south for three sold out shows in Philadelphia.

Back in New York City, John and Yoko gave the *Soho Weekly* an interview at the Record Plant. Yoko did her vocal overdubs for "Walking on Thin Ice" as the song was near completion. John had just gotten word that "Starting Over" had sold over 200,000 copies in the UK. He was pleased by the news although it surprised him. He had long harbored some resentment at the UK for the way they treated Yoko, and he cited it as one of the reasons they left. Still, with the buzz from overseas, John found one more incentive to look forward to a trip abroad. The two artists together along the trajectory of John's post-Beatle years had never received as much positive attention as they did during that first week of December, and they were both riding high amidst a wave of promotional interviews. The next day was no different. Friday, December 5 saw the couple begin an interview with *Rolling Stone* inside the Dakota that evening. From there, *Rolling Stone* reporter, Jonathan Cott accompanied John and Yoko to the Record Plant where they were to do some mixing. Cott brought up perceived similarities in the new album with older songs like "Strawberry Fields Forever," and a new song like "Watching the Wheels," where much like his Beatles work, he continued to question reality and illusion. Lennon made it a point, however, to distinguish between past and present positions. At first, he echoed the past John. If you broke down *nothing*, it became *no thing*. No thing is real. Hindus and Buddhists called it an illusion. We all see the same thing, but how we perceive it is different. *Rashomon*. Facing himself was the hardest thing for him. Socialists, communists, fascists, Christians, Jews...they had all been doing something to him. It was a state of mind he was in for a long time when he was much younger. The world was doing it to him and the world fucking owed him something. But then at some point, you face yourself...and at 40, that sort of shit just doesn't fucking work anymore.[140]

Critics were on John's mind that night in the studio as he talked about the negativity and often destructive potential of the myths that rock writers create. Once again, the dead were on his mind. Sid Vicious...James Dean. Hero worship. He didn't buy it and he had no interest in being a dead hero. He admired the critics who picked rock stars apart though. Lester Bangs. Jon Landau. He was sure Landau, like Bangs, must have shit on him at some point, counterbalancing equal parts love and hate in his years as a rock writer. Perhaps the height of John's concern coming out to the press again was presenting himself as an artist who had gone through a profound maturation and was attempting to bring adulthood into rock and roll at a time when his peers were all adjusting to it differently, thus being treated differently. What about Mick Jagger? What praise was he getting at 37? "Emotional Rescue" was a beautiful song, John thought, and it was fucking number one. Lots of people, including him, enjoyed it.

And then there was that younger generation...Baby Boomers who had grown up to John and Mick's music...some of whom who were already on a rock icon trajectory themselves. Bruce Springsteen in particular was on John's mind.

"God help Bruce Springsteen when they decide he's no longer God," he exclaimed. He hadn't seen or met Bruce, but he had heard all about him, and such good things. The concern seemed genuine as he acknowledged his escalation in popularity since *The River* had come out. The fans were happy. They were getting songs about cars and being drunk and chasing girls, pretty much falling into the generalizing stereotype of Bruce's music often displayed by his worst critics…but John was making a point. At some juncture in Springsteen's career, he was going to piss off his audience…perhaps with a drastic evolution in musical direction…or maybe the content would change. Maybe his characters would grow up and become adults. But wasn't that what had already happened on *The River*? Well, regardless, he foresaw critics turning on Bruce and expressed hope that Bruce would be able to handle the backlash when it happened. All he had to do was look at John or Mick. They survived. And just what did the critics want with the guy anyway? Or the fans who expected things from him? Did they want him to fucking kill himself onstage or something? Did they want John and Yoko to fuck onstage or kill themselves? John wondered these things. How do you evolve as an artist without getting shit for it and suffering some sort of backlash?[141]

The interview continued well past midnight as Yoko got some sleep on a couch while John and Cott kept talking. Bob Gruen who John called earlier in the day was also on hand in the studio. John had gotten a new Yamamoto jacket that he wanted to be photographed in, so Gruen stayed up all night with him until they all left the studio after the sun had come up. Out on the street, Gruen snapped a series of pictures, said goodbye and went home. In the early morning light, John and Yoko retreated back into the Dakota. It was Saturday morning, December 6.

With Sean and Helen visiting a farm in Pennsylvania, John was left on his own for much of the day. He phoned Mimi at around 9AM to tell her he was planning a trip to England. Then he wandered aimlessly around the Dakota for a while. John's thoughts that morning were on the *Two Virgins* album, and how it occurred to him that it was a sort of precursor to *Double Fantasy*, and how both served as bookends. It hit him that it would be a collector's item if it wasn't already, so he asked an assistant to go out and purchase all of the copies of *Two Virgins* he could find. Around noon, he went to La Fortuna for a cappuccino and then headed to the barber for a haircut. He spent the rest of the day rummaging around the Dakota with nothing on the schedule until night time. He and Yoko spent Saturday night at the Hit Factory talking to Andy Peebles of the BBC for a lengthy interview around a table of untouched Chinese food from Mr. Chow's. Peebles remembered John being extremely happy and energetic, but looked alarmingly thin from the macrobiotic diet he had been on. Long after the interview ended, the discussion went on until the early hours of Sunday. Finally, at 3:15AM, Peebles walked the couple to the elevator and posed for a few pictures. Before saying goodbye, John asked Peebles if he thought anyone in Britain would be interested in promoting him, leaving the obvious hint of an upcoming tour.

Earlier on Saturday in the afternoon, a cabbie named Mark Snyder picked up a young man also named Mark on Eighth Avenue. Over the course of the ride, Mark, no older than his mid twenties, had Snyder's ear.

"Do you like rock and roll?" he asked.

"Yeah," Snyder replied.

"Do you like the Rolling Stones?"

"Sure."

"Well, I just have to tell you something. I have to blurt this out."

The kid was anxious and Snyder was humoring him.

"I was just at a recording session with John Lennon and Paul McCartney!" the young man emphatically said to him. "I'm the engineer. They just recorded together for three hours straight. They met me and they told me how much they admired my work as an engineer."[142]

Cabbies, like bartenders, are often haunted by the unwritten part of their job description that states overhearing people's private conversations, taking part or being brought into conversations and sometimes just dealing with nutcases talking shit while pretending to be mildly interested. Then

Mark began to shake his head in a whirling frenzy, smiling to himself as if he knew something that nobody else knew. He offered Snyder some cocaine. Snyder politely refused. Then the kid began to rant about successful rock stars in what seemed a fit of jealousy. He then introduced himself and told his driver to remember him if he ever heard his name again.[143] To Snyder, the encounter was innocent and harmless enough so he really thought nothing of it as he pulled up to the Sixty-Second Street YMCA where Mark paid his fare, said goodbye and got out of the cab.

10

DECEMBER 8, DAYTIME

Among all those who were in New York City on December 8 and have recounted the events through their own eyes, many make it a point to recall the unseasonably warm temperature reaching a balmy 62 degrees, uncharacteristic of early December. From the top of the Dakota, John Lennon sat in a window looking out over Central Park West. This was very often part of his morning routine as he reflected on life, past, present and future. It had been 20 years to the date when a much younger version of himself and his former band were returning to Liverpool after being kicked out of Hamburg. On December 8, 1960, a hungry and disillusioned Lennon returned to his Aunt Mimi's house after traveling alone by train through Germany and Holland. Some speculate on whether the Beatles could have ended there. The picture would have been much different then. Three weeks later however, the band regrouped and played at Litherland Town Hall in Liverpool, where the performance became known as their first major breakthrough at a time when the people in Liverpool didn't even know they were from Liverpool, thinking they were from Hamburg. They were amazed at how well the group spoke English. It was the first time they were cheered and they finally began to think they were actually good. In Hamburg they weren't feeling so great about how they sounded as a band. That all changed upon returning to Liverpool.[144]

Twenty years later with the legend and all that became of that band already ten years behind him, along with a sporadic solo career that only resulted in a sprawling soul-searching quest to cut out the noise, raise his son, enjoy family and home, find himself, possibly address demons and make some open wounds alright, even if some of them still lay across the ocean, he was finally at peace going public again. After years of talking about peace, he was probably as close to being at peace with himself as he ever would be, and possibly the most content he had ever been in his life.

The day's schedule was by far the fullest and busiest the Lennon's would see since promotion of *Double Fantasy* began. There is very little record of John's activity on Sunday, December 7, except that he did not leave the Dakota. Given the grueling hours he kept between Friday morning and Sunday morning, he had gotten very little sleep, so it is highly probable that he spent the day resting and recovering. Monday morning, however, they were up bright and early once again. The day began with breakfast at La Fortuna. Knowing they had a *Rolling Stone* photo shoot with Annie Liebovitz in a few hours, John must have been self-conscious of his looks, and for whatever reason decided to go back to the barbershop for a second haircut. The question of the haircuts has been a mystery to some over the years, but the answer is quite simple. Accounts including Yoko's have John getting a haircut on the morning of December 8, while other accounts have him getting a haircut on the morning of December 6. Photographic evidence between Saturday and Monday is clear indication that John had cut his hair twice. Pictures from Saturday show his hair much shorter than it was on Friday, while pictures from Monday, show that he had it touched up and trimmed a tad bit shorter.

The Lennon's were back at home by 11:15 AM for the photo shoot that would accompany Friday night's *Rolling Stone* cover story interview. Leibovitz had been shooting pictures in and around rock and roll for the past decade, had become *Rolling Stone's* chief photographer, and was a respected veteran in the art whom the Lennon's were quite comfortable with. Initially, she only wanted to photograph John, but he insisted Yoko be on the cover as well. There is no understating the lengths John was going to during that week to help raise Yoko's star level. Once he read a few positive reviews, he was on a mission to put her in the spotlight. It would have been easy to sit back and enjoy the successful run of *Double Fantasy* as it was happening. The album was expected to reach number one, and "Starting Over" had hit number six the day before…two spots above Springsteen's "Hungry Heart." He could have simply done a little more promotional press and rested on his laurels for a while, but instead he used the momentum as a reason to strive further for Yoko. The plan was to get another album out as soon as possible…a Yoko album, and just as he said to Bob Gruen two days earlier, put a tour together. It was a rather uncommon scenario for an artist with a successful new album only three weeks old to be working tirelessly on the next album, and it was under his own self-imposed deadline that John kept returning to the studio with Yoko even while promoting *Double Fantasy*. So it was important to him that Yoko share the spotlight. Leibovitz was fine changing her plan and immediately thought of the two in a nude embrace for the cover. Yoko didn't want to remove all of her clothes although she did offer to take off her top. Disappointed, the photographer told her to remain fully clothed. John, however, completely disrobed and lay down on the floor curling up to Yoko and wrapping his arms around her while Leibovitz recognizing it as a poignant moment quickly snapped it with an instant camera, giving birth to the most revealing picture ever taken of the artist…revealing in that it exposed the true nature of his desperately co-dependent relationship with Yoko, snuggling up in a fetal position to her detached and indifferent demeanor. For anyone who ever had any doubts about what John and Yoko's relationship was like, it's one picture that says it all.

Downstairs, a crew from RKO Radio began to set up in the Lennon's first floor office in preparation for the afternoon's scheduled interview. RKO was the first radio network to operate through satellite distribution and hosted many syndicated specials. After being promised the interview by David Geffen over the summer, Dave Sholin was finally contacted by Yoko who set up the date according to her astrological readings. Having to fly in from San Francisco, he was hoping for a weekend interview, but Yoko was convinced that Monday, December 8 was the right day and insisted he be there. Sholin arrived with his team, Laurie Kaye, Ron Hummel and Bert Keane at around 12:30 and were led through the office and into a plush living room-type space with carpeting and couches where they removed their shoes and made themselves comfortable. Sholin and Hummel had produced specials for RKO before, and Keane was the national promotions director for WB. Kaye was a student at Berkeley who was able to get into the newsroom at KFRC. Through Sholin she was put on assignments interviewing musicians and writing specials. This was obviously a momentous occasion for all of them.

Yoko came down first and spent a half hour talking with Sholin and Kaye while John got dressed, threw on his leather jacket and took some last pictures sitting in the window where he so often sat looking out over the park. Before he and Leibovitz parted company, he requested she shoot the photos. When the session was over, he headed downstairs to greet the guests with an apology for being late. Given the schedule the Lennon's had that day, Sholin asked if it was a basic day or if he could describe what the usual day might be like for them.

John described what he called a basic day, which began at six when he got out of bed. He goes to the kitchen to get coffee and drinks his coffee while coughing a little. After coughing, he has a cigarette. By seven, the newspapers arrive and he's going through them. Sean gets up around 7:20, 7:25, and John tends to his breakfast, making sure he knows what his son is eating.

DECEMBER 8, DAYTIME

Yoko is already downstairs in the office, right where this interview happens to be taking place. Some days, the stars align and she and John manage to have coffee together. Sometimes he'll fix her up with an espresso to take downstairs while he and Helen tend to Sean. John hangs around the kitchen until nine after it's been decided what Helen will do with Sean for the day. Mornings have their television shows, and he has no issue with Sean watching TV, although he tries not to let him see the commercials. If John can help it, Sean watches mostly *Sesame Street* and PBS programs. He does get to see cartoons occasionally, but with commercials censored. After nine, John disappears back into the bedroom where he has everything he needs to survive a nuclear blast and mass extinction. Around noon, he buzzes down to Yoko to see what she wants to do for lunch, and the two manage to get together for a bite to eat. Sometimes Yoko is too busy to meet with John, so he remains on his own, often tending to his errands outside the Dakota. More often than not, he'll check in with Helen to make sure Sean is getting a good lunch, and if he's still at home, he'll sit with them even if he himself is not eating. From around one to five, it's more of the same. He spends most afternoons reading, writing or strumming an acoustic guitar. Some days he'll go to the Plaza for tea while Helen is out somewhere with Sean. By five, he checks back with Yoko who is still in the office. If Yoko is back upstairs by six, they eat dinner together. Most nights she is still tending to business and remains downstairs, going well over twelve hours. Sean's bath time comes at seven while John watches Walter Cronkite. Sean watches some TV from 7:30 until eight, and this time it's usually commercial programming. Once the advertisements come on, John hits the switch and it goes to radio. He doesn't want Sean seeing the shit being sold, and the last thing he wants is his son asking for junk food...especially given the fact that he's on a health food diet. Ice cream is permitted once a week, although John prefers that it be Haagen-Dazs. McDonalds is allowed occasionally, but he doesn't want him going there every day. To be clear, he is not an authoritarian when it comes to diet...he just tries to do what he thinks is the right thing. He is well aware that Sean is a

181

kid and naturally wants the things that kids want...sugar. In a nutshell, it's the sugar John doesn't want him to have and it's the sugar they are selling. He also admits to eating sugar himself, but only when he's making records because it gives him energy. By eight, he's kissed Sean goodnight and Helen sees him off to bed with a bedtime story. Mother is still downstairs.

What the hell is she still doing down there? Is she even down there?

He buzzes her.

He explains her long hours to the RKO interview team, not sounding very convinced of them himself, but with resignation in his voice. Any marriage counselor would sense the rift and that the husband just wasn't really sure what the hell his wife does all day long.

If he's lucky, maybe she'll come up and they'll do something. But Yoko is a workaholic...she can go on for hours and hours. Some nights she'll finally come back up at ten, rest a few hours and then go back down at midnight. According to John, that's when she's calling the West Coast or England or Tokyo or some Godforsaken place where the time zone is different.

On the subject of *Double Fantasy*, they spoke about the origins and themes of the album's title, first detailing his encounter with the Double Fantasy orchids in Bermuda that inspired it. The couple expanded on the "double" theme, pointing out the obvious...that there were two of them...John and Yoko, and the symbolism along with the dualities entailed...man/woman, husband/wife, reality/fantasy. John sounded the more sincere of the two. Yoko chimed in every so often, sounding more juvenile if not completely pretentious. John has his own fantasy and she has hers. And that's absolutely alright, you see. Their thoughts don't have to be totally unified. But there's a common plan they have...this dream they share, and that is what the big picture is really about. It wasn't really all that different from life's paradoxes, and the same dualities Springsteen spoke about while discussing *The River*. John stressed that the material wasn't all love songs. Relationships were fucking hard work and not everybody in a relationship was artistic enough to be able to express something so complex in a song. So here were the Lennon's finding out in their forties what Bruce Springsteen already knew in his late twenties.

John and Yoko weren't aiming at 16-year olds on the new album. If teenagers dug it, great. But as John was writing, he was visualizing the people of his own generation who had gone through the 1960s with him and were now in their thirties and forties. He saw it as part of a continuing conversation with that audience...with that period of history...with that generation that had watched the death of a dream at the end of one decade and then stumbled out of the next decade. They were adults now. They were parents. Many saw the world differently. Then came the part of the interview that seemingly every human being on planet Earth has heard, containing one of the biggest sound bites of John Lennon's life...the gist and summation of *Double Fantasy* being this old friend checking in with the people who weathered the storm with him. And here he was in 1980...all grown up and speaking with the concerns of an adult and seeing how everyone else was doing. How were they? Did they make it through? Weren't the 1970s a drag? Let's all work on making the new decade a whole lot better...that sort of thing.

Lennon had reached a stage of life and career where he could look back on the demoralizing turn of the decade ten years earlier when the dream was over. The Beatles were over. The Sixties were over. Peace and love were over while Richard Nixon and the Republican Party prevailed. He could look back on it with a sense of equanimity and a clearer understanding of himself, where he had been and where he was going. In between the turn of the decades were the dreaded Seventies. He'd state how we "survived" Vietnam and Watergate and all of the upheaval of a changing world, but also noted that "we" were the "hip ones" during the Sixties, but the world obviously was no longer like the Sixties.[145] The conservative backlash was in full swing...nowhere near the extent that it would tear the country apart three decades later, but unlike the pervading sense of defeat that opened the Seventies, Lennon was finally acknowledging that as long as there was life, there was hope. John had grown up to finally be able to dream again.

Sholin addressed the taboo subject of artists playing rock music as adults. The art form, still only a quarter of a century old, still carried the weighty stigma that rock was made *for* the young and *by* the young, and many believed it as the Baby Boomer generation was about to enter its forties during the 1980s. Were they expected to trade in Little Richard for Barry Manilow? Lennon did not believe that all adults wanted to listen to Barry Manilow. The original sounds of rock and roll still appealed to him and he heard its influences across the spectrum of new music. He had dropped out of paying attention, but having been turned onto bands like The Pretenders and the B-52's, he was starting to listen again. With the latter, he still insisted as he had all summer, that Yoko was the precursor to the new wave sound. But he also heard the Fifties in the early Eighties. And Springsteen was still on his mind. He loved "Hungry Heart." It was a great record with the same period sound as "Starting Over." He was especially tuned in to newer music that had obvious roots in older and familiar sounds and styles. He also liked "Touch and Go" by The Cars because it sounded straight out of the 1950s. He felt a lot of music on the charts was completely derivative of the Fifties, but with an Eighties approach.

They spoke inevitably of politics. But John didn't believe politics was the only answer. It was absurd to think that any elected leader was going to go into office and perform miracles. So, Reagan was going to go in, and all of the so-called rightists were going to be waiting for him to do everything they wanted him to do, completely naïve to the fact that the office of President of the United States was far fucking bigger than any one man or group of right wingers or left wingers could ever truly influence. It would always remain the status quo. Of course, this was 1980, an era still informed by moderation, bi-partisanship and to a great extent, respect and decency. John could not possibly have envisioned a president who would one day attempt to use the Supreme Court to fight his own personal battles or hire an Attorney General who would serve as his own personal protector. Nor could he ever foresee a Senate majority leader that would literally bend, break and reverse rules to his party's advantage without shame or consequence. It is clear that Lennon in December 1980 did not believe much in the political system as the optimum vessel of positive change, but he also didn't see it as anything that could tear down the foundation of American values. In other words, the long-term damage later caused by villains of the American tradition like Mitch McConnell, Donald Trump and William Barr were not even in John Lennon's capability of imagination.

The Lennon's also spoke of a holistic approach to the future, applying it not just in the health field, but in politics as well as the entire global outlook. Together they addressed the role of their influence and how they saw the future as transcending the negativity of the past into something positive for the days to come. They were fully aware of their "power," as Yoko called it, referring to their influence as famous people. Yet, even John Lennon, a member of the biggest rock band in the history of eternity was not nearly as powerful and influential as the Republican Party had made him out to be when the FBI file was opened for political reasons and he was followed and treated as a dangerous criminal for the better part of a decade, even as he was fighting to become a citizen of the United States, the country he loved and chose to spend his life in. Regarding the power Yoko spoke of, everybody had it. Not so much the power of fame and influence on large numbers of people in the same way that maybe she and John had…but she insists that we all have that direct power of communication and mutual awareness of the big picture, and the interconnectedness of it all. In essence, the dream was over for a while. For some, there may have been a naivety to this dream in some capacity, but now it was a dream they felt had died. The ugly side of the counterculture was revealed by way of the Manson murders and Altamont, as the Sixties came to a screeching halt, not necessarily ending as much as being interrupted by dark and dreary negative shit, followed by resignation, acceptance and complete demoralization. The music that followed in those first few years of the Seventies all wreaked of that sentiment, and the key players, Lennon included, believed it to be true as they all retreated with their heads up their asses for the next decade, naïve now to the fact that the dream never died, nor did it go anywhere. The Sixties were merely an idea. It planted the seed. It was the flowering of the feminization of society…meditation…positive learning. But it wasn't the answer. It merely pointed the way. Now we had the Eighties. It was all still ahead of us.

After a two and a half hour interview, the Lennon's signed a few items as the RKO team packed up their equipment. One of the things they signed was an original copy of Yoko's *Grapefruit* book that Kaye brought with her that they were stunned and pleased to see. Sholin randomly asked John his opinion on the band Rockpile, and John briefly mentioned his love of Dave Edmunds. All in all, the interview accomplished what all involved had intended. For RKO, it was an in-depth invitation into the past five years in the life of an artist the world had sorely missed. For John, it was a chance to get the world up to date on where he stood, publically make his peace with the past and talk about where he was going. In short, it echoed what he talked about to Jonathon Cott and Bob Gruen just two nights earlier. Gruen's account sums it up: "I was at the studio for most of the night and we sat on the floor and talked about his plans. He was planning to take a little break for the holidays, come back and finish the album in January and make some videos, get a band together by the end of February, rehearse in March, and by April he was planning to go on a world tour. He was in a position of great strength at that point. From '75 to '80, he was staying home and raising Sean, and he learned about the responsibility of raising a family and the joy you can have…the human joy of seeing your family grow and taking responsibility for that…controlling the intake of alcohol and drugs, paying attention to a healthy diet…those are the things he was concentrating on at the time that he was going to talk about and bring around the world on that tour."[146]

DECEMBER 8, DAYTIME

The creeping menace of the Dakota's exterior loomed hauntingly over Central Park West. The overcast gray of late autumn wasn't much a contrast against the dark and dreary macabre of One West Seventy-Second. But the outside of the Dakota was not all that haunted people. There was always fear among tenants…a fear about the interior. Throughout the labyrinthine floor plan existed numerous dark storage spaces, random closets and rooftop lofts. It would be quite easy for someone to hide out and remain there for a long period of time without being discovered. On the flipside, however, it would be awfully difficult for that person to find his or her way out of the building. One of the concerns of tenants was that if someone got into the building and actually penetrated the security system, how that person would ever be found. Some girls managed to get in once and pulled it off. Neighbor David Marlowe opened his door to them after they rang his bell. They were searching for John Lennon's apartment. Referring his own apartment, he told the girls it was John's but he was away in Europe. They bought it, and it was enough to get them to leave. Things like that did happen.[147]

Somewhere between 4:30 and five, the Lennon's walked out of the Dakota with Sholin and the RKO team. The approaching darkness of late afternoon early in December was draining from the sky what little traces of daylight remained. A limo at the curb was waiting to take the RKO crew back to the airport, but John's car wasn't yet available. There weren't too many people situated outside waiting as they got to the sidewalk. Out of the small crowd, John recognized only Paul Goresh, a fan he had befriended a year and a half earlier who occasionally accompanied him on walks around the neighborhood. Goresh is forever tied to Lennon for several universally famous photographs he took of the artist. The first of which, being the Lennon's walking out of the Dakota on the way to their first session for *Double Fantasy* back in August. The shot was later used on the cover of the 45-rpm

187

"Watching the Wheels" single. The other pictures would be taken within the next few minutes.

Paul had some other photos that John was expecting to see. As John thumbed through them, he sensed the awkward presence of someone standing at his side. It was a young man in an overcoat and a scarf, seemingly in his early to mid-twenties. Paul only knew him as "Mark from Hawaii" who had been there all day waiting to get his album signed. The two had spoken throughout the day.

John looked at Mark, but Mark said nothing, nor did he approach. He simply held the album out to John.

He gave Paul an odd glance and then turned back to Mark.

"You want that signed?"[148]

Mark from Hawaii nodded and extended the record. John reached out and took it, shooting Paul the same odd look as if to say *what's wrong with this guy?* Paul, camera in hand, snapped a few pictures of John signing the album as Mark from Hawaii stood beside him. He took the pictures randomly and spontaneously, maybe thinking they'd make a great souvenir for the autograph recipient once they were developed...a nice gesture on his part. The approaching rush hour was filling the streets but none of the passing cars were for the Lennon's. John, not wanting to stand around waiting, handed the signed record back to its owner and asked if there was anything else he wanted. Mark from Hawaii responded by asking John if there were any jobs available at the Dakota.

"Send us your resume," John told him, and then turned to Sholin whose limo was waiting a few feet away.[149]

"Well, our car isn't here. You're going to the airport? Would you mind giving us a ride?"

The Record Plant on West Forty-Fourth Street was on the way downtown.

"Hop in."[150]

Paul took a few more pictures as John got into the car with Sholin, Hummel and Keane. Kaye was staying in New York City to meet a friend and wouldn't be returning to San Francisco just yet. John waved and the limo drove off leaving behind the few scattered fans remaining on the sidewalk in front of the building...Paul and Mark from Hawaii among them. It was nothing unusual, and was in fact quite common. The time to catch John was when he was coming or going and everybody knew that.

Laurie Kaye waved to John and Yoko as the limo took off up West Seventy-Second. She was on such a high from the entire experience of the day that she didn't even mind when Mark from Hawaii walked up to her and began chatting her up asking all sorts of questions.

Did you talk to him?

Did you get his autograph?

What did he say?

What's he like?[151]

Something about him bothered her, but she stayed a few minutes to talk before leaving. Eventually, Paul would leave as well, never imagining this mysteriously brooding figure might hang around for the next five and a half hours.

On the way toward midtown, Sholin realized he had a few more minutes to ask what may or may not have been a touchy subject for John over the past decade, but since the mood had been relaxed and optimistic all afternoon, he causally asked about the artist's relationship with Paul McCartney.

"Well, he's like a brother," John said without hesitation. "I love him. Families...we have our ups and downs, but at the end of the day when it's all said and done, I would do anything for him, and I think he would do anything for me."[152]

As the late afternoon gave way to darkness, the temperature hadn't changed much. It was a damp warmth, the kind of weather that nobody who knew any better could trust because it was after all early December, and this kind of shit made you sick once it got cold again. Nevertheless, it probably allowed for more activity in the form of people on the streets and in the park just a quarter block away from the Dakota. It wasn't July…it was December, which made the reports of fireworks in the park early that evening a little unique to the goings-on for the average late autumn night. Some fifty blocks downtown on the East Side, Ronald Reagan arrived at the Waldorf Astoria Towers. The President-Elect had a busy schedule for the next 24 hours, meeting with black civil rights figures that had supported him, as well as a dinner party the next evening with some elite journalists and financiers. In front of the Dakota, security guard, Jose Perdomo settled in for a long and quiet shift, kept company by the same kid who had been hanging around, gotten his album signed and yet somehow remained. As full night crept in, Mark from Hawaii talked on and off to Perdomo, and walked on and off back and forth across the sidewalk, and sat down on and off with his book…and against the backdrop of the Dakota must have seemed a shadow sliding undecidedly along the angles of the stone and curves of the building, returning time and again to wait under the infamous and consequential archway as if standing inside the mouth of an awaiting monster.

11

DECEMBER 8, NIGHTTIME

The WNEW-FM Christmas concert had become an event that marked and encapsulated the festive joy of the holiday season in New York City every December. The station, one of the pioneers of freeform radio during the 1960s had become the city's premier location on the dial for album-oriented rock music, and was hosting its annual benefit that Monday night at Lincoln Center's Avery Fisher Hall with the Marshall Tucker Band headlining the party. The Spartanburg, South Carolina band had become a staple to the rock station's format and had a good history in the city going back to their Beacon Theater gig five years earlier. In between, they'd seen success both on rock radio as well as the pop charts with their hits, "Heard It in a Love Song," "Take the Highway," and "Can't You See," and established themselves as a major touring act. Outside in the lobby, veteran DJ, Scott Muni dressed as Santa Claus, greeted concert-goers who left their gifts in one of the many boxes that were quickly filling and then overflowing with toys. Much of the station staff was in attendance while Vin Scelsa manned the controls back in the studio for the evening. In Philadelphia, another rock and roll party was taking place inside the Spectrum as the Boss and the E Street Band were plowing through another 35-song set for the second of three nights. "Santa Claus is Comin' to Town" would mark the occasion with its traditional encore spot that had become a regular in the set whenever the band played during the Christmas season.

At the Record Plant, John Lennon recorded a guitar solo for "Walking on Thin Ice" and then he and Jack Douglas mixed the song. With their goal of having the song out by the holidays, they were making pretty good time and made a plan to bring the tape to Sterling Sound in the morning after they'd meet for breakfast. During the recording process of *Double Fantasy*, and now these sessions for Yoko, Douglas and the Lennon's established a routine of having breakfast together at La Fortuna and riding home together at night. This wasn't the case on this particular evening as Douglas had one more session following John's. They talked a little more about John's upcoming plans...finishing Yoko's album, doing a Ringo album, a world tour in 1981... he had a full agenda mapped out, was positive about it and was embracing the future. In the meantime, the immediate plan was to meet in the morning to master the song they'd just completed. They said their goodbyes and the Lennon's were off. Getting into the elevator, John told Douglas he'd see him in the morning...a smile on his face, and nothing but a productive future ahead. It was shortly before 10:30.

At 10:30, Alan Weiss, a 29 year-old producer for WABC television left work, got on his motorcycle and rode off to pick up a date. On his trip, he took a routine turn into Central Park, using one of the park drives that connect the West Side to the East Side. Since he was only riding through the park, he didn't bother to put a helmet on. When a taxicab hit him, sending him flying off his Honda 650, bouncing off the car's windshield back into the air, and finally to the ground with his head making contact with the concrete about five times, Weiss realized it might have been better to have worn a helmet.

During the ride from the Record Plant, Yoko entertained the thought of first grabbing a bite to eat. John wanted to see Sean off to bed, so he declined, opting to go straight home as the Lennon's car made its way up Central Park West in the unusually warm December night. Outside the Dakota, the man known as Mark from Hawaii sat against the wall of the archway near the sidewalk guard booth. He had been talking to Jose Perdomo for a good portion of the night. Perdomo was walking the sidewalk out in front of the building just steps from where the man was sitting. As the limo turned left onto Seventy-Second Street, Jose knew it was Lennon's car and went out to meet it. Mark stood up near the driveway entrance under the arch. The limo stopped in the street next to a cab letting out a passenger. It was 10:45.

Nearby police officers in the park sent for an ambulance that quickly got Alan Weiss over to Roosevelt Hospital where it was a rather slow night in an unusually empty emergency room. That allowed him immediate attention where he found himself lying on a gurney in a hallway, being examined by an attractive surgical resident whose company he enjoyed.

Yoko got out of the car first. As she approached the archway, she made eye contact with the man that she may or may not have recognized from earlier in the evening. Mark from Hawaii. He nodded as she walked past. She didn't respond. John was several steps behind her, carrying a tape recorder and some tapes. Whether or not he recognized the man will also always remain as speculation. As John walked by, the foreboding presence stepped down off the curb that ran along the wall of the driveway. Crouching down into what police would call a combat stance he aimed a Charter Arms 38 caliper pistol at John and pumped four bullets into him. Five shots were fired. Four went through Lennon while the fifth went astray striking the window and door of the vestibule. The shots along with the bloodcurdling screams of Yoko Ono could be heard across West Seventy-Second Street and beyond Central Park West, sparking the first wave of curiosity shown by passer bys in the area, suddenly lured in the direction of such distraction and disruption in an otherwise calm New York City night. In that very instance, John Lennon took the final few steps of his life, stumbling up the six stairs that led to the security office where he told security guard Jay Hastings, "I'm shot" before collapsing face down on the floor. Outside the door, Jose grabbed the shooter's arm forcing him to drop the gun onto the pavement where the guard kicked it across the driveway. The cab outside that had just was dropped somebody off sped away after witnessing what had just happened. The passenger also took off. Scattered pedestrians began to emerge curiously from both sides of the block and from out of the park.

"Do you know what you've just done?" Jose screamed into the shooter's blank and lifeless stare.[153]

In the security office, Hastings quickly rushed to John's side where he realized the extent of his injuries. All he could do was cover John with his jacket and quickly call for an ambulance while alerting police from behind the desk. Outside the door and down the driveway, the shooter began to pace.

"Yes, I just shot John Lennon," he answered Jose.[154]

The shooter walked over to the sidewalk just outside the archway and took off his coat, sweater and scarf, placing them down on the pavement. He then leaned over to pull out a copy of *Catcher in the Rye* from the coat pocket and began a back-and-forth series of actions consisting of sitting on the curb, pacing the driveway under the arch, or simply standing still…all while reading his book.

Steve Spiro and Peter Cullen were radio car patrolmen assigned to the 80th Precinct when they heard the initial report of shots fired at One West Seventy-Second Street. The officers happened to be in their car on West Seventy-Second and Broadway, just two blocks from the Dakota, which Spiro knew to be the address of the given report. Within two minutes, the officers were the first to arrive on the scene, first noticing someone standing in the middle of the street almost flagging them down and waving them into place as their vehicle pulled up, front end facing the building. Spiro got out and approached from just west of the sidewalk guard booth where the man in the street was pointing toward the archway of the building.

"That's the one doing the shooting," the man yelled from the street, still pointing.[155] 20th Precinct officers Herb Frauenberger and Tony Palma were also in the immediate area when they heard the call, racing toward the Dakota to provide backup. As they pulled up, Spiro and Cullen were approaching the archway. Spiro, whose initial thought upon hearing the radio report of gunshots was that it was probably more of the fireworks that had been set off in the park earlier in the evening. He knew there and then that there were no fireworks as he cautiously scaled the guard booth and peered around the corner into the driveway where the shooter was standing with his hands in the air. As Spiro grabbed him and threw him up against the wall, Jose began screaming about somebody being shot, motioning toward the security office vestibule. Cullen went inside. Frauenberger and Palma were just running into the archway as Jose was directing Cullen inside. The two officers followed behind and went up the stairs into the vestibule to see a man lying face down, arms outstretched in a pool of blood and a woman crying beside him. Outside, Jose addressed the shooter to Spiro.

"He just shot John Lennon!"[156]

Assorted people from all directions had converged on the Dakota. There were at least a dozen.

"You *what*?!" Spiro exclaimed in disbelief at what he had just heard.[157] The shooter, against the wall, begged, "Please don't hurt me."[158]

In the vestibule, Frauenberger checked for a pulse, which John had, but it was faint.

"I think this is John Lennon," he said to Palma.[159]

Palma disagreed.

It wasn't Lennon.

Hastings then confirmed it was John and that he lived in the building. Their surroundings also gave away that something on another level of importance had happened…additional police and the continued calls over the radio for officers needed at the Dakota. Then Cullen recognized the woman as Yoko. He ran down the stairs and stuck his head outside the door.

"You better cuff this guy," he yelled to Spiro.[160]

For a brief few seconds Cullen, Frauenberger and Palma assessed the situation knowing the ambulance was eight minutes away and decided they couldn't wait. Unlike the documentaries and re-enactments, police were not standing around talking about what they should do. The decision not to wait for an ambulance was made immediately within seconds of their arrival on the scene. A copious amount of blood trailing out and around John's body was a clear indicator that they needed to get him the hell out of there as quickly as possible. Palma grabbed John's arms and Frauenberger took his legs, hoisting him up off the ground, carrying him like a sack of potatoes out of the vestibule and down the stairs. Yoko pleaded hysterically for them to be careful with him.

Outside, Spiro cuffed the shooter and led him toward his police vehicle. As they walked out of the archway, across the sidewalk and to the car, the shooter noticed the gathering crowd of onlookers.

"Don't let those people hurt me," he said to Spiro as the officer put him into the back of the car.[161]

Frauenberger and Palma carried John Lennon through the archway. Spiro closed the door of the backseat on the shooter to see the other officers carrying out the victim, which he indeed recognized as John Lennon. He then saw Yoko among several other officers accompanying them. And then it all hit him, and he became livid…seething, in the sense that here one minute ago, the shooter asked him not to let anyone hurt him, and now suddenly Spiro was doing everything in his own power not to kill the guy himself. Yoko, being led out by additional officers broke away and approached Spiro's vehicle. The shooter in the backseat, Mark from Hawaii, became mortified as Yoko peered through the window, looking him square in the face.

Another police car pulled up toward the curb. Officers James Moran and Bill Gamble saw police walking a body out to the sidewalk and toward their vehicle. Frauenberger and Palma's car was blocked in, so they approached Moran's car, opened a door and laid the victim face down on the backseat, telling Moran and gamble to get to Roosevelt Hospital with scattered onlookers in the street saying "that's John Lennon!" Moran, without question or hesitation, sped away west on Seventy-Second Street, made a left at the light and sped down Columbus Avenue in a frantic race against time. A few seconds into the ride, he turned around in the front seat looking at John with a need to be sure.

"Are you John Lennon?"

John slightly nodded, and barely audible, gurgled through the bloody reservoir in his mouth what could have been a "Yeah."[162]

In New York City, the avenues run wider than the streets, and with multiple lanes, Moran couldn't get to Roosevelt fast enough. Along Columbus Avenue a trail of buildings and establishments that were regular fixtures to John Lennon's line of sight every time he took a walk around the neighborhood. His favorite was La Fortuna, approximately 20 yards off Columbus on West Seventy-First, and anyone standing outside the café that night would have heard the sirens and seen Moran's vehicle speed past in what would have seemed just another speeding police car in just another incident in a city where crazy shit happens. So it would have been the type of thing that nobody thought anything of. But in the car was John Lennon, and unlike his other rides down Columbus in the back of a limousine, where he could take in the sites, the people, the restaurants, fashion shops, antique stores, dry cleaners, the ABC building, Lincoln Center and the eventual break in Sixty-Fifth Street where Broadway cuts diagonally through Columbus to intersect in its own decorated and well-lit rush downtown, this time he was slouched face-down bleeding to death on the cold unwelcoming leather seat of a Plymouth Volare.

Yoko Ono got into the back of Frauenberger and Palma's car...Palma still not completely sure of who they were dealing with. Frauenberger dug his way out of being hemmed in, and took off to catch up with Moran who by circumstance, timing, and through no fault of his own, carried with him a man, an artist, somebody's husband and father, and one of the Beatles in his backseat bleeding out, barely clinging to life.

Alan Weiss lay on a gurney in Roosevelt's ER talking to the doctor when the phone rang at the nurse's station just steps away. Assistant Head Nurse, Dea Sato answered and was told that the police were bringing in a gunshot and it was bad. Weiss, caked in mud and leaves, was in a fog and his ears were ringing. He felt like someone had beaten the shit out of him. Upon hanging up, Sato sprung into action in preparation with the second-nature response of any veteran nurse who flawlessly knew her role and had seen enough of this sort of thing before. New York City was notoriously a violent place at the turn of the decade, and by the coming winter of 1980/81, crime had reached a record level. Shootings and stabbings were the norm, and expected on an almost nightly basis.

"We have a gunshot coming in, gunshot to the chest!"[163]

Over the loudspeaker, senior resident Dr. David Halleran was paged to the ER.

The doctor with Weiss, who has never had her identity revealed, asked when the victim was arriving, obviously thinking in terms of an ambulance. Sato told her the police were already coming in the door with the victim.

Wait.

The police?

Weiss was no longer a priority and was told he'd have to wait. He understood the situation and was fine with that.

For having happened long before the age of the Internet, social media and 24-hour cable news, word of the shooting spread quickly throughout the city within minutes. The gathering crowd outside the Dakota was helping push the event in a chain reaction of spreading news throughout the streets. Shortly after eleven, Jack Douglas received a call at the Record Plant and was told John had been shot.

Shot?

"He just left here!"[164]

John Lennon died on the backseat of the police car on the way to Roosevelt. The ride took five minutes, and when Moran and Gamble arrived a few minutes before eleven, a team was waiting at the doors with a stretcher. More police had arrived by the time the doors burst open in the ER. Alan Weiss lay flat on his gurney as the team of cops staggered up in back of him carrying the body on a stretcher into the trauma bay in Room 115 which was just behind his head.

It certainly caught Weiss's attention.

Why cops?

Shootings were not unheard of in an emergency room. But then...

What set of circumstances would send a bunch of cops frantically carrying a body into the ER?

Weiss, on his gurney wondered about the unusual situation racing past him.

Unless the victim is somebody important?

That's also what Dr. David Halleran was thinking when he was paged to the ER, which never happened. Doctors summoned to the emergency room were usually called and later paged on a beeper, but never directly paged over a loud speaker. When he arrived in 115 awaiting the arrival of the patient, he too found the frantic rush of police carrying the body to be peculiar. Amidst the madness was nurse, Barbara Kammerer who was just walking in to Roosevelt to begin her shift. Most nights, she came in a little earlier to coincide with Sato's break and the two would work on a crossword puzzle together. But upon arrival, she barely had her coat off when she immediately found herself in 115 where a scrambling team of doctors and nurses were cutting the clothes away from a bloody body, and a group of shaken police officers watched helplessly.

Two officers then walked out of the room and were just behind Weiss when he overheard one of them whispering.

"Can you believe it? John Lennon."

Stunned yet unsure of what he'd just heard, he raised his head.

"Excuse me, officer. What did you just say?"

"I didn't say anything," the officer murmured, walking away.[165]

Weiss eased himself up on his elbow, turned on his side and poked his head into the room where he saw a body surrounded by doctors and nurses. He couldn't tell who the person was but knew it had to be John when he saw a woman he recognized as Yoko being led by Nurse Kammerer into a separate room. Weiss was becoming a pain in the ass and the nurses knew it, prompting administrator, Saundra Shohen to instruct a security guard to move him out into the hallway. That did not deter Weiss's inquiries.

In the trauma bay, the body had no vital signs…no pulse, no breathing…four entrance wounds over the left chest, three exit wounds over the left back. Halleran and his nurses had no idea they were dealing with one of the Beatles. A comment was made regarding the body looking like John Lennon.

"This is not John Lennon," Halleran contested.[166]

As they cut his clothes off, Lennon's wallet contained the revelations of his identification.

Halleran, in his third year, knew the situation was grave but he tried anyway. All of the major vessels were destroyed. He opened up Lennon to massage his heart as all hell began to break loose outside Roosevelt.

Dr. Richard Marx was serving as advisory in offering support to residents. His presence was not always mandatory if a resident doctor took a patient into surgery, although it was not uncommon. Marx happened to live near the Dakota and was returning home from his shift when he saw Lennon being put into the back of the police car, prompting him to return to the hospital. As he entered the room, Halleran was still in doubt of who he was working on, to which Marx upon walking in confirmed that it was in fact Lennon. Shortly after Marx arrived, it became clear to Halleran that Lennon had desanguinated, and there was no possibility of survival. He had bled to death before he even entered Roosevelt. Just before the team of doctors and nurses had exhausted their effort, Dr. Stephen Lynn entered the room while the Beatle's "All My Loving" played in the form of Muzak over the hospital P.A system, adding insult to the now eternal injury stemming from what had just shockingly transpired over the past fifteen minutes. It was Lynn's duty to go break the news to Yoko Ono that her husband had passed away. Nurse Kammerer would accompany him. The time of death was recorded as 11:15PM.

Out in the hall, Weiss, now unattended and still trying to piece together what the hell was going on, watched the team leave the room covered in blood while Lynn and Kammerer walked toward the small office where Yoko was waiting. Kammerer, still in her boots, told Lynn she wanted to change into her more appropriate hospital attire before they went in to see Yoko.

"You're covered in blood," Lynn snapped condescendingly. "Do you think she's going to be looking at your feet?"[167]

Seconds later, Weiss heard the screaming and crying, all but confirming what he thought he knew. As the reporter in him instinctively took over, he carefully jumped off the gurney and limped his way to a payphone where he contacted Neil Goldstein, the assignment editor at ABC. The details were sketchy at best: He *thought* John Lennon was shot and brought to Roosevelt, and he *thinks* Lennon *may* have just died. As it turned out, ABC already had some information from the police radio regarding a shooting at the Dakota. Given all of the banter and communication between police in between repeated calls over the radio, the network sent someone to Seventy-Second Street to check out the scene, which by 11:15 while Lennon was officially being pronounced dead in Roosevelt, news footage on the street was already being filmed as reporter Rita Sands began questioning witnesses. It was enough to conclude what had happened even before any major announcement was made. By that time, word was also spreading on the ground and throughout the streets. But nobody was saying the word *dead* yet. That was the predicament ABC found itself in as the thin line between responsibility and breaking a story began to blur.

Most people who first heard the news, got it from Howard Cosell on *Monday Night Football* during the crucial late minutes of a close game.

ABC ran the risk of reporting something that potentially wasn't true since there had been no official announcement yet. Trusting Weiss's word with an urgency to get the news out before anyone else ABC in New York called Bob Goodrich in the production truck. Goodrich called ABC right back and they confirmed it. He then contacted Roone Arledge, President of ABC Sports who advised him to be careful how he presented the news to Howard because he and Lennon were friends. Cosell took Goodrich's call during a commercial break late in the game's fourth quarter. Hanging up the phone, he told his co-announcers Frank Gifford and Fran Tarkenton that Lennon was killed. The transcript highlights Cosell's distress over coming to a decision on reporting the news:

COSELL

Fellas, I don't know. I'd like your opinion. I just can't see this game situation allowing for that newsflash. Can you?

GIFFORD

Absolutely. I can see it.

COSELL

You can?

GIFFORD

You betcha. You've got to. If we know it, we've got to do it.

COSELL

Alright

GIFFORD

Don't hang on it. It's a tragic moment and this is going to shake up the whole world.[168]

After the commercial break, the New England Patriots ran a play and called a timeout before a field goal attempt in the final three seconds of the game. With the camera focused on Patriots kicker John Smith, Gifford addressed the game situation but took a turn that nobody in the country watching could ever have anticipated or imagined.

"Three seconds remaining, John Smith is on the line…and I don't care what's on the line Howard, we have got to say what we know in the booth."[169]

"Yes, we have to say it," Cosell dutifully responded. "Remember this is just a football game no matter who wins or loses. An unspeakable tragedy... confirmed to us by ABC News in New York City. John Lennon...outside of his apartment building on the west side of New York City...the most famous perhaps of all of the Beatles...shot twice in the back...rushed to Roosevelt Hospital...dead on arrival."[170]

Around a half hour after Cosell's announcement, a formal and official statement was given to the press by Dr. Stephen Lynn who was the hospital administrator chosen to be the public face and voice of Roosevelt concerning Lennon's death. While an understandably shaken Dr. Halleran did not want any part of the press or his name mentioned in connection with John Lennon's death, Lynn was in the circumstantial position of having to claim himself as the doctor who worked on Lennon. Lynn would later exploit and abuse this claim for decades whenever an anniversary of the murder came up and the media wanted to talk to him. Rather than retreating back into obscurity, he not only talked to the press every time, but he often appeared animated in demonstration of actions that turned out to be lies, such as having massaged Lennon's heart while holding it in his hands. Not only was Lynn not the doctor who worked on Lennon, but by all accounts of anyone who was there, he was never even in the room until the final minutes. It wasn't until 2013 when Dr. David Halleran went public with the truth about what really happened in Roosevelt that night.

By the midnight hour, the story was all over the radio. Just a half hour earlier, the WNEW Christmas concert was winding down and it was kept from the musicians onstage until after the show was over. Dan Aykroyd fresh off the success of *The Blues Brothers* film did a guest spot with the Marshall Tucker Band and the energy of the evening was tangible and unmistakable. The aftermath of the show was quite the opposite.

Back at the radio station, Vin Scelsa had just begun to play Springsteen's "Jungleland" when word of the shooting had come in. At first, he was hesitant to say anything on the air, but after it was confirmed that Lennon had indeed been taken to Roosevelt, he interrupted "Jungleland" to tell listeners that John had been shot and there was no further information. From there, he went back into "Jungleland." Within minutes, Lennon's death was confirmed and a devastated Scelsa was back on the air.

"This is WNEW-FM in New York…I have the extremely sad task of… informing you that John Lennon died tonight. He was shot, and a…and fatally wounded in front of his home at the Dakota. This report has now been confirmed by all of the other wire services, and…this is a New York City police report. I…I'm at a loss for words…I think for the first time in my career on the radio I don't have anything to say."[171]

The other local rock station WPLJ was under the watch of a young Mark Goodman who was equally distraught, and struggled to navigate his way through the broadcast. In Philadelphia, Bruce Springsteen and the E Street Band got off stage just after midnight. Just as with the Marshall Tucker Band, the news was kept from band members until after the show. Fans high off the past three and a half hours inching along slowly in parking lot traffic outside the Spectrum turned on their radios to find the dreadful news all over the dial, and little by little, the country began to collectively mourn its way through the long remainder of an evening that had gone from the highest highs to the lowest lows.

Outside Roosevelt Hospital, a crowd was growing just as large as the one at the Dakota. Innocent onlookers mixed with every possible facet of media and fans crowded doors on Fifty-Eighth and Fifty-Ninth looking for answers. Freaks and disciples knelt down to pray, one man inviting everyone around him to join in as he was "praying the rosary" while the final 60 minutes of December 8, 1980 and into the witching hour saw the streets outside Roosevelt as one giant clusterfuck of humanity...a circus of outpouring ranging from grief to greed. Various mobs of differing intentions...fans hoping for a miracle...news reporters legit and tabloidesque arriving by the dozens, some respectful and some stretching their long obtrusive necks into the personal space of anyone they thought they could get something from...orderlies trying to extort twenty dollars to reveal information...more cops arriving. Just outside the ER, reporters fought over the two available telephones while some scumbags offered money to staff for anything that had Lennon's blood on it. Inside the ER, the regular patients remained waiting. On any given night in Roosevelt in the New York City of 1980 was a regular assortment of shooting victims, stabbing victims, overdoses, jumpers and all kinds of people who had fucked themselves up and needed to be put back together. Whatever just had happened in 115 and the surrounding area needed to wrap up soon in order for the night to go on...even as all the bloody remnants...sheets, scrubs, clothing were being properly collected and dealt with accordingly so as not to be exploited or sold. The nurses had been instructed by Dr. Lynn not to sell their blood-soaked uniforms, which didn't sit very well with Nurse Kammerer. Not as if she would have sold her uniform, but the nerve of him to even go there enraged her.

"If he had been in front of me, I swear I would have punched him in the nose," Kammerer said to me in a 2019 phone conversation. "And people did try to buy our clothing, and of course we just walked right past them. But for him to say something like that was so derogatory of the nursing staff."

For the most part, the cameras were kept at bay, and to our knowledge, nothing of the horror inside Roosevelt was captured and documented visually except for what was experienced and seared permanently into the psyches of those involved. When Officer Frauenberger emerged from a doorway on the hospital's Fifty-Eighth Street side to accompany Yoko Ono and David Geffen to a car, photographers managed to capture the moment, etching the images into eternity, as they came to represent what little was handed down to history, and so those pictures largely told the story. Once the official announcements were made to the press and Yoko had left the building, the shock began to set in. Moments later at 1:11AM, when police cars pulled out of the basement drive to escort the morgue vehicle downtown, there was a sense of permanence and an overall collective forced exhalation of the wind being knocked out of society and humanity itself. And then there was nothing left to wait for outside. Traffic down Ninth Avenue, blocked for a period of time, was once again moving freely, and John Lennon would not be coming out of Roosevelt alive. In fact, he had just ridden past those who remained on the sidewalks and streets…just some pale and sullen faces of those still holding out for some hope in the spirit of something… something intangible. But something they always knew was still somewhat alive until that moment…the 1960s. But now they were faced with the sudden knowledge that the dream, this time, really was over.

Across the dial phone lines were jammed as fans called into radio stations, many calls taken on the air as listeners and DJs alike tried to process what had happened. Vin Scelsa with his voice trembling spoke slowly and tried desperately to work through his grief live on the air.

"John Lennon was…I don't know how to say this without it sounding mundane…but he was not just another person in the public eye. He was not just another star or rock star or movie star or politician or whoever. The enormous amount of grief that is being expressed tonight by people…certainly…picking up the telephone and listening to phone calls here at the station is incredible. The man had touched the hearts and minds of us all…as a Beatle…still as a Beatle, and as John Lennon, as he fought so hard to gain his identity as John Lennon. It's almost as if…I'm just flashing back to the day that John Kennedy was shot and killed, and I feel a similar loss and a similar grief. Ya know, it's something that, again, goes above and beyond the public figure to somebody we all dearly loved…and who gave us so much. And we gave it back to him too. We loved him, and we let him know it a thousand different ways. Particularly here in New York, he was one of us. He has been a New Yorker for so many years now, and you'd see him walking on the streets and stuff, ya know, and you'd wave and say 'Hi John.' I've heard so many stories from cab drivers who've picked him up and refused to let him pay, ya know…just because they said 'Hey…thank you for all that music…thank you for all those years.' And what a sad and terrible thing that he was to meet his end in this violent, damnable fashion. So if you believe in prayer, say a prayer for John Lennon. Say a prayer for Yoko Ono. And say a prayer for the rest of us."[172]

12

THIS LAND IS YOUR LAND

As the shocking news of John Lennon's murder completely engulfed television and radio on the morning of December 9, Steve Van Zandt couldn't conceive of going onstage that night. Later on in the day, he'd call the tour manager to ask what the status on the show was. He was certain it would be postponed.

But that was not the case.

Springsteen wanted to play.

Night three, the last of the Spectrum run would go on as scheduled.

On television, the overnight reports of the shooter as a "local screwball" turned into much more detailed information. By the time ABC's *Good Morning America* went on the air at 7AM, the name Mark David Chapman was all over the media. Over the course of a few hours, the unknown irrelevant nobody, who only a few people on West Seventy-Second Street knew as Mark from Hawaii, was now a famous irrelevant nobody with his entire life story circulating around the world. At the Eighty-Second Street station house, he'd calmly go through his story and his motive, which included his official "statement," marked inside his copy of *Catcher in the Rye*, which he spoke about in depth, attempting to validate his actions by way of the book's main character, Holden Caulfield. Caulfield is disgusted with all the phoniness in society and uses words like "goddamn" a lot. In one of the more significant passages, Caulfield talks about saving innocent children from being corrupted by the big bad phony world; i.e. superficiality, selling out and every other negative quality that only fake people exhibit. In his testimony to police, Chapman sees John Lennon as an innocent about to be corrupted. Much worse, he sees himself as Holden Caulfield, but in order to save Lennon, he kills him, somehow forgetting, or never even stopping to consider anywhere within his twisted fucked up mind that Holden Caulfield never hurt anybody. Following intensive questioning and discussion for several hours, Officer Spiro brought Chapman downtown to One Police Plaza at 6:30 AM for booking.

A few hours later in midtown, Ronald Reagan, accompanied by William Casey met with Terence Cardinal Cooke, and was approached by reporters who asked for comment on the murder of Lennon.

"Well, what can anyone say?" Reagan offered, seemingly caught off guard. "It's a great tragedy. It's just further evidence of what we have to stop happening."

"Could you stop that with handgun legislation, governor?" a reporter cut in.

"I don't believe that. I believe in the kind of handgun legislation we have in California. Someone commits a crime and carries a gun when he's doing it that will add five to 15 years to the prison sentence."[173] Reagan appeared somber and not his usual smiling self. Lennon's murder would not be made an excuse for gun legislation.

The president-elect's meeting with Cardinal Cooke lasted an hour, and the two spoke about "the world and everything" including situations in Poland and El Salvador. Reagan's schedule also consisted of lunch with his son

Ron. Amidst all the speculation since Ron Reagan quietly married Doria Palmieri a week earlier, a top aide told press that the lunch date would only be a father and son occasion with no pictures or media allowed. Going into the Waldorf wearing faded jeans, a black polo shirt and a gray windbreaker, Ron was also asked to comment about Lennon's murder and was less forgiving of the question.

"What would I have to say about that?" he asked reporters. "That's disgusting."[174]

Reagan's visit to New York City during this transitional period when the media began to grow restless amongst speculation over his eventual cabinet picks might have seemed a major story on any other day…and it was…but it was no means the biggest story. That story was happening uptown.

While the president-elect's public response to Lennon's death seemed detached and uninterested, President Carter issued a more thoughtful and reflective statement:

"John Lennon helped create the music and mood of our time. His spirit, the spirit of the Beatles—brash and earnest, ironic and idealistic all at once—became the spirit of a whole generation. In the 1960s, John Lennon and the Beatles captured the imagination of the world. Their greatest success came when they conquered America; and in recent years, it was in America that John Lennon chose to live, because he valued the atmosphere of freedom and ferment he found here. His work as an artist and musician was far from done, but in the songs he composed, both in partnership with Paul McCartney and in his own right, he leaves an extraordinary and permanent legacy. I know that I speak for many millions of Americans when I say that I am saddened by his death, and distressed by the senseless manner of it. It is especially poignant that John Lennon has died by violence, though he had long campaigned for peace. Rosalynn and I extend our deepest sympathy to Mr. Lennon's wife, Yoko, and to their young son, Sean."[175]

Julian Lennon flew from overseas to New York City where he went to the Dakota to be with his half brother Sean, Yoko, and to witness the collective sadness of the experience for himself. Ringo Starr also flew in, having to be snuck in through the back of the building before later walking through crowds of reporters and grieving fans upon leaving the Gothic structure.

Inside, Yoko broke the news to Sean, telling him his daddy was now part of God. Her biggest concern before leaving Roosevelt the night before was that Sean find out from her rather than the TV news. For this reason, she asked Stephen Lynn to delay the announcement to the media as long as possible in order to allow time for her to get back home to her son. But the announcement came and so did the crowds, and from the seventh floor windows, Sean Lennon, just two months past five, could see that not everything was right with the world.

Outside, it was another overcast day with rain on and off. Traffic had opened up again on West Seventy-Second, but the crowds on both the north and south sides of the street in front of the Dakota and closer to Central Park West were packed to the point where pedestrians had to literally walk into the street to go around them. The driveway gate, covered in flowers, remained closed with police still rummaging around behind it, and fans, onlookers and newly-established lost souls staring into nothingness in front of it. Different crowds came and went throughout the day.

Lennon was taken from the morgue to the Frank E. Campbell Funeral Chapel at Eighty-First and Madison, and then to the Ferncliff Cemetery where his body was cremated. Yoko quickly issued a statement that there would be no funeral service. Instead, a vigil in Central Park would be held later in the week, and she invited the rest of the world to join in and "pray for John's soul."[176]

Steve Van Zandt was beside himself and unable to get it together. Shortly before show time, he went into Springsteen's dressing room and told him he didn't feel right playing the show given what had just happened. Bruce understood, but reminded him of why they were there in the first place. Lennon inspired them to do what they did and now it was their turn with a venue full of people counting on them. Today it was Lennon. Tomorrow it could be Springsteen. The idea was literally to live each day and play each show as if they were the last. That was Bruce's attitude and Van Zandt considered himself lucky to be close to him during moments like that.[177]

Around the Spectrum the mood was obviously somber compared to the previous two nights. The collective sadness was universal, and one Springsteen would share with his audience. When the lights went down, the band appeared dressed mostly in black. Gary Bridges of Philadelphia's AOR station WYSP-FM did the introduction, and normally after being introduced, Bruce would immediately launch into his "one, two…" or "one, two, three, four" countdown to the first song…usually either "Born to Run," or "Prove it all Night." Instead, he stood at the mic and tried to get the crowd quiet.

"Um…I'd just like to say a quick thing. I'd appreciate it… (the crowd grows silent) That it's a hard night to come out and play tonight when so much has been lost. The first record that I ever learned was a record called 'Twist and Shout.' It was a Beatles record." The crowd cuts him off in approving cheers. He continues after a few seconds. "And if it wasn't…if it wasn't for John Lennon, we'd all be some place very different tonight. But it's…It's an unreasonable…world… and you get asked to live with a lot of things that are just unlivable. And…it's a hard night to come out and play, but there's just nothing else you can do."[178]

Of the performance, Fred Schruers wrote, "I've seen people digging firebreaks to save their homes, and I've seen some desperate fist fights, and, God knows, I've seen hundreds of rock & roll shows, but I have never seen a human being exert himself the way Springsteen did that night in Philly. His delivery of the last verse of 'Darkness on the Edge of Town' was raw with a mixture of anger, grief and determination. I'll remember "Promised Land" for the way the silhouettes in the top tier of the 18,500-seat arena were standing, striking the air with their fists. The crowd sang the refrain of "Thunder Road" so hard you could feel your sternum hum."

Van Zandt had heard these songs a million fucking times. In Philly, night three, it was like he was hearing them for the first time and living inside Springsteen's mind, heart and soul just as he was writing them. Spirits were elevated inside the Spectrum at a time when it counted most. The fans needed Springsteen that night, and he needed them. It was a re-affirmation of the connections he often spoke about in his music and through the growing number of lengthy stage raps in between songs. These connections sealed the bond between artist and fan, and demonstrated the heart, soul, joy, celebration and healing in the power of rock and roll.

A few days later, Helen Thomas of United Press International asked Nancy about her opposition to gun control in relation to Lennon's murder. Mrs. Reagan maintained that she would be against any sort of gun control because guns could possibly end up in the hands of the "wrong person." Despite the hypocritical nature of the comment, she never explained what she meant, opting instead to say she favored stricter penalties for criminals who use guns.

He told Thomas that she had a "little gun" that she kept.[179] It was a revelation unexpected, and one that would be of consequence. Ronald Reagan throughout his political career had been away a lot. So he had given his wife a small hand gun. She didn't know anything about it. When pressed, she couldn't say much more. The comments coincided with reports of Mrs. Reagan wishing the Carter's would move out of the White House and into Blair House during the transition so she could move her belongings in sooner and begin redecorating. The media shit storm happened quickly, and the comments were attributed to her press secretary, Robin Orr. Orr was in attendance during the gun statement, and although Mrs. Reagan was responsible for spontaneous gaffes that came out of her own mouth, the incident became the last straw in what her superiors believed to be the press secretary's inability to do her job. Orr became the Reagan Administration's first public casualty after serving only 28 days. She was hired by Deaver who told her it would often be a 24-hour a day job. When she asked if she should move a cot into the White House, he took it as a joke. Then the same joke found its way into the press, and Orr was verbally reprimanded. In her new position, many felt she was still acting as reporter instead of protector, and so, in the case of the First Lady's comments on guns, Orr took the fall.

Also pressed on the gun issue was the man who sold Chapman the weapon he used to kill Lennon. Steve Grohovac, owner of J&S Sales where Chapman purchased the gun, told news reporters that he immediately started getting death threats.

"Sure, it bothers me," he told a reporter. "Not what they're saying about me, but the incident itself. Any time somebody gets blown away, I don't feel good."[180]

Very little was said again onstage regarding Lennon's murder as Springsteen finished out the final shows of the tour's first leg. In Providence, he dedicated "The Promised Land" to the slain Beatle and addressed the events one last time before 'Badlands." Most versions of "Badlands" opened with Roy playing Sergio Leone's "Once Upon a Time in the West" before the escalating E chord rises out of the ashes and Max kicks into the concert anthem. Bruce had only spoken before the song one other time on the tour, and that was to address the election of Ronald Reagan. Now he was speaking about Lennon.

"This past week we've been reminded again how we gotta live in a world with things that are just sometimes unlivable…and how easy it is to lose that human part of you…"[181]

The news was still fresh and hovered over every show. Still, the concerts became longer and longer, more celebratory and much greater statements of purpose. Subtle differences did take place though. Bruce was more vocal about his usual concern that everybody straggling around the aisles get to their seats safely. He also dropped the "goin' downtown" rap during "You Can Look." There were no more references to guns which he began ad-libbing during the song in early November. The lines would appear again during the 1981 leg, but it seemed that in the wake of Lennon's killing he was making a conscious effort not to sing them in the final days of 1980.

At 2 PM on Sunday, December 14, the vigil took place. The global sadness and fusion of negative and positive energy was palpable. 100,000 mourners gathered in the center of the noisiest and perhaps most violent city in America to express grief, bow their heads and stand in silence. The music was plentiful at the outset, with thousands singing along in reluctant celebration to "Give Peace a Chance," and echoing the ghosts of the counterculture, but with the youthful optimism now turned dour, deflated and defeated. Rarely, if ever, had the entire world shared such collective sorrow. In America, the last time had been following the assassinations of Martin Luther King Jr. and Robert Kennedy. In his fine biography of Lennon, Tim Riley compared it most appropriately to the tension and turmoil of the 1960s suddenly flowing back to fill a "countercultural void" that had been left by the election of Ronald Reagan.[182]

When the music and singing stopped, the silence began, and it was the silence that grabbed everyone's attention. It was the silence that news reports stressed as the most remarkable occurrence even though that's what they were there for. It was nevertheless easy to be taken aback by how quiet the world became for ten minutes. It was long-winded and sustained absolute deafening silence where the city could not be heard aside from the network helicopters that hovered above. Public areas around the world saw the same scene unfold simultaneously.

When it was over, "Imagine" played…the opening chords striking an emotional nerve across the crowd as if being slapped in the face unexpectedly while reminded of John. From silence and deep reflection on whatever focal point one personally needed to remember, celebrate, mourn and say their own private, silent goodbye to John…to "Imagine," perhaps his most universally profound piece of art to signify the end of the vigil and thrust the world once again into the sobering realization…John Lennon was gone. At various spots around the perimeter of the vigil location though, capitalism prevailed. Buttons with John's face sold at "three for five dollars" while the John Lennon Tribute Collector's Issue sold for $2.50. "The Legend Lives" t-shirts took six dollars each, and framed pictures of The Beatles, some 200 of which sold in under an hour, were a whopping twelve dollars apiece.[183] Among the dispersing crowd, the message of peace persisted for the most part until an argument between two people escalated into a fist fight. Ultimately, a man drew a small caliber pistol similar to the one that killed Lennon, and shot the other man in the chest. The 22-year old assailant was quickly arrested and charged with attempted murder. Coming out of Central Park there was nothing significant in the symbolism of peace that pervaded over the event. Nobody was feeling the spirit of the Sixties. The air was bitter and the mood somber. Up in the sky, snow flurries began to blow aimlessly over the city. Reagan's 1980s were beginning.

Amidst the public devastation of Lennon's murder were also the inevitable suspicions that arose almost immediately, questioning the lack of an investigation outside of the seemingly ready-made police report that said next to nothing. John Lennon was shot and killed by Mark David Chapman outside the Dakota. Period. The police were satisfied. Chapman confessed and that was all they needed. Open and shut. But the conspiracy theorists thought otherwise, and many made the point that Lennon had long been a target for the U.S. government. There was the FBI file taken out on him during the Nixon years while he was at his most politically active. With the new Republican administration coming into Washington, hardcore conspiracy personalities like radio host, Mae Brussell pointed at Ronald Reagan and the assumption that hawks on the right were well aware of Lennon's return to the public eye and were expecting him to become an active voice of the left again. Brussell charged that the same monster in place to do assassinations during the late 1960s was back in place in the Beltway, and its first target was John Lennon. While all of this is plausible, it is, at the very least, highly unlikely, not because it is not possible, but because the concrete circumstances of the murder do not add up to the speculation that conspiracy theorists offer. Those who questioned the immediacy and vagueness of the police report raised many questions about the role of Mark David Chapman and many feel he did not even do the shooting. There remain questions as to just how many shooters there were, and where in the Dakota driveway they were standing or hiding. There remains the question of the broken glass in the vestibule door, and many insist that Chapman could not have hit that glass from the angle he was supposedly firing from. The questions arise over poorly-drawn diagrams, one of which from the *New York Times* suggesting where those involved in the tragic event were standing and how it took place. The most commonly-known story, accented by the inaccurate drawing, is that Chapman stepped down off the curb under the archway and into the middle of the driveway where Lennon was walking. He shot Lennon in the back and Lennon staggered to the vestibule door and then stumbled up six stairs into the security office. From that version came the many questions of how the glass was hit, and some explanations go as far as to suggest extra shooters camped out on the other side of the driveway in the entrance to a service elevator and possibly even in the courtyard…none of these people were ever accounted for, nor has there ever been a single shred of worthy evidence suggesting these people even exist. Taken at face value, a simple understanding of the layout of the Dakota driveway on the night of December 8, 1980 is all that is necessary to understand the shooting. Let's look at two facts that are usually always ignored. One fact is that John Lennon was never shot in the back. John Lennon was shot in the chest. All doctors and nurses involved in the events that night who have spoken out confirm that Lennon's body had four entrance wounds in the left chest and three exit wounds in the left back and shoulder area. The second major fact is that the vestibule door faced the driveway entrance and was (with the exception of a slight angle) almost parallel to the sidewalk and Seventy-Second Street. The door was not flush with the walls of the driveway as a *Daily News* drawing suggested. The glass could not have been struck from the locations that these theories place non-existent shooters in. Couple this with a very early account by Chief of Detectives, James T. Sullivan that night that Lennon was actually approaching the door. With this in mind, it is far more likely that Lennon was not *still walking* through the driveway when Chapman fired, but may have already stepped onto the curb to go through the door. Whatever the case, Lennon had already reached the door and was standing in front of it when he was shot. He was not in the middle of the driveway as most accounts depict. There is also the report from eyewitnesses that Chapman called out "Mr. Lennon" before he started shooting. This piece of information remains hotly-debated as Chapman denies saying anything at all before shooting Lennon. That Chapman was clearly not in his right mind during the event is enough reason to allow the possibility that his memory of this particular detail is unclear. Regardless of whether or not Chapman called out "Mr. Lennon," there still remains the fact that Lennon was shot in the chest, which means something got his attention for him to turn around. He was not *spun around* by a bullet as some explanations suggest. Lennon was facing his shooter. Why (despite the initial reports of Roosevelt Hospital, which clearly stated entrance wounds in the chest) the narrative still insists Lennon was shot in the back, is really the only inconsistency. Regarding the broken glass, there is no other explanation that is solidly supported by facts. John Lennon, standing in front of the vestibule door, was facing Chapman. Chapman fired five bullets. Four hit Lennon in the chest and three exited his back. One bullet missed Lennon completely. Between the three exiting bullets and the bullet that missed Lennon, the glass behind him was struck three times.

Springsteen and the band did a quick pair of marathon shows in Boston before returning home for the holidays and two more local engagements. First, they were back at Madison Square Garden on December 18 and 19 with the concerts now stretching to three hours and 45 minutes. On both nights, "Drive all Night," rarely played two nights in a row, was dedicated to Bruce's girlfriend, actress, Joyce Hyser for her twenty-third birthday.

Over the holidays, Bruce had been reading journalist Joe Klein's biography of Woody Guthrie when he picked up his guitar to rework one of the folk legend's classics. In the book, Bruce got immersed in the Midwestern American landscape of the 1930s and Dust Bowl era Depression. He drifted with Woody to California and eventually across a very different America that he himself had traveled during the 1970s. Yet the sentiment seemed the same. The questions he had…age-old questions through time that never get answered…it all seemed a direct conduit back to Woody's music and before…a trek through American history itself and the universal truths and untruths that make clear as well as distort our understanding of where we come from. The book sparked an interest in a further study of America and a quest for information. The election of Reagan nagged at him and he needed to understand why.

Three days after Christmas, the second local engagement began out on Long Island. Three shows at the Nassau Coliseum would close out the year. The general structure of the average *River* show was kept, but key song slots were shuffled around. "Born to Run," normally one of the two openers, was moved to the encore, and the shows opened with "Merry Christmas Baby" on the first night, and "Night" during the second and third. On all three nights, Bruce approached the mic halfway through the first set and waited for quiet. He strummed chords as he so often did when introducing a song.

"There's a book out now, it's called *Woody Guthrie: A Life*," he began. "It's by this fellow named Joe Klein. And a…it's really a great book. And this song was originally written as an angry song. It was an answer to Irving Berlin who just wrote 'God Bless America,' and…and this song was written as an answer to that song. And a…it's just about one of the most beautiful songs ever written. Anyway…I'll do this for you…"[184]

And as the crowd broke into polite applause, knowing they were getting a slow song…knowing they were getting something he hadn't written, they were with him as they were now seeing a side of him they hadn't yet seen, and they watched him evolve right in front of their very eyes as he blew into a harmonica to sing "This Land is Your Land."

The third night at Nassau, New Years Eve, was a 38-song blowout that scraped the edges of the one AM hour. That last week of 1980 saw Springsteen closing out the year with the number five song in America, as "Hungry Heart" reached its peak on the pop charts, just four positions away from the new song at the very top, "Starting Over," which came off the album *Double Fantasy*, also at the top of the charts. John Lennon, posthumously, was number one.

By Christmas Day, President-elect Reagan broke his silence on the hostage situation as Iran's negotiations with President Carter began to anger him amidst new demands being made toward the United States. As guarantees for the return of Iranian assets that Carter had frozen, Iran wanted 24 billion dollars deposited in various escrow accounts in Algeria. In the meantime, Algeria was sending intermediaries to Washington to assist with a formal response to the request.

"There's another Christmas going by," Reagan told reporters beside his Christmas tree in his Pacific Palisades home. "They're still there in captivity, and I think all of us deep down inside have an anger at the idea that their captors today are still making demands on us for their return, when their captors are nothing better than criminals and kidnappers who have violated international law totally in taking these innocent people and holding them this long."[185]

As Jimmy Carter saw the clock ticking away with less and less of his presidency remaining, the Iranians knew Reagan would shortly assume the role. Both saw Inauguration Day as a deadline before which the hostages should be released. By the second week of January, a deal seemed to be reached as the Iranians were requesting meetings with the Majlis in order to authorize negotiations through Algeria in an attempt at resolving the hostage issue. White House Counsel, Lloyd Cutler reported back to Carter however, that the Iranian national bank as well as 12 American banks could throw a monkey wrench into the situation. The root of the problem the banks were presenting, at least from the American side, went back to the seizure of the U.S. Embassy in November 1979, when in retaliation, the United States froze all Iranian funds in American banks, confiscating some 12 billion dollars of Iranian money and around two billion dollars worth of gold. Now that Carter was ready to use the frozen assets as leverage in his negotiations with Iran, a handful of greedy bankers were holding on to the deposits and trying to milk more profit by making last minute changes to the interest. Iran's national bank also needed to approve the deal.

Carter's Farewell Address on January 14 emphasized Human Rights, the environment and the counterproductive nature of special interest groups…

most of the same concerns he spoke about in his inaugural speech four years earlier. Added to his speech, however, was the threat of nuclear destruction, quite fitting to the coming new era. He didn't mince words and he painted a dire picture. He expressed his sincere thanks to the country as well as his support for the incoming president and then said farewell.

A few days before being sworn in, Ronald and Nancy Reagan went to the White House to see the family quarters for the first time, and the rooms where they would be living. The Reagan's expected that the Carter's would give them a tour of the White House. After briefly greeting the incoming president and First Lady, the outgoing president and First Lady turned them over to the staff and abruptly walked out of the White House.

PART THREE

CROSSED SWORDS ON THE KILLING FLOOR

13

INAUGURATION DAY

While Bank of America and some smaller banks continued to give Carter problems by withholding the 4.8 billion dollars needed to complete the hostage deal, a solution came from the other side, as Iran suggested the U.S. transfer eight billion dollars to the Bank of England. Iran in turn would refund all of it except three billion, release the hostages immediately and deal with the interest rates and claims in the future. Critics of Carter, and years later, Barrack Obama, would claim weakness and submission on the part of the two Democratic presidents, suggesting that they paid a ransom to Iran, when it was, in fact, Iran's money. For historical purposes and clarity, it is important to note that meeting this part of Iranian demands had the full backing of Ronald Reagan as well, as he told his supporters back in September, "We can and should agree to unfreezing the Iranian assets held by us, cancelation of any and all claims against Iran and nonintervention in Iranian domestic affairs."[186]

The hostage deal was getting down to the wire during Carter's final weekend in the White House. With Inauguration Day breathing down their necks, the administration was ironing out the last minute details when by Sunday, the U.S. banks finally agreed to pay full interest into the escrow account. Despite Reagan's decision not to be briefed, Carter still phoned him with the update. As Sunday spilled into Monday, the president pulled an all-nighter making and waiting for phone calls. The next 24 hours would be met with last-minute nail-biting delays related to technical instructions of transferring the deposit and debt payments. While Carter was well-embedded in what became another sleepless night, his last in the White House, the Reagan's were flown by helicopter to the Capitol Centre in Largo where Johnny Carson hosted a two and a half hour inaugural gala for television. The evening was filled with entertainment by Frank Sinatra, Dean Martin, Jimmy Stewart, Bob Hope, Ethel Merman, Ben Vereen and Charlton Heston.

At 2 AM on Tuesday, Carter received word that Iranian Bank Markazi had given the final approval and the money was immediately transferred. Four hours later, the Bank of England confirmed that they had received the correct amount. Within minutes of the news, Carter phoned Reagan at 6:47 AM, but was told he was sleeping and didn't want to be disturbed.

"Are you serious?" the president asked Reagan's aide, said to be Deaver.

"Yes I am," he was told.[187]

An hour later, the planes were on the runway in Tehran. Even Mike Deaver thought it peculiar when he found Reagan still in bed at 9:15 with the inauguration less than three hours away. According to Deaver's book, Reagan returned Carter's call at 8:30, so he must have phoned the president and then went back to bed.

Aside from a few catnaps on the couch in the Oval Office, Carter had not slept much since Saturday night. At 10:15 AM Rosalynn came in to tell the president that the Reagan's would be arriving by eleven and that he needed to get ready. After being up for almost two straight days, he now had to sit down to a barber who was brought in to cut his hair and give him a shave.

Then his wife brought in a rented suit for him to change into. Carter recalled the moment: "I looked in the mirror as I put on the rented clothes, and I wondered if I had aged so much as president or whether I was just exhausted."[188] When the Reagan's arrived, the president-elect greeted the president's news of the hostage deal with a joke about Khomeini's beard as well as a series of other jokes. Carter was perplexed by Reagan's lack of interest or engagement in the situation. In one final assessment of Reagan, Carter wrote: "I consider him to be affable and a decent man, remarkably old in his attitudes. His life seems to be governed by a few anecdotes and vignettes that he has memorized. He doesn't seem to listen when anybody talks to him. He'll have my support and my sympathy when he's president. It's a tough job and I think he'll have to rely heavily on his advisors and subordinates to make the ultimate policy decisions."[189]

Needless to say, Carter's last day as the president was bittersweet. He had become preoccupied with the hostage crisis to the point where it consumed his last year in office and he didn't rest until it was over. And even then, he didn't rest because of his obligation to stick around for the changing of the guard as the new president who had just had a full night's sleep was sworn in.

Carter's obsession with the hostages saw him pouring over their entire lives over the last year of his presidency. He knew all their names, careers, backgrounds and visited their families. Now with their release, he was never more figuratively alone as he spent those last few hours in the Oval Office. It was a moment when to those who can sympathize with Carter could see him perhaps hoping for some vindication or validation on a presidency that was otherwise going to be judged as a failure, and that the day would center around Ronald Reagan as the hostages were freed, and mythology would make Reagan the hero. Reagan would later gloat about it in his personal White House diary. "Word is that last two weeks of hostage negotiations were completely dominated by Iranian fear they'd have to negotiate with our administration. I couldn't be happier."[190]

As the Reagan's and the Carter's met briefly at the White House, Nancy was struck by how pale and exhausted the president looked. She felt for him knowing he had been through the mill on Iran and the ordeal he struggled through right up to his very last hours in office. It was a bittersweet ending and she knew it. Rosalynn looked uncomfortable and unhappy, saying hello to the Reagan's but barely saying anything else.[191] For the limousine ride to the Capitol, Nancy and Rosalynn rode together with John Rhodes, the House minority leader. In what Nancy described as an awkward situation, she was thankful Rhodes kept conversation going through the short ride as Rosalynn remained silent and stared out the window.

The event marked a first in the inaugural activities at the Capitol. Ever since 1929 when Andrew Jackson became president, the swearing-in ceremony was held on the steps of the East Front of the building. For Reagan, a new tradition was born when the ceremony was moved to the West Front facing the Mall and its view of the Washington Monument and Lincoln Memorial in the distance. Guests arrived and were seated to the sounds of the Marine Corps Band playing "Yankee Doodle," and "The Battle Hymn of the Republic." President Carter, Vice President Mondale, majority leader, Howard Baker, the Supreme Court justices, family and friends all gathered in the gray overcast late D.C. morning. Nancy's parents flew in from Phoenix, neither of them in good health. Her brother Dick and his family came in from Philadelphia. The Reagan children were all in attendance, Patti flying in from California, Maureen and her finance Dennis as well, Michael and his wife Colleen and their son Cameron, and Ron Jr. and Doria who shuttled down from New York City. Reagan himself remained inside the Capitol with Deaver, Rhodes and Senator Mark Hatfield.

At 11:39, the president-elect walked out to the strains of "Jubilant" on trumpet. Bush was sworn in first, Justice Potter Stewart administering the oath with a Bible from Billy Graham, given as a gift to the incoming Vice President. Reagan was sworn in by Justice Warren E. Burger, using Nelle Reagan's Bible. The inside cover contained his mother's writing which read

"You can be too big for God to use, but you cannot be too small."[192] The book had been filled with little folded pieces of paper and marked with words that Nelle had jotted down throughout the years of its worn use. His mother's influence was with him that day. It was interwoven into his speech in the religious tone and sentiment that so often graced his gift of communication and attracted people to listen. The Great Communicator was in his element.

Although the president-elect had seemed unengaged on the release of the hostages, at least in the company of Carter, he had it in the back of his mind as the hours dwindled toward noon. In the holding room at the Capitol just before being sworn in, he told Deaver to pass him a note if he received word that the hostages were released...even if it was during the speech. And for as miserably defeated as Carter was on that morning, Reagan was just as giddy and eager to be the one to make the announcement. For the television, the networks cut back and forth from the inauguration to the hostage situation, sometimes with a split screen. With the realization that Iran had in fact waited until Carter was officially out of office, he approached the inaugural podium.

And just as with the transforming symbolism of the snow that briefly fell for a few minutes following John Lennon's vigil a month earlier, the dark clouds parted ever so slightly to reveal enough of the sun to beam through the hole in the sky and down over Reagan's head. And as the new President of the United States spoke, a ray of light flowed out over the crowded Mall, seemingly from Reagan himself.

He approached his address from the foundation of a crisis that had its roots in government. The mantra that government is the problem would become his longest-lasting legacy, and unfortunately appeal decades later to the most extreme versions of anti-government sentiment. On January 20, 1981, however, there was still a backbone of rational thought to the American presidency and most of the Republican side of the aisle, save for a few decrepit ultra-right wing hardliners who were living on borrowed time.

"In this present crisis, government is not the solution to our problem… government is the problem," he told the massive crowd that swarmed the suddenly-sunlit Mall. "From time to time we've been tempted to believe that society has become too complex to be managed by self-rule, that government by an elite group is superior to government for, by and of the people. Well, if no one among us is capable of governing himself, then who among us has the capacity to govern someone else? All of us together, in and out of government must bear the burden. The solutions we seek must be equitable, with no one group singled out to pay a higher price. We hear of special interest groups. Well, our concern must be for a special interest group that has been too long neglected. It knows no sectional boundaries or ethnic and racial division and it crosses political party lines. It is made up of men and women who raise our food, patrol our streets, man our mines and factories, teach our children, keep our homes and heal us when we're sick…professionals, industrialists, shopkeepers, clerks, cabbies and truck drivers. They are, in short, 'we the people.' The breed called Americans."[193]

He vowed an objective to produce a healthy and vigorous economy that was conducive to the needs and lives of all Americans. His tone was optimistic, chastising the pessimistic realism of Carter.

"We're not, as some would have us believe, doomed to an inevitable decline. I do not believe in a fate that will fall on us no matter what we do. I do believe in a fate that will fall on us if we do nothing. So with all the creative energy at our command, let us begin an era of national renewal. Let us renew our determination, our courage and our strengths. And let us renew our faith and our hope."[194]

And then he appealed to the working class, a great percentage of which, was already in his corner, so he spoke with just enough conviction not to sound like a sales pitch.

"Those who say that we're in a time when there are no heroes, they just don't know where to look. You can see heroes everyday going in and out of factory gates. Others, a handful in number, produce enough food to feed all of us and then the world beyond. You meet heroes across the counter, and they're on both sides of that counter. There are entrepreneurs with faith in themselves and faith in an idea who create new jobs, new wealth and opportunities. They're individuals and families whose taxes support the government and whose voluntary gifts support church, charity, culture, art and education. Their patriotism is quiet, but deep. Their values sustain our national life."[195]

Several of the aforementioned such as culture, art and education would be progressively devalued by the Republicans over the course of the next few decades and into the next century, as social programs would not be the only areas where funding would be slashed or gutted completely. These, however, are later consequences, and not totally attributable to the Reagan years. Reagan, in speaking to America needed to keep a united country and project unity at least in rhetoric, which meant speaking and appealing to everyone and not just his base, whatever his base was. If we have to pinpoint and illustrate specifically what his base was, it seems to have grown from multiple areas of conservative interest and a little beyond. Reagan had a growing number of constituencies making up a *new right*...a collective conservative movement consisting of supply-side economists, evangelical Christians and hardline warmongers. The 1980 election resulted in the Republican Party being pushed farther to the right by these three entities that would inevitably consume the entire GOP. Depending on which faction of extremity, each had their eyes on their own prize. The "Moral Majority" set their sights on the overturning of Roe V. Wade and their obsession with having complete control over women's reproductive rights. The hardliners set their sights on the oil supply of the Middle East, and years later, would face the karmic retribution dealt to them in the form of dictators and terrorists who the Reagan Administration would soon align itself with. And the economists and law makers guided by the new conservative playbook, salivated at the thoughts of gradually dismantling the New Deal one piece at a time. Reagan also appealed to Democrats who maybe weren't particularly thrilled with such rapidly-spreading social change, and still had one foot in the past…who felt their party had embraced the 1960s counterculture and therefore had become synonymous with it. Put in the context of its times and up against the Democratic Party's past history, particularly in the South, the phenomenon known as the Reagan Democrat doesn't seem all that unusual. So while he appealed naturally and logically to the evangelicals and conservative hardliners, he also appealed to the working class. So on Inauguration Day, he seemingly spoke to everyone. With respect to the evangelicals that he personally endorsed, he did not make any political promises, but nonetheless highlighted his sincere and unshakeable beliefs, which were undoubtedly at the root of his personality and core of his soul.

"I'm told that tens of thousands of prayer meetings are being held on this day, and for that I'm deeply grateful," he told an elated and growing Christian right.[196] "We are a nation under God, and I believe God intended for us to be free. It would be fitting and good, I think, if on each Inaugural Day in future years it should be declared a day of prayer."[197]

Questions remained.

How free could God have intended for us to be if the evangelicals were doing God's work?

Did God endorse politicians?

What did the Christian right want from Washington anyway?

To outlaw abortion?

To ban art exhibitions that were considered offensive?

Perhaps impose school prayer?

And if school students were expected to pray as one nation under God, which God did they mean?

And if there were multiple Gods, would all Gods be accepted and respected?

INAUGURATION DAY

Just what did they want from Reagan?

Whatever it was, he was now expected to deliver it.

Between the parade and the Inaugural Ball, the Reagan's went home…to the White House. It was a momentary break before they'd race around town to attend nearly a dozen parties between nine and midnight. They were pleasantly surprised to see all their furniture and belongings had already been put in place as if they had always been there. They had hoped to get some rest before the approaching long evening began, but the activity was nonstop as family and friends arrived from Blair House to share in a champagne toast. They stayed briefly and then everybody had to be on their way in order to put the coming long evening into place. It had been a long day, a long transition, a long campaign, a long road and a long journey altogether. The new First Couple found themselves alone for a few minutes and suddenly it was a long way away from big town Hollywood, small town Middle America, and everything they had lived in between. They were together not unlike any other usual night they'd spend at home by choice. But that night, they'd have to go out, and out again, and out again, and repeat the ritual over and over again as night faded to dawn. As a new and budding couple well over thirty years earlier, they were homebodies, opting to stay in most nights at Nancy's apartment watching movies on television and making popcorn. If by any chance they went out, it was usually to spend time with Bill and Ardis Holden. It wasn't an exclusive relationship at first, and neither was in a hurry to get married. Nancy felt Ronnie needed time after his painful divorce to even consider marrying again. He was also still living the life he'd had with Jane Wyman and taking a lot of trips for the Guild. In addition to this, Nancy had been reminded by her mother, possibly to turn her off to the idea of tying the knot, that Loyal Davis had been "badly burned" in his first marriage and was wary of making another mistake. Ronnie's divorce with

Wyman had come suddenly and unexpectedly. Since he wasn't very close to anyone, he had nobody to really confide in, not that he probably would have. For a while, he stayed with the Holden's, but that did nothing to help him mentally or emotionally. When he finally married Nancy, the Holden's were the only witnesses at the small non-eventful wedding at the Little Brown Church down in the Valley on March 4, 1952. They wanted no press, family or friends to mark the occasion and were powerful and discreet enough to have those wishes met. Nearly 29 years later, it was precisely the press, family and friends who they were surrounded by, as they had stepped into a new world and a new life that was much bigger than them. Alone upstairs in the White House for a few minutes in preparation for the night of inaugural festivities ahead, there was no turning back.

As it grew dark outside and the guests downstairs left for the Ball, the popping and cracking sounds of explosions in the distance, prompting the Reagan's to step out onto the Truman Balcony for the first time where they saw the sky over D.C. completely illuminated. The new First Lady of the United States remarked to the new President of the United States that it looked as if they were welcoming him with fireworks.[198]

Did she really think so?

When Jim Baker was tapped to run the Reagan White House, it surprised most people except for those who really knew and worked with Edwin Meece. Meece, having been with Reagan for the past two decades serving as Legal Advisor to the Governor, Executive Secretary, and Chief of Staff, was the obvious shoe-in for Reagan's White House Chief of Staff. But despite Meece's commitment to Reagan and the Republican Party, everyone around him seemed to agree that he lacked organization and the stern manner they felt a Chief of Staff needed to possess. Meese was notorious for his chaotic and downright sloppy organization habits, so much so, that they became a running joke in the Reagan camp. His briefcase had two nicknames that everyone seemed to know about…the "Black Hole" and the "Meesecase."[199] Reagan also wanted someone who was well-versed in the ways of Washington, and Baker, although having been against him, had been a key member of the Ford team, helping him get elected in 1976. He had also managed the primary campaign for Bush. Still, despite the consensus, everyone assumed Meese was going to get the job, even Reagan himself at one point. Reagan recognized and acknowledged loyalty, and was therefore loyal to those loyal to him. Often pressured into certain moves at the influence of those around him, he didn't like to disappoint people, and he knew Meese was disappointed, not just in the appointment of Baker, but in the fact that Baker's office was much closer to the Oval Office than his. It was Deaver who ultimately suggested Baker. Feeling bad about the decision, Reagan's appointment of Meese as counselor to the president also came with a promotion of the position to a cabinet rank. Meese would stick around through both of Reagan's terms in office as well as nearly a decade of being under scrutiny for various scandals and ethical shortcomings. Meese would later serve as attorney general, remaining untouchable through the Reagan years until his resignation in the summer of 1988. Baker's appointment upset not just Meece, but several of those among Reagan's inner circle…namely Lyn Nofziger who didn't believe Baker was a conservative, based on his preference for Ford and Bush during the past two presidential elections. He also bluntly felt that Baker was in it for himself.

Michael Deaver became Baker's deputy…another chosen for his commitment to the Reagan's over the long haul of their life in politics, and was perhaps closer to them than anyone else. Nancy felt he was the only choice for his understanding of how and when to approach her husband. They both also admired his willingness and unwavering insistence on telling the president-elect when he thought he was wrong. Not that he disagreed with him all that often, but you want honesty from those closest to you.

Alexander Haig, an army man, was chosen as Reagan's secretary of state. Haig had an impressive and respectful military history, serving in the Korean War with Douglas MacArthur, the Vietnam War, and later headed NATO forces in Europe. In between, he served as Chief of Staff under Richard Nixon during the turmoil of Watergate.

Reagan didn't believe military experience was a requirement for a defense secretary. He wanted a numbers man, and that's exactly what he got in Casper Weinberger. Weinberger was Reagan's budget director in Sacramento, ran Nixon's Office of Management and Budget, and then the Department of Health, Education, and Welfare. He became known as "Cap the Knife" for his unapologetic desire to cut social spending. When it came to the Pentagon, however, Weinberger wanted to increase spending so significantly, that when he got his way, it became the biggest defense buildup in American history, thus playing a significant role in taking on the Soviets in a re-escalation of Cold War fear and paranoia that had not been seen since the early 1960s.

The plan was to cut taxes and the administration needed an effective Treasury secretary. For this, Reagan looked no further than Wall Street and came up with Donald Regan, the head of Merrill Lynch. Regan joined Merrill Lynch in 1946, helping to transform it into one of the largest and most powerful banking firms in the business, with innovations beyond just offering securities, but also real estate, consulting, checking and credit cards by the time he left in 1981 to join Reagan's cabinet. Regan was known often to a fault for being engaging and ruthlessly blunt, and was precisely the kind of salesman the president would need in pushing his tax cuts, which would for better or worse, come to define and symbolize the Reagan Era.

For the Office of Management and Budget Reagan chose a bright young fiscal conservative serving as a congressman in Michigan, named David Stockman, who saw the establishment and it's penchant for the demand side economics of John Maynard Keynes that had been a staple going back to FDR, as a problem. To the Republicans, he seemed an economic golden child whose swift precise knack with big numbers intimidated the old guard in Washington and produced a large range of proposed cuts in the hopes of implementing Reagan's agenda and achieving his goals as president. Stockman wasn't the first neoconservative who transitioned out of liberal roots, but he also wasn't an ideologue that fit in perfect lockstep with the Republican Party. He was still somewhat socially liberal but saw social issues as a distraction from what he believed to be the country's biggest problem, the economy. He strongly cautioned Reagan very early on about cutting social programs. In addition to what Stockman saw as hindrance issues to the right, he didn't give two shits about the Moral Majority, school prayer or unisex bathrooms that were going to cause the fire of God's wrath to rain down on America. With the exception of being fiscally conservative, he did not align himself with the pre-occupations and obsessions of the new GOP and those whose social hang-ups were about to redefine the Republican Party for the next several decades by slowly but surely attempting to take it back in time a century and a half. Being part of the Reagan presidency surprised even him. He saw Reagan as a cranky relic of the past and believed his ideology too be much more ancient than his age.[200] Initially, Stockman supported Jack Kemp and was shocked at the candidate's early surrender to candidate Reagan. He saw Reagan's campaign as an alignment "with Jerry Falwell, the anti-gun control nuts, the Bible-thumping creationists, the anti-communist witch-hunters, and the small-minded Hollywood millionaires to whom 'supply side' meant one more Mercedes."[201]

If anyone couldn't be happier about the incoming Reagan Administration, it was the Central Intelligence Agency. Carter purged the agency through his director, Stansfield Turner in the fall of 1977, a mass firing that became known as the "Halloween Massacre." Carter wanted a more moral foreign policy, and the CIA was known as anything but that in its shadowy, creepy existence. Discontentment within the crisis-ridden agency broke out into the open when a class-action lawsuit was filed against Turner who fired some 200 agents in a move to scale down controversial covert operations. The reality of the situation was that the organization existed precisely for that type of activity. Turner, at 56, was a retired four-star admiral, systems analyst, Rhodes Scholar, and probably much more of an intellectual and humanist than the CIA cared to have leading it. Newspapers had been reporting Casey as the number one possibility to take over, although Reagan had stated several weeks earlier that Casey would be going back to his private law practice. Everyone Turner spoke to at CIA headquarters all foresaw him being replaced. Turner, however, through his own personal outlook, or perhaps naivety, had reason for optimism in how Reagan would handle the role of director and believed he would remain in the position. Not only would Reagan give him the ax, but Casey would indeed take over, restoring all things Carter criticized about the agency and far beyond. Casey would wield absolute authority, becoming possibly the most powerful director in the history of the CIA, and the Reagan years would become accented as an era of covert wars and clandestine relationships among areas that would become obsessions for him and the president, such as the Nicaraguan Contras, Iran, Libya, terrorists and a blurred line between espionage and foreign policy.

The first few days in office were what Reagan described as long and hard. He had daily cabinet meetings and talked with congressional leaders. The sense of business-as-usual didn't really pick up until his second week where on Monday, January 26, he found himself in a meeting with members of Congress talking about raising the debt ceiling after starting off the day on terrorism with the heads of the FBI, CIA, Secret Service and the Secretary of Defense. A ceremony for the returning hostages was held the next day on the South Lawn of the White House where thousands of people attended including the families of the eight men who lost their lives in the rescue attempt.

While preparing for his first weekend at Camp David, Reagan found the debt ceiling issue imperative and met again with members of Congress.

He knew the United States would be out of money by February 18 and with Congress going on recess from the fifth of February through the twelfth, he needed the bill passed by the fifth. He found Camp David peaceful and appreciated being able to open the door and just walk outside. The first weekend was spent sitting by the fireplace reading intelligence reports consisting of evidence showing that Nicaragua was sending hundreds of tons of arms from Cuba to El Salvador.[202] He also prepped for a visit with Korean President Chun.

Reagan came into office with a prejudice against the U.S. tactic agreement with the Soviet Union regarding nuclear missiles. What he called the MAD policy (mutual assured destruction) wasn't very reassuring for peace of mind…the idea of two countries aiming nuclear missiles at each other reminded him of two people in a saloon permanently aiming guns at each other's head. That both countries would be destroyed was obviously enough for deterrence, but still, there had to be a better way.[203] His bottom line was that agreements couldn't be based on trust alone.

Just as Reagan had struggled to contain the drama within his team during the campaign, more drama found its way into his cabinet in the form of paranoid insecurity and petty jealousies. Al Haig was usually at the center of it, and by late March he was threatening to resign when he got word that George Bush was to be chairman of the Crisis Council. Historically, the chairman was the National Security Advisor, who happened to be Dick Allen whom Reagan knew Haig wasn't crazy about, hence the selection of Bush. Haig, however, saw it as an invasion of his turf.[204] It wouldn't be the first time Haig's insecurities surfaced over other cabinet members. On one occasion he became livid over Bill Casey's decision to bring a Saudi Arabian prince to the White House. The prince wanted to see Reagan, and Casey didn't have the patience to go through the usual channels of setting up such a meeting. But that was part of Bill Casey, and Al Haig didn't like it. Rather than going through protocol or dealing with large White House meetings where he was just one of a handful of cabinet members competing for the attention of their boss, Casey preferred a direct channel to the president and would simply call him in the Oval Office. Regarding Secretary of State Haig, Casey felt such matters of the CIA were too sensitive for State to be privy to, and therefore kept the department out of his encounters with Reagan, much to the chagrin of Haig.

The Reagan's found it difficult to exist in the White House, quickly longing for the open seemingly-unlimited space of their ranch where they could take long walks. Camp David was therefore a godsend that became part of their regular routine practically every weekend. Neither Ronnie nor Nancy had lost their want or need of nature. Want of nature, however, really had nothing to do with their situation, as they were now public figures of the highest level. Every move would be planned, choreographed, accompanied and documented.

One time soon after moving into the Governor's mansion and losing the ability to go freely in to public, Ron Jr. dared his parents to go on a backpacking adventure. Nancy believed her son needed some assurance that they still enjoyed the outdoor life, aside from just wanting to go on a trip with his parents, not exactly taking into consideration that this sort of thing wasn't possible for such public figures. The three of them did it anyway…a four-day long horseback trip in the High Sierras with nothing but sleeping bags and limited supplies. But that was as First Family of California. The White House was a completely different monster.

The new president's schedule was full but not always packed with work and obligations. Reagan still made time for entertainment, taking in at least one film a week and an occasional show. During his first two months in office, he saw *Sugar Babies* in New York City, *Little Foxes* at the Kennedy Center, and he and Nancy watched *Tribute*, *Tess* and *9 to 5* in the White House screening room. He found *9 to 5* to be a funny movie, but was literally angry over the pot smoking scene in which Jane Fonda, Lily Tomlin and Lily Tomlin share a joint during a sleepover. He thought the scene would not only have worked better if the girls had played drunk instead of stoned, but he also saw it as an endorsement of marijuana.[205]

While in New York City, his motorcade cut through traffic-free streets that were lined with people cheering and clapping as he passed. That night, he went to bed thinking about it. The people's love affair with him couldn't continue much longer. It all seemed so genuine, their love and affection, almost too good to be true. So he prayed. It was a prayer he had most likely grown accustomed to, asking God to see to it that he doesn't let the people down.[206]

On Saturday, March 21, the Reagan's stopped by the Georgetown Club where the press was doing a roast for Press Secretary, James Brady. Brady was very well-liked, and the president was happy to see him receiving such warmth and affection. Afterwards, he attended a benefit at the Ford Theater. He'd later remark how powerful it was to see the flag-draped Presidential Box where President Abraham Lincoln was shot, and though it was not his first visit to the theater, it raised certain feelings within him as he was seeing it for the first time as President of the United States himself.

14

LET ME TAKE YOU DOWN

The autumn of 1980 seemed far in the past. The smiling friendly face of that election season and the all-encompassing candidate who swore to represent all Americans, as so many candidates often do, had quickly revealed himself as the vehicle through which the Republican Party would attempt to steamroll its agenda, once piece of inequitable legislation at a time. But what should have been a period of welcome across the board, the presidential honeymoon of Reagan's first two months were marked by the lowest approval rating of any modern president serving that same brief amount of time. Reagan had very specific political and legislative plans, and already, he was being met with criticism over his proposals to drastically cut federal programs...something seen as his war on the country's poor. Democrats also objected to sending military advisors to El Salvador where a civil war was taking place. Vietnam was still a fresh collective wound on America, and many feared El Salvador might become another Vietnam.

The transition coming out of 1980 and the election of Ronald Reagan saw those who took note of eerie historical coincidence light up with concern as they were cautiously aware of the new decade. There seemed to be a curse on the presidency way back to William Henry Harrison in 1841 that followed a trajectory of the President of the United States dying in office every two decades. With the exception of Zachary Taylor who died in 1850, each President who died in office was elected some 20 years apart, and four out of those seven presidents were assassinated. This was not lost on the historical nor the superstitious mind as Reagan took office in 1981. So when the would-be assassin's bullets came at him 69 days after taking office, it wasn't hard to be reminded of that pattern.

John Hinckley Jr., the same man who purchased a couple of guns in Dallas just a week after being arrested in Nashville where President Carter was campaigning, was once again waking up in a cheap hotel, this one for $45 a night and this time in D.C. Hinckley was the son of a wealthy oil executive and had grown up around the suburbs of Dallas and Denver. After some college and what he considered a failed attempt at being a musician in Los Angeles, he was at the end of his rope and the end of his bank account. His mother gave him $100 before he left for the West Coast, and he thanked her for everything she had done for him as if it were a farewell encounter and he was never going to see her again. With his last few hundred dollars, he trekked across the country by Greyhound after giving up on his music dreams. Suicide was a constant thought. Very often he'd play out different scenarios in his mind of how he might end his life. One of them involved Jodie Foster, the actress he became obsessed with and stalked after seeing the film *Taxi Driver*, and one plan was on its way to being acted out as his stop in D.C. was merely on the way back to New Haven, where Foster was attending Yale University. During the four-day bus trip prior to Washington, he read *The Catcher in the Rye*, prompted by reading about John Lennon's killer. Lennon had been Hinckley's favorite musician, but on this bus trip he felt he identified more with Mark David Chapman in terms of the alienation he was feeling. Hinckley had 130 dollars left and was ready to move on to New Haven where he was plotting to possibly kill Foster and then himself. In his suitcases were photographs and magazine clippings of the actress, a book on Ted Bundy, six Devastator bullets, the RG14 he had purchased with zero obstruction in Dallas, and 37 rounds of ammunition. That morning, he briefly left the hotel, walked out on K Street to get breakfast at McDonald's, and on his way back picked up a copy of the Washington Star. Back at the hotel, his plan for New Haven got sidetracked as he flipped through the paper to see President Reagan's schedule for the day printed on page A4. Hinckley would no longer be going to New Haven.

After lunch on March 30, the president prepared for a speech that he would be giving within the hour to the National Conference of the Building and Construction Trades Department of the AFL-CIO at the Washington Hilton Hotel. Presidents had come to the Hilton since 1972 so it wasn't an unusual stop. Jim Brady had just finished briefing the press about a message from the president that would be shown during the TV broadcast of the *Academy Awards* that night. Larry Speakes asked him which of them should go to the Hilton with the President. Speakes was concerned when Brady asked him to have lunch that day. It was the first time he and the press secretary had eaten together, and as Deputy Press Secretary, Speakes wondered if Brady wanted to discuss something related to the job. Brady simply told him he thought they should have lunch more often. After lunch, he told Speakes to stay at the White House and that he would accompany the president to the Hilton. Assistant Press Secretary David Prosperi would also be accompanying the president to the hotel, so there was already enough coverage. Speakes would be better off at the White House.

At 2:00 PM, the motorcade pulled up at the Hilton where John Hinckley Jr. was still at large, but this time casing another president. Secret Service blocked the way for Reagan to enter. From the curb to the door was about 23 feet with two velvet ropes forming an aisle the entire distance. A crowd had gathered behind the ropes with reporters and police officers down front as the president walked into the hotel. He was escorted downstairs into the ballroom which was set up for the AFL-CIO's Building and Construction Workers Union. The room was made up mostly of Democrats who were unsympathetic to the president's seemingly anti-union views. As he spoke, he reminded them that he had been the President of the Screen Actors Guild and was a lifetime member of the AFL-CIO. He told them, "We've been left with a legacy of almost eight million people out of work, 666,000 of them construction workers. The annual inflation rate has soared to nearly 12 percent making a mockery out of hard work and savings. And our national debt has grown to more than 950 billion dollars despite taxes that eat up an ever-increasing share of the family dollar. If we don't get control of the budget and stop wild and irresponsible spending..."[207]

Still, the audience afforded him a respectful applause, even if unenthusiastic as he spoke for twenty minutes and finished with the words, "Together we will make America great again."[208] The bullet that went through him a few minutes later ricocheted off the rear passenger side window of the limousine and pierced his left side as he walked out of the hotel.

To a mild applause following the speech, Reagan left the platform and walked with Deaver, Brady, Prosperi, and Secretary of Labor Raymond Donovan down a long corridor to an elevator. After reaching the ground floor, they walked out into a misty rain.

It happened in a matter of seconds. Reagan smiled as he walked out of the Hilton, acknowledging the TV crews. Brady, Prosperi, and Deaver moved toward their cars as the President stopped for a moment, recognizing Sam Donaldson and waving. There were about 100 people in the crowd trying to catch a glimpse of the president as he left the hotel. He then carried on toward the car with Secret Service agent, Jerry Parr at his side. As they approached the limo, the door was open with another Secret Service agent, Dennis McCarthy standing next to it. Questions from reporters bounced off each other. Donaldson and Mike Putzel of the Associated Press both tried to get the president's attention.

"Mr. President. Mr. Reagan," Putzel called out.[209]

At which point Brady was tapped on the shoulder by Deaver to go take the questions. Deaver continued toward his car, while Brady approached the rope, and John Hinckley Jr., who had infiltrated the press section, stepped out, crouched down and fired six bullets out of a 22 caliber pistol aimed at the President of the United States and whoever else was in his path.

Pop pop pop pop pop pop

Reagan thought the sounds were firecrackers.

Turning he exclaimed, "What the hell's that?"[210]

At the first instance of the sounds, Parr and Secret Service Agent, Ray Shattuck grabbed Reagan, bending him forward at the waist. Parr then pushed him into the limo in what he described as a tremendous lunge. Reagan landed on the transmission hump in the middle of the floor with Parr directly on top of him. He landed face down and he landed hard. Shattuck slammed the door behind them, and as quick as the door was shut, Parr screamed at the driver, Drew Unrue, to get them out of there, and instantaneously the car was moving.

Reagan was furious. He railed at Parr to get off of him. Parr got up off the president and sat down on the backseat. As the president did the same, he felt excruciating pain, almost paralyzed by it. The entire incident from the first bullet fired to the president's limo speeding off, happened in less than ten seconds. All six bullets were fired in less than two seconds. The president and Parr were in the car within the next two seconds, and the car was moving within five seconds after that.

In the limo, Unrue made a left onto Connecticut Avenue as Reagan was telling Parr he might have broken a rib when landing in the backseat. Then Parr saw the tiny mark on the window next to him where a bullet had bounced off. He turned to the president and examined him, running his hands under his coat and all along his body. He radioed to Shattuck in Secret Service code language suggesting the president was fine and to go to the White House.

"Rawhide's okay…head for Crown."[211]

As they approached Dupont Circle, Reagan pulled out a napkin from his pocket as he began to cough. When Parr saw the frothy blood covering the napkin, he ordered Unrue to go to the hospital. The Secret Service called the Emergency Room to give them a heads-up to be ready when they got there. In an imposing burst of noise and maneuvering, an ambulance sped past them going in the opposite direction on its way to the Hilton where three bodies lay on the sidewalk.

Amidst the gunfire, Jim Brady was hit first, as the bullet went into his head, sending him straight to the ground facedown, just inches from the shooter. The second shot fired hit police officer Thomas Delahanty who had briefly turned away from the crowd for a single moment to see where the president was in proximity to the limousine. He therefore took the bullet in his back, falling to the ground next to Colonel Jose Murrati and landing on Murrati's leather briefcase containing the Gold Codes to launch a nuclear war. Murrati had ducked for cover and was unharmed. The third shot sailed over Reagan's head. Secret Service Agent, Dennis McCarthy was hit by the fourth shot just a fraction of a second after spinning around in a blocking position, opening his arms in protection of the president, thus taking a bullet in the chest. The fifth shot nicked off the bulletproof window of the limousine as Parr shoved Reagan into the backseat, not knowing that the bullet had hit the President. The sixth and final shot sailed across the driveway.

It was extremely rare that the white Trimline phone on the secretary's desk of the ER in George Washington University Hospital ever rang. When it did, it was a wrong number. That phone was a direct line to the White House, which is why, when nurse, Wendy Koenig answered and was told by Secret Service that a motorcade was on its way, she knew something big had happened. In the waiting room, an ER attending physician entered in a state of panic and screamed at patients without explanation to get out.[212] When the phone rang again, it was well understood that more bays would need to be cleared as three more people were on the way.

The president's limousine arrived at GW within three minutes after leaving the Hilton. Given the condition Reagan was in as the car pulled up to the curb outside the ER, it was marveled at for years by those closest to him what the president did next. As Parr opened the door and held out his hand to help him get out of the car, Reagan got out on his own, stood up straight, pulled his pants up at the belt, buttoned his suit jacket and walked 25 feet to the emergency room door. Bleeding from his mouth and in excruciating pain, still unaware he had been shot, Reagan was walking in on his own terms…as the President of the United States and with dignity, and unless he was unconscious or dead, he wouldn't have had it any other way. He knew that people may have been out there who could turn this into a worldwide story within minutes. He knew how important it was to walk into the hospital unassisted so as to project strength and not rattle or alarm the country. Something was clearly wrong though. His face was a grayish pale and there was a distance in his eyes. As a team of doctors and nurses met him at the entrance, he was fading. He told them he was having trouble breathing and then his legs began to buckle at the knees. As he fell, they caught him, and lifted him with his Secret Service agents. They all carried him at shoulder height and ran toward a trauma bay. A few of them began to remove the president's clothes to save time as he was carried through the air, so when they placed him on a gurney in trauma bay five, he was completely naked.

The ambulance they saw going past them on the way to the hospital was headed for the Hilton where all hell was breaking loose and the sidewalks were spilled with blood. What remained outside after the president's car pulled away were three bodies on the ground and a pile of Secret Service, police and union representatives on top of the shooter.

Reagan passed out as the doctors and nurses got him on the gurney. His blood pressure was down to 78 from his usual reading of 140. It was Nurse Kathy Paul and Dr. Wesley Price who first saw the half inch mark under Reagan's arm, and what hadn't yet been clear to Parr on the way to the hospital suddenly became clear to everyone, as they realized the President of the United States had in fact been shot.

Back at the White House, Speakes took a call as his secretary handed him the phone saying it was David Prosperi. Speakes answered. Prosperi was frantic and out of breath. He told Speakes that shots had been fired and that Brady was down. He wasn't sure about the president.[213]

Speakes hung up.

Fuck.

He could easily have gone to the Hilton instead of Brady.

That could have been him.

He went to Baker's office.

Baker had already heard from Deaver, as well as Secret Service.

Baker's phone rang.

It was Deaver.

The president was alright and headed back to the White House. That became the first TV report.

Then the phone rang again.

Baker, Meese, Nofziger and Speakes jumped into the same car, one with sirens and flashing lights, and cut across D.C. afternoon traffic to GW. When they reached Reagan's room, the chaos of uncertainty pervaded over the trauma bay, doctors still unsure of what had happened and why the president was bleeding. In the minutes from not knowing what was happening to discovering the flattened Devastator bullet to wheeling the president into surgery, many thoughts of outcomes had flashed through the minds of the Reagan's staff…that he was bleeding to death and they were going to lose him. Then they knew it was a bullet and the doctors made it sound more promising once they knew what they were dealing with. In the meantime, blood transfusions and intravenous fluids would stabilize his condition. Everything forward would be uphill though.

As the president was wheeled into surgery, Nancy walked beside him.

"Honey, I forgot to duck," he said to her, his ever-jovial persona still present even in this most dire of moments.[214] He then passed by his staff members who remained. Baker, Meese, Nofziger and Laxalt all stood by, but none would be allowed in the operating room. Speakes had been sent back to the White House to handle the press. The news would be coming from the hospital, and there were already enough staff to handle the press at GW. As Reagan went by on the gurney, he turned to his men asking who was "minding the store."[215]

Deaver called Jim Baker at 2:38. Baker called several cabinet members and within minutes, a mob scene in the Situation Room.

Once the incident hit television stations whereby "Special Report" flashed on soap operas and game shows across the dial, it was initially reported that the president was unharmed in an assassination attempt. But with the truth so far off and a White House Briefing Room filled with reporters, Assistant to the President, David R. Gergen walked in to clarify what was known, and it began with the president being shot at 2:25 PM, just an hour earlier.

"Good afternoon," Gergen began at 3:37. "This is to confirm the statements made at George Washington Hospital that the president was shot once in the left side this afternoon as he left the hotel. His condition is stable. A decision is now being made whether or not to operate to remove the bullet. The White House and the vice president are in communication, and the vice president is now en route to Washington. He is expected to arrive in the city this afternoon. Mrs. Reagan is currently with the president at the hospital. I would also like to inform you that in the building (the White House) as of the moment are the Secretary of State, the Secretary of the Treasury, the Secretary of Defense, and the Attorney General as well as the other Assistants to the President."[216]

Speakes returned to the White House and echoed to the press what Gergen had said…that the president was shot and was in stable condition, and that Jim Brady was also shot with a head wound and no other information was available yet. He also made it known that Lynn Nofsiger would be keeping the White House posted as information became available. Leslie Stahl wasn't satisfied with that and gave the deputy press secretary the full treatment of a hostile media, pressing him for information, audibly frustrated that he didn't have any new forthcoming details. He was not afraid to say "I don't know" to certain questions, simply because he didn't want to create even more confusion if he wasn't sure of the facts, and he stressed that point to Stahl. The reporter persisted when Speakes said he couldn't say definitely if the president was in surgery. Stahl seemed to already know Reagan was in surgery and that his brother had been called and that there had already been blood transfusions. Speakes reiterated that he couldn't confirm those details. He was then handed a note and told to return to the Situation Room. Stahl pressed him.

"What does the note say, Larry?"[217]

As Speakes walked into the Situation Room, Al Haig was panic-stricken and clumsily running out, shoulder-bumping him. It was 4:14 PM.

In the Briefing Room, Haig arrived out of breath and clearly shaken. He immediately confirmed that the president was in fact undergoing surgery, the vice president was on the way, and that there were absolutely no causes for concern. He then answered a question related to who was in charge in the White House, and what he said would inadvertently ruin his political career, become part of his legacy and attach itself to his name for the rest of his life.

"Constitutionally, gentlemen, you have the president, the vice president, and the Secretary of State, in that order, and should the president decide he wants to transfer the helm, he will do so. He has not done that. As of now, I am in control here in the White House, pending return of the vice president and in close touch with him. If something came up, I would check with him, of course."[218]

Caspar Weinberger begged to differ.

So did everyone else.

When Haig returned to the Situation Room and Weinberger took issue with the outrageous claim, the defensive Secretary of State boldly told him, "You'd better read your Constitution, buddy."[219] White House Counsel Fred Fielding wasn't about to support the claim either, although Haig sought out the support.

"Right, Fred?"

"No, Al, not right," Fielding informed him, confirming what everyone else knew…that the Constitution puts the Speaker of the House next in the line of succession following the Vice President, not the Secretary of State.[220]

At 6:30 PM, Vice President Bush arrived at Andrews Air Force Base where he was immediately met and taken to the White House.

At 7:00 PM, Vice President Bush arrived in the White House Situation Room where he met with a crowd that included Ed Meese, Richard Allen, Secretary Lewis, Attorney General Smith, Secretary Weinberg, Secretary Regan, Admiral Murphy, Jim Baker, Secretary Haig, Secretary Block, Secretary Vodridge, Secretary Watt, Bill Casey, Martin Allen, David Gergen, Max Friedersdorf, and Fred Fielding. The meeting lasted for a half hour, after which the vice president prepared to give a statement to the press.

At 8:20 PM, Vice President Bush arrived in the Briefing Room to address reporters.

"Well, I have a very brief statement that I would like to read. I am deeply heartened by Dr. Leary's report on the president's condition that he has emerged from this experience with flying colors and with the most optimistic prospects for a complete recovery. I know I speak on behalf of the president and his family when I say that we are very grateful to all the many people from across the country who've expressed their concern at this act of violence. And finally, let me add our profound concern on behalf of two brave law enforcement officers who served to protect the president, and then, of course, for a friend of everybody here, dedicated public servant, Jim Brady. We're going to watch their progress with all our prayers and with all our hopes."[221]

ABC, NBC, CBS and CNN, only a year old at the time, had been running several bits of video collected at the scene…the president waving and then reacting to the gunshots as Parr pushed him into the limo, and then the frantic scramble of bodies piling on the shooter. The networks ran the footage on a continuous loop for the remainder of the afternoon and then nonstop in the evening. Only the sporadic reports from the White House clarified what was going on. But up until Vice President Bush finally spoke, the anchors reporting the news knew as little as the public did. Sketchy-at-best reports from all directions of who was hit, who wasn't hit, who died and who was still alive were unreliable, leaving the nation in limbo for several hours. At one point, Dan Rather reported that James Brady had died, prompting a White House spokesman to quickly respond with a statement that the report was false. Rather had been around for years, but the shooting was his first major event to cover as an anchor of CBS News. On ABC, the only thing that was clearly certain was the confusion. Sam Donaldson had since returned to the news desk with a slip of paper. Sitting down next to Frank Reynolds, the miscommunication between what was going on in front of the camera and off camera was apparent. This was at a point when the nation was told that the president had not been hit. That changed very quickly.

"He *was* wounded!" Reynolds exclaimed on the air. Then he put his hand to his head. "My God, the President was hit. The typed information I have is that he's okay." Looking to his side at someone off camera, he was livid.[222]

"Speak up!"[223]

Realigning himself, he turned to the camera again to acknowledge the inaccuracies of what they had been telling the nation.

"All of this that we've been telling you is incorrect. We must redraw this tragedy in different terms."[224]

What we've learned from such an event that has an effect on the White House, is that not much changes. Policy is already out, everything is in place and everybody knows their jobs, roles and expectations. Martin Anderson, interviewed for the Miller Center of the University of Virginia, spoke to the subtlety of changes following the time period where nobody quite knew all of the facts yet.

"You find out what the situation is. You don't rush off and assume 'oh my God, he's been shot, we're going to put the vice president in charge,' or you don't say 'well, he's been shot but he's in charge, so let's talk to him and see what he is going to do.' You wait and say, 'well, let's see what happens.' And people were very calm and they just settled down."[225]

The White House and government remain functional and in complete operation.

"It is amazing how much goes on in the government, in the White House, without someone 'controlling' it," Anderson said. "It works. People do things…life proceeds. They were just very careful."[226]

In the early moments and hours following such a potentially tragic occurrence, the White House is leaving no stone unturned, even as information about the shooter is being unearthed, the administration is already looking elsewhere, scouring for every possibility of a plot, checking things out.

Russia was checked out.

Soviet submarines had been slightly closer to American shores than they normally were and there were more of them than usual. As it turned out, the end of the month meant that the Soviets were changing battalions which meant more submarines at that particular moment.[227]

It was evident that Soviet submarines had no hostile intentions, but the situation had to be investigated for every possibility. Other investigative measures were taken in response as Weinberger instructed Strategic Air Command to be on alert. As details began to emerge on John Hinckley, it became apparent that he had acted alone and was not part of some larger assassination plot.

While Americans were feeling both sympathetic toward the president as well as relieved he had not died, the shooting of Ronald Reagan was immediately used by the GOP to pass tax cuts, increase defense spending and cut domestic spending. The next day, Donald Regan went on *Good Morning America* to push Reagan's tax cuts for the rich in a feel-good attempt to "win one for the Gipper" while everyone was feeling so warm and fuzzy about him. Paul Laxalt, Reagan's closest friend in Congress sounded like a smarmy used car salesman when he put forth the idea of selling the idea of tax cuts through another political campaign formulated to seem as if they were selling a product rather than a candidate.[228]

At the hospital, Nancy Reagan was furious over Strom Thurmond's ability to talk his way past security and work his way into the president's room where she did not want any visitors. Sometime after the president's surgery, Max Friedersdorf who served as Assistant to the President for Legislative Affairs arrived to find Jim Baker who told him to remain on watch. A few exceptions were made, namely Howard Baker and Tip O'Neil. One night during the president's stay, Nancy had stepped out when O'Neil came in and got down on his knees at Reagan's bedside. Heavily sedated, Reagan was still aware of his surroundings and knew it was the Speaker. O'Neil held his hand and recited the 23rd Psalm, and then sat down next to the president. In a twenty-first century climate, it is difficult to fathom such a scene...that there once existed an America before the division of identity politics, when Americans were just Americans and not judged on their party association...when political differences merely amounted to the squabbling of disagreements within one giant dysfunctional family, rather than the ideological war between two opposing sides. It was a time when two political opponents served together for the good of their country. And so the Democratic majority leader held the Republican president's hand and they remained in silence and reflection until the president spoke, his voice labored and weak.

"I appreciate you coming down, Tip."

"God bless you, Mr. President," the speaker said, crying. "We're all praying for you."[229]

Agent McCarthy was the first to be discharged from George Washington University Hospital after having been there some ten days. Before walking out the door, he was called to Reagan's room. When the president heard he was leaving, he wanted to thank him for saving his life, which he did while keeping a brief exchange slightly humorous and lighthearted.

"Ya know," he said to McCarthy, sense of humor still intact. "It was McCarthy, Reagan, Delahanty and Brady. What the hell did this guy have against the Irish?"[230]

To which McCarthy only offered a polite smile.

Officer Delahanty suffered difficulties after release with the bullet in his back causing long-term nerve damage that prevented him from returning to duty. He'd retire on full disability seven months later.

Of all the organs in the human body, the brain is the only one that cannot repair itself, nor is it replaceable or transplantable. That is why James Brady was not as lucky as Ronald Reagan in the aftermath of the tragic events of March 30, 1981. While doctors were tending to the president amidst his unfolding situation that afternoon, James Brady lay comatose in bed 5B. The bullet wound in his left-center forehead produced a contorted expression on his face. The wound was more of a shatter, which in effect, destroyed the top of his face, and opened and exposed the inside of his head with part of his swollen brain visible. His inflated eyes were sealed shut. Beneath the eyelids, air bubbles had formed from the impact of the bullet. His breathing was shallow and rapid, and his blood pressure was elevated to an astronomical 240 over 160. Like Reagan, his clothes had been cut away, and the initial attempts at stabilization were successful. But unlike the president, the press secretary would not get by on just one surgery, a recovery and quick release. The initial surgery, a bi-frontal craniotomy saw a post-operative period where Brady was plagued by seizures, pneumonia, pulmonary emboli and cerebrospinal fluid leakage, which made numerous additional procedures necessary. Given that nobody who had seen Brady on arrival in the ER believed he would make it, his recovery was miraculous. That he survived was astonishing, but what caused doctors to marvel over time, was that his cognitive functions and personality traits were nearly at the same level as they were before the shooting. Permanent weakness on the left side of his body, however, left him partially paralyzed and confined to a wheel chair for the rest of his life.

Reagan was back home on April 11. In the early stages of his return, he remained in the residence where he worked steadily to regain his strength. Meetings were therefore held in the Reagan's personal quarters, often with the president in jeans and a t-shirt or riding an exercise bike. The president spent Easter Sunday in bed watching TV where he saw Gloria Steinem "rake me over the coals for being a bigot and against women." Reagan didn't mince words in his written entries of his diaries. "Either she is totally ignorant of my position which I doubt or she is a deliberate liar."[231]

Sometime after returning to the White House, the president received a call from Billy Graham who told him he knew the family of John Hinkley Jr., and stressed they were "decent, deeply religious people who were completely crushed by the sickness of their son."[232] Soon after, Reagan wanted to meet face to face with Hinckley. He wanted to be able to look him in the eyes and let him know he forgave him. At Camp David, he consulted with White House physician, Dr. Daniel Ruge on the idea, and following their conversation, Reagan reached out to Dr. Roger Peele of St. Elizabeth's Hospital where Hinckley was under observation. Peele and Reagan spoke several times, once over lunch at the White House, but Peel ultimately advised against such a meeting, stressing that such an encounter might empower Hinckley and diminish the magnitude of his actions. His concern was that Hinckley, a narcissist and sociopath that felt no empathy, sympathy or sense of wrong-doing should not have what little he understood of his sense of responsibility reduced.

When James Brady did come back to work, he would no longer perform his job as press secretary, although he retained the position in name and kept his office in the Reagan White House. There was speculation from the outset of the shootings that the press secretary job would be between Speakes and Nofziger. The two had had a history of hostility since the 1976 campaign. Nofziger had been a longtime Reagan loyalist whereas Speakes had worked on Ford's campaign. But that was only expected with Speakes having been part of the Ford White House. This was 1981 though, and his job as deputy press secretary made him by position the logical choice for the job, and even Nofziger acknowledged this as well as the fact that he did not want to be press secretary. The two made their amends in a brief encounter initiated by Nofziger where he pledged his support to Speakes in his new role, and Speakes expressed his appreciation to have that support.

Nancy Reagan, who seemed to have an influence over who got hired and let go, didn't feel Nofziger was the right person for the job anyway…this due mainly to his lack of meeting the physical criteria of what the image for a press secretary should be. Words like "rambunctious," "profane" and rumpled have been used to describe his personality and appearance. Perhaps it was the Mickey Mouse ties that he often worn with the top button of his shirt undone, but he didn't fit the mold. The story around the White House was that Nancy wanted someone who was young and handsome in front of the cameras, often referring to Brady as "Y&H," just as her husband was known as O&W (oldest and wisest).[233]

When people lose loved ones to gun violence, or if a loved one's life is profoundly altered, they've often come out for sensible gun legislation. In the wake of Lennon's murder, not too much was said or focused upon with respect to gun control. Someone who should not have had a gun had gotten hold of one, and another person was dead. Simple as that. Just one more life taken in the ever-turning wheel of senseless acts. Ronald Reagan sure didn't have much to say, and we know Nancy's response was to mention the "little gun" that she kept for protection. Three months later when her husband was shot, Nancy did not call for more gun laws, nor did she invest in more firearms. Instead, she contacted an astrologer who she'd consult for the duration of the Reagan presidency. Years later, as she put her memoirs together, Nancy's omission of Lennon's death as a significant example in a line of gun violence remained. She'd remark how the world seemed to be inundated with violence around the time of her husband's shooting, citing the attempt on Pope John Paul II's life just six weeks later…then President Sadat being killed during a parade in Cairo. She'd write how three world leaders were shot within a nine-month period.[234] But John Lennon was not a world leader. He probably wasn't even a leader. He was just some guy in a band…just one more in the statistic box of those who get shot and killed in the street…just some guy who ended up in the *Well, What Can Ya Do* pile. For Nancy, the fear of such an act against high-profile people seems to have begun with the attempt on her husband's life, as if prior assassinations weren't cause for notification. But then again, she didn't seem all too concerned with gun violence. She just didn't want her husband shot again.

In the weeks following Ronnie's shooting, Nancy was talking to her friend, entertainer, Merv Griffin who told her about his friend Joan Quigley, an astrologer. Quigley had told Griffin that she foresaw and predicted the shooting and felt like she could have stopped it from happening had she been in contact with the First Lady. Quigley was relatively well-known as an astrologer having published several books and frequently appearing on the *Merv Griffin Show*, where she and Nancy had met once earlier in the 1970s. The First Lady got in touch with Quigley and shortly afterwards, she was hired as the White House astrologer. The president showed some concern at first and cautioned his wife to keep her association with Quigley under wraps due to the potential embarrassment it could cause in the event of the public ever finding out. For the remainder of his time in office, Nancy Reagan would strongly influence her husband's schedule based on Quigley's readings, determining whether or not it was safe for him to be in a certain place on a particular day, or if planned events needed to be rescheduled. There is no overstating how profoundly shaken up the First Lady was by the shootings, but it was to the extent that she would allow the world of astrology to become the hand that turned the key, much like Yoko Ono had that same firm grasp on her own husband's decisions. For the most part, Nancy's association with Quigley was kept a secret from the public until 1987 when Donald Regan's book was published with the details of that association spilled inside its pages as a personal vendetta against the First Lady. Regan, who would serve as Secretary of Treasury during Reagan's first term would literally swap positions with Jim Baker and become Chief of Staff for half of the second term until Nancy would force his resignation. Within the Reagan camp, Regan's combative relationship with the First Lady was well-known and eventually well-documented in the press. The events that would play out in the early months of 1987 culminating in Regan's departure are far from the focus of this book, as is the First Lady and Regan's mutual dislike of each other, though it is significant in these pages to merely consider mentioning in illustration of Nancy Reagan's influence over the president. To sum up these points, the presidency, for the remainder of the 1980s, would be informed by tarot cards.

While Nancy Reagan was playing with tarot cards in response to her husband's near assassination, Sarah Brady, whose husband's life was interrupted irreparably, was fighting for effective gun legislation to no avail. With the National Rifle Association dumping millions of dollars into Washington, Republicans continuously squashed the proposed Brady Bill, which would have required background checks for gun purchases. Sarah Brady argued that such a background check could have stopped John Hinckley Jr. from obtaining the weapon that altered her husband's life and nearly killed the President of the United States. It wouldn't be until twelve years later, when Democratic President Bill Clinton took office with a Democratic majority over both houses of Congress when the Brady Bill would be signed into law. At the signing, James Brady would reflect on the long road toward arriving at the much-needed law.

"Twelve years ago, my life was changed forever by a disturbed young man with a gun. Until that time, I hadn't thought much about gun control or the need for gun control. Maybe if I had, I wouldn't have been stuck with these wheels."[235]

The assassination attempt on the President of the United States on March 30, 1981, much like the return of the American hostages coinciding with his inauguration, contributed immensely to the mythology of Ronald Reagan as an American hero. Whereas his approval rating was at a record low during the first few months of his presidency, his popularity soared following his recovery from the shooting. In his first speech upon returning back to work, he introduced the spending cuts that he had promised in his campaign, seemingly picking up with the pre-election vigor and enthusiasm of candidate Reagan, right where he left off in the autumn of 1980.

15

BORN IN THE U.S.A.

Bruce Springsteen was spending his last week off from an unexpected extended break when President Reagan was shot. The European leg of the River Tour was scheduled to begin in Brighton, England on March 17, but coming offstage at the Market Square Arena in Indianapolis on the night of March 5, the artist was beyond exhaustion and needed some time off beyond the week and a half he'd have to rest before embarking on another two-month run of shows. The European dates were postponed and pushed up one month as he took the remainder of March off. It was the same week just two years earlier when the events at Three Mile Island took place as he was just about to begin work on *The River*. Now two years later, he was halfway through a tour in support of the work he began that spring of 1979. He finally made it overseas when the band landed in Frankfurt, Germany on April 5, 1981. It had been six years since the *Born to Run* hype, and he had not forgotten his overall experience in Europe. Once again, he was on trial. Reminiscent of the feeling on the Darkness Tour, he once again had something to prove. By the time of "Tenth Avenue Freeze-Out," the third song in Hamburg two nights later, he succeeded in getting the rigid crowd off their asses and onto their feet. During Clarence's extended sax solo, he made the nightly leap into the German crowd. This was the norm for him back in the States, but was unprecedented in Germany. The one-to-one contact with the audience…touching people, high-fiving them, telling stories about his life and making the extra effort to learn certain words of whatever language he faced, all counted immeasurably in Europe. Let's be clear: Springsteen is not the only artist to do some of these things, but he put an unrivaled personable and human face on the image of the "rock star" in ways perhaps no other artist did before or since. And that was the idea…for the fans to look at him and be able to see themselves. Stars like Mick Jagger and Freddie Mercury, both royalty in Europe, were larger than life and unattainable…their performances, spectacles…their presences, kingly. Springsteen on the other hand, looked like he just walked out of an auto body shop…a normal guy in jeans and a t-shirt busting his ass for rock and roll. Elvis, the Beatles and the Stones all made people love rock and roll. Springsteen made them believe, as he tore through Germany, France, Spain, Belgium, Holland, Denmark, Sweden and Scotland, followed by three weeks jumping from town to town around England and giving European audiences a rock and roll experience unlike anything they had ever taken part in.

In Europe, Springsteen trimmed the set down to an average of 28 songs per night, cutting some of the excess material that made for a particular weighty show during the autumn 1980 leg of the tour. Songs like "Fade Away," "The Price You Pay," "Jackson Cage" and "Drive All Night" were rarely played if at all. "Crush on You" never even made it to Europe, having been dropped in December. All five songs would completely disappear, never to be played again until well into the 2000s. Cover rarities were a staple to the Europe shows, however. Elvis Presley's "Can't Help Falling in Love" appeared in several encores, while a reworked version of "Follow That Dream" suddenly showed up early in the first set of many shows. "Johnny, Bye Bye" a new song about the death of Presley seemed to have come out of nowhere. Introducing it, Springsteen told audiences about sneaking into Graceland in an attempt at meeting his hero, and remarked about how he could never get over how someone who had been such a winner "could lose so big in the end."[236] While in the Netherlands, a spooky version of Creedence Clearwater Revival's "Run through the Jungle" began opening the shows and then suddenly never appeared again. In Amsterdam, he purchased a Jimmy Cliff tape featuring a song he'd never heard before called "Trapped." He liked it so much that he re-worked it into his own version and premiered it soon after at his London gigs. Throughout Europe, two self-conscious anthems, "This Land is Your Land" and "Who'll Stop the Rain," songs he had toyed with toward the end of the U.S. leg became staples in the show.

In the spring of 1981, Springsteen began reading *A Pocket History of the United States* by Henry Steele Commager and Allan Nevins, as well as Howard Zinn's *People's History of the United States*. He'd remark to a Paris audience, "I'm 31 now, and I just started to read the history of the United States."[237] The books, which influenced him greatly, would be mentioned through most of the tour and even into the coming U.S. summer tour. The publications opened his eyes to much of the bloodshed and inequity that is so much a part of American history, but otherwise left out of the standard sanitized textbook version taught to school students in order to start them off with a subjective positive view of their country. As Springsteen became more informed and educated on his government over the next few years, he'd later comment on how that very same blind patriotism "could get you killed," when referring to the Vietnam draft.[238] Although he always stayed one step away from partisan politics, it eventually became obvious which side he was on. His silence at the M.U.S.E concerts didn't reveal much, but his statement in Tempe about the election outcome during the autumn of 1980 spoke volumes. He spent a great deal of time talking to European audiences about his own country. Someone…something…some combination of events had flipped a switch in his conscience, beginning perhaps on election night while he was in Arizona. These revelations hinted at shades of what his artistic purpose would be and how effective the power of his voice through his music could be. Two examples of what was going through Springsteen's mind in Europe come from two onstage monologues from the same Stockholm show on May 8, 1981. The first is his introduction of "This Land is Your Land."

"In America, there's a promise that gets made. And it's...over there...I guess...it's called...they call it...the American Dream, which is just the right to be able to live your life with some decency and some dignity. Over there, and in a lot of places in the world now...that dream...it's only been true for very few people. It seems if you weren't born in the right place, or if you didn't come from the right town, or if you believe in something that's different from the next person...ya know...right now there's a lot of...in the States, there's a lot of hard times, and when that happens, there's always a resurgence of groups like the Ku Klux Klan and white nationalists...and it seems like hard times turn people against each other. People that don't understand that... that the enemy is not the guy on the street that looks different from you."[239]

The crowd applauds loudly in approval and cuts him off.

He waits.

They settle down.

"But it's hard...it's hard in the States because the enemy is something you can't see. It's something that's invisible, and it's something that works on you, and it eats away inside you every day of your life...and it turns the good things that you have in you...into...into nothing. So this is a song by a guy named Woody Guthrie."

The crowd cheers in recognition.

"He understood what it was about, and...it's just a song about livin' free... about the land that you live in...it should belong to each and every one of you, and that...you got a right and a promise to life...to fulfill yourself inside."[240]

The audiences in Europe showed Springsteen an unexpected warmth and respect that in some ways he hadn't even experienced back home. The

U.S. audiences demonstrated a loyalty that was messianic, but in a selfish manner. European crowds could get much rowdier, but there was also a polite attentiveness to them. Perhaps the best example of this is the complete silence during the slow songs. When he asked for silence on "Stolen Car" and "Wreck on the Highway," the European crowds sat down and complied, taking in as much of the experience as they could. When he did the same songs back in the States, the American audiences began talking or got up to go for more beer. This became on ongoing problem in America from every tour forward. In 1978 before the mainstream had really caught on to Springsteen and he was still performing to his largely cult following, his song, "Factory" was a quiet tribute to his father, and the audience, still made up of loyal fans, silently soaked in every word. By the 1980s, the song became an excuse to carry on a conversation or get up to take a piss. The element of rudeness and inconsiderate behavior has long been part of an underlying tension between Springsteen and his audiences in the States ever since the firecracker hit him in the face during the opening seconds of 1979. But whether he was struggling with people in the crowd occasionally setting off firecrackers or just blatantly talking through quiet songs, he has expressed his disgust on more than one occasion. In the Eighties, as he got more and more popular, he became one of the mega artists whose shows became events for a very particular portion of the American population with excessive disposable incomes that go to concerts just to have an elaborate background for their quarterly meetings, if not just to say they were there and have the t-shirt to prove it. This wasn't so much a problem on the River Tour as it would become on the Born in the U.S.A. Tour and beyond.

Before "Point Blank" in Stockholm, he addressed the crowd one more time.

"This song I wrote three or four years ago I guess, and um…it's about… There's this Marvin Gaye and Tammy Tyrell song…it's called 'It Takes Two,' and in the song Marvin Gaye sings, 'It takes one to dream, but it takes two to make a dream come true.'":[241]

The crowd applauds and quickly goes silent again.

"I guess that's why we're here tonight talkin' to you and you guys are talkin' to us. And because it's…it's funny, ya know, because…on this tour… since we've been over here…this is our last night on the continent…and I've learned…I've learned a lot over here. I've learned the importance of the audience…the importance of *you* in the show…because we come out and we play, and we play hard, and try to tell you about the things that mean a lot to us, and when you respond the way that you have tonight and last night…it's like a big…like 'me too'…ya know?"[242]

The Swedish fans rise into the loudest cheers and applause of the evening. He waits until they once again settle into total silence.

"It's in a bunch of little things. I want you to know that it means a lot to us just how quiet you've been on the slow songs, and I wanna thank you for doing that. This song is about two people that once had that kind of connection, and for some reason, it got broken apart. And…it's like…a song ain't no good until somebody hears it…and like…by yourself, you can't have effect… you know…ya have to…ya have to reach out. This is a song about someone who loses that power…which is the most powerful thing in the world…your ability to affect your friends' lives…and my life…and maybe I could do something for you."[243]

Firecrackers exploded in the middle of "Factory." The Boss was pissed. A song that had opened a few shows over in Europe and held audiences captive saw nothing but disrespect in America. The crowd noise was tolerable. It was the firecrackers that got under his skin. He was three nights into an otherwise successful six-night stand in East Rutherford, New Jersey at the Brendan Byrne Arena. The opening of the summer leg of the River Tour on July 2, served as the grand opening of the new 20,000-seat addition to the Meadowlands sports complex. It was the end of Fourth of July weekend by the third show (July 5), when the firecracker incidents began, ironically just before his opening monologue to "Independence Day."

"I'd just like to make one announcement," he said sternly some 25 minutes into the show. "If by any chance you brought any fireworks with you, please don't set them off in the hall. Keep them in your pocket or throw them away. If you see somebody settin' them off, tell the usher or tell the security guard because I want them thrown out. 'Cause you're gonna hurt yourself or hurt somebody that's around ya."[244]

A few bars into the keyboard intro, he regained what he was going to talk about in the first place.

"We just spent a couple months over in Europe. And I found myself thinkin' of home a lot more than usual, from being away. I'd never been away from the States for so long. And I started to read this book called *History of the United States*. And in it, I found a lot of things that were important to know, because they helped me understand how when I was a kid all I remember was my father worked in a factory, his father worked in a factory...and the main reason was that they didn't know enough. They didn't know enough about themselves, and they didn't know enough about the forces that controlled their lives. I started to read this book, and the thing that most impressed me was the idealism. It was like when you were a kid and you leave home. You leave home because you believe in yourself or you think you're gonna do something. And because you wanna be different...you wanna be different than your old man was. And that's what happened here. The idea was that there'd be a place for everybody no matter where you came from, no matter what religion you were or what color you were, you could help make a life that had some decency and some dignity to it. But like all ideals, that idea got corrupted. And as I read through the book and I got up into the Sixties and Seventies...in the Seventies, I was in my twenties, and I was in my teens in the Sixties, but I felt like I was sleeping all the time through all those years. 'Cause I didn't know what was goin' on. I didn't know what the government that I live under was doing. It's important to know about yourself, that's all...and know about the things around you. So if you get a chance, read that book, *History of the United States*, it's good."[245]

It became clearly evident just by the way he was addressing his audiences that summer that something had happened to him in Europe. To the hometown crowds, he spoke much more than he did at the previous Garden and Nassau shows over the holidays. But it wasn't how much he talked to the crowd that was noticeable...it was what he was saying. By the time the next round of firecrackers went off during "Racing in the Street," he was infuriated. The complete ignorance of a select few in the Jersey crowd reminded him of the beautiful harmonious experiences with the Europeans. And here were the ugly Americans. It was a foreshadowing of the future when his popularity would reach its peak during the second term of the Reagan years, and his audiences would become too big to manage on any meaningful level. Once again, memories of Cleveland came to mind.

"When I was over in Europe," he began with the tone of a lecture, "one of the things that I hadn't thought about that much before, that I started to think about, was the importance of the audience in the show. And I just want to say that I'm proud that everybody's come down to see us. And whoever it is...and there's only one person or two out of, I guess 20,000 people here tonight...that has to set off a firework in the middle of a song, the only thing I can say is, you can do me a favor and never come back to one of my shows ever again. Because if you don't have the respect for yourself, you should at least have respect for the people around you. And if you don't have that, you should at least have the guts to do it where I can see you."[246] But the danger didn't exist in the form of firecrackers only. Security concerns at rock concerts were substantially raised a year and a half earlier when a stampede at a Who concert killed 11 people outside the Riverfront Coliseum in Cincinnati. Springsteen went out on a limb every night when he entered the crowd, a measurement of his relationship with his fans and his trust in them. Stage diving itself was common at punk shows, but for an artist of Springsteen's magnitude and fame to put himself in a situation where he was held in the air over a dark crowd of people in the middle of a sports arena floor…was risky. The cold-blooded murder of John Lennon on the street and the reality that nobody was safe no matter who they were, unleashed a new paranoia in the music world.

John Lennon!
A fucking Beatle!
Instantly snuffed out and extinguished.
And if they could kill John Lennon…

Later in the summer, Paul Simon would have a brief scare as an erratic fan would come climbing onto the stage under a dark sky over Central Park, charging at him. The firecracker incidents occurring throughout the Meadowlands engagement were disruptive and annoying, but however ugly they were, they didn't dominate it. Overall, the shows served as a triumphant victory lap in his home state before embarking on the final leg of what had become the biggest year of his life.

While Springsteen was in the middle of his Meadowlands run, President Reagan announced Sandra Day O'Connor as his nominee for the Supreme Court. Associate Justice Potter Stewart announced his retirement in early July, angering a lot of Republicans, which paled in comparison to the angry response to the president's pick of the moderate judge. At the outset, it was the liberals who were dreading an ideological fight over the pick, as conservatives were expecting Reagan to deliver on choosing an opponent of *Roe V. Wade*, and someone who was ready to help eliminate the legality of abortion in America. Some may challenge the labeling of O'Connor as a moderate or centrist at the time of her appointment, though it is precisely how she was viewed in light of her support for the Equal Rights Amendment and the fact that conservatives questioned her commitment to overturning women's rights to their own body. In choosing O'Connor, Reagan fulfilled his promise to appoint a woman to the Court, and he offered a much more pragmatic side of himself, easing some fears that he would merely be a puppet for the ideological right that was increasingly trying to wage war on the countercultural progress of the past decade and a half. If we approach the counterculture and "countercultural progress" as comprising the totality of Civil Rights, Women's Liberation, ERA and everything that challenged and ran contrary to accepted behavior in America prior to the 1960s, it becomes much clearer why conservatives were threatened by it, simply equating it with the anti-war movement and a bunch of hippies doing drugs. What the Republicans and Democrats would find out over time, beginning with Sandra Day O'Connor, was that Reagan was in fact a pragmatist and not an ideologue, though right-wing ideologues love to attach themselves to his name.

The Vietnam War comes back into the picture during the summer of 1981. Springsteen had read *Born on the Fourth of July* three summers earlier, and had a chance encounter with Ron Kovic, the book's author. Kovic, a paralyzed Vet, spotted Springsteen sitting poolside at a Los Angeles hotel. He noticed the book he was reading and went over, introducing himself. Springsteen, who failed his physical, labeled 4-F because of a leg injury in a motorcycle accident some time before, got to stay behind while he saw friends go off to Southeast Asia…some never to come home. Kovic's story never strayed too far from his mind, and probably rose back to the surface as he read *History of the United States*. Between Europe and the summer tour in the States, he had run into Kovic again at the Hollywood Bowl in June. Kovic introduced him as he went onstage joining Jackson Browne and Gary US Bonds at the Survival Sunday anti-nuclear benefit. Soon before the summer tour began, Bruce started making inquires, initially with the intention of gaining whatever information he could. Having read Joe Klein's book on Woody Guthrie, he'd contacted Klein, who had also written a book on Vietnam Vets. Klein referred him to Bob Muller, the President of the Vietnam Veterans of America Foundation.

Bob Muller served in the Marine Corp as a lieutenant during the Vietnam War. Injured severely in 1969, he was left unable to walk. He saw combat during what were perhaps the ugliest years of the war. Angered like millions of other Americans over Richard Nixon's failure to end the war and letting it drag on for another four years, he joined the anti-war movement. Soon after Muller was thrown out of the Republican National Convention in 1972, Nixon was re-elected in a landslide. Feeling betrayed and rejected by the very country he was told he was fighting to protect, his anger turned to bitter resignation.

"What do you do?" he asked Jonathan Pont in a 2001 interview for *Backstreets* magazine. "1973, 74, you go to the racetrack and get fucking high, because fuck this country."[247]

Completely disillusioned with the United States, he decided to leave. On the night of August 8, 1974, as Richard Nixon was resigning from office, Muller was on a plane to Switzerland. He suggests that it was boredom that ultimately brought him back to the States and that is highly believable. It is often said that Americans very often don't appreciate what they have in their country until after they leave and return. That is not to suggest this was the case with Muller. But as for the "anti-American" label that the *My Country Right or Wrong* people would tag on the protesters and some returning Vets, this sentiment was more along the lines of simply feeling disgusted toward the ideologies that dictate the atrocities that are committed under your country's name and under its flag. When convictions are strong enough and deep enough, the power of the human spirit will always make some sort of difference. That is always the idea. Although one person can usually never change anything, numbers often can. Bob Muller would go for the numbers, and try to turn one giant negative into a positive.

Soon after returning home to the United States, Muller got married and began working for the Eastern Paralyzed Veterans Association, handling legislative and legal affairs. In 1978, he helped put together the Vietnam Veterans of America in the interest of Vet's issues that were largely being ignored by the government. In D.C., he received some help from Phil Geyelin, the editor of the Washington Post's editorial page, who gave the VVA some 35 editorials over the next year. Some of their concerns entailed a revamped G.I. Bill that would allow Vets the chance to attend college. Muller spoke at length to *Backstreets* magazine in 2001 about the G.I. Bill, the distribution of benefits and how the "older with these non-service related programs were sucking up all the bucks...we had nothing that compared with what previous generations had gotten in a G.I. Bill. We were getting shut down left and right."[248] The G.I. Bill that the Vietnam Vets got was inadequate when compared to what the World War 2 Vets received. Other concerns consisted of employment opportunities, counseling centers, Vet's centers and the controversial long-sought recognition of Agent Orange as something of detrimental consequence. It seemed promising at first when a caucus was put together by a young member of Congress, David Bonior of Michigan, a Vet himself. Members such as Al Gore, Tom Daschle and Leon Panetta were freshmen in Washington and had no real clout. Any legislation they tried to pass was continuously blocked by older members of the House and the Senate who seemed to have an allegiance to the older Vets. Some even equated Vietnam Vets with the anti-war movement and saw the entire thing as an embarrassing stain...one they did everything they possibly could to cover up and ignore. By the summer of 1981, the VVA was thousands of dollars in debt, with no money coming in and virtually no support.

    In late June, the telephone rang in the VVA New York office. Muller, who happened to be there, answered. It was Jon Landau who told him he was Bruce Springsteen's manager and that Bruce had been following the Vet's movement, and was interesting in setting up a meeting to talk. Muller wasn't a fan, but did know who Springsteen was. He agreed to come to one of the shows at the Meadowlands engagement a week later. When he showed up at the newly-opened arena, Springsteen was in mid-performance. Largely unfamiliar with the rock and roll world, Muller was taken aback by the power of the show as well as the communal artist-to-audience energy dialogue. After the show, the two met and spoke for 45 minutes. The next day, Landau called Muller again to ask him if he could go out to Los Angeles in August. Bruce was interested in helping, and wanted to do a benefit concert. Knowing the impact Springsteen had on his very large audience, he agreed to come out, knowing it could serve as the boost that the movement needed. The six-night stand at the Sports Arena would see extra attention placed on its opening night on August 20, being billed as "A Night for the Vietnam Veteran."

In Los Angeles a month later, Springsteen met with Muller who took him to a Vet's counseling center. There he got a chance to meet and talk to some people. He was then shown a powerful documentary on Vietnam Vets made by Muller's friend David Monroe. The reality and responsibility of the situation that Springsteen had taken on must have begun to sink in for him that day. He had been asked before to participate in benefits, but these were events that had been set up by others where all he would have to do is show up. In the past, he had only done M.U.S.E. It was a situation that was brought to him and left for him to decide on doing it. This one, however, was his own doing. Breaking the silence surrounding the Vietnam Vet by using his influence as a rock star had gone from a mere thought in his head to a reality.

Meeting the Vets that day proved to be a moving but intimidating experience. These were people who had their lives forever altered because of the lies and deceit of their own government...people betrayed and forgotten by their own country. People who put their lives on the line, had their hopes, dreams and spirits crushed, first by the draft and then by America itself. What could Springsteen possibly say to these guys? How would he even look them in the eye? Years later he'd carry that message to an audience in Zimbabwe. Speaking about Vietnam, his hostility and rage still present, he'd tell a crowd that the Vets went to the other side of the world "because their government told them it was the right thing to do. And now there are

50,000 names on a black wall in Washington D.C...names of good people who fought a bad war."[249] Two decades earlier, the drummer of his first band never returned home. He had been personally affected. His convictions were as strong as his words in this respect. In Los Angeles, he'd look them in the eyes. He'd listen to their words. And on the next day after a long sleepless night, he'd take their fight to the rest of America.

At the Sports Arena, Springsteen had two platforms built on both sides of the stage to accompany wheelchair seating for Vietnam Vets.

"They were sensitive to doing the right thing," Muller said in 2001. "It was great. We had the best view you could ever want to have of the event. To have these guys elevated...when are you ever going to go to a concert and have a seat like this? It was a special night for us. We celebrated."[250] Springsteen nervously stayed up the night before, preparing to address the audience, but not quite sure what to say. He also approached Muller about speaking to the audience before show time. Before the lights went down, Springsteen had some tips for him.

"If you think they're booing you, they're not," he told Muller. "They're just saying Bruuuuuce. And Bobby, it's a rock and roll audience...keep it short!"[251]

When the lights went down, Springsteen did something he had never done before. He walked onstage without his guitar. Amidst the cheers, he took the microphone off its stand and waited for silence. Muller waited in the wings as Springsteen began to speak.

"Tonight, we're here for the men and the women that fought in the Vietnam War. Yesterday, I was lucky enough to have met some of these guys, and it was funny, because I am used to coming out in front of a lot of people, and I realized that I was nervous and I was a little embarrassed about not knowing what to say to them. And it's like when you feel like you're walking down a dark street at night, and out of the corner of your eye, you see somebody getting hurt, somebody getting hit in a dark alley, but you keep walking on because you think it don't have nothing to do with you…you just want to get home. Well, Vietnam turned this whole country into that dark street. And unless we're able to walk down those dark alleys and look into the eyes of those men and women that are down there, and the things that happened, we're never gonna be able to get home. And then it's only a chance. You guys who are out there who are 18 or 19 years old…it happened once, and it can happen again. So, I guess all I'm saying is, you gotta go down there and you gotta look. And we got the easy part. Because there's a lot of guys here tonight that had to live it…live it everyday. And there's a lot of guys that made it home to America but died and didn't make it down here tonight. So, what I want to ask you to do, I want you to give a few minutes of your attention and listen to a friend of mine, a Vietnam Veteran named Bob Muller."[252]

 He leaned over and handed the mic to Muller who was now onstage.

 "Thank you," he began. "It's very exciting to be here tonight. It's a great night for Vietnam Veterans. You may have been hearing about Vietnam Veterans and not really understand what it's all about. Very simply, there was a lot of controversy and a lot of pain surrounding the tragedy of Vietnam. And because of that, a lot of people are trying to forget it and pretend it never happened. That doesn't do much for the families of the 55,000 Americans that were killed in Vietnam. It doesn't do much for the 300,000 that were wounded fighting that war. But tonight is the first step in ending the silence that has surrounded Vietnam. It is the beginning of thanking all the people that have worked so hard for these years all over the country. People like in L.A.…the Shad Meshads, the team leaders from the Vet centers, the Center for Veteran's Rights, all the Vietnam Veterans…it's bringing us together. And by that it'll make sure that the Vietnams aren't allowed to happen again. The last thing I'm going to say…it's a little bit ironic after the years that we've been trying, when the businesses haven't come behind us and the political leaders have failed to rally behind us, that when you remember the divisions within our own government about the war, that it ultimately turns out to be the very symbol of our generation...rock and roll...that brings us together. And it is rock and roll that is going to provide the healing process that everybody needs. So let's not talk about it, let's get down to it...let's rock and roll!"[253]

And with that, Bruce Springsteen and the E Street Band launched into an audacious version of "Who'll Stop the Rain." In Denver just three nights before, the rain fell heavily over Red Rocks as the same song kicked off the set with a tongue-in-cheek attempt at acknowledging the weather. In Los Angeles, the song was stripped to its purest intention...an outcry against war and injustice...a song that John Fogerty wrote to mirror the betrayal and shame his generation felt during the Nixon years.

In 1981, the wounds from Vietnam were still fresh. In the years prior to the benefit concert, three major anti-war Vietnam films, *Coming Home*, *The Deer Hunter*, and *Apocalypse Now* all came out of Hollywood. The immorality of the war had always been an issue, and yet conservatives weren't happy with the harsh realities portrayed in the films, and dismissed them all as liberal propaganda, as acclaimed as they were. As reprehensible as the government's silence was, along with its failure to not only acknowledge one big shitstorm of a mistake, it took the rock and roll community, often as always, to step up and break the silence. Within a month of Springsteen's concert, both Pat Benatar and Charlie Daniels did benefits for Vets as well. The following Memorial Day would see the dedication of the long-awaited Vietnam Veterans Memorial...something not every Vet thought was a priority over the benefits and useful government support they needed. Nonetheless, it was a bittersweet occasion. Within a few months, inspired by the plight of the Vietnam Vet, Springsteen would pen a brand new acoustic ballad called "Born in the U.S.A."

Springsteen wrapped up the River Tour in Cincinnati in mid-September, eleven months after the album's release. When he arrived back in New Jersey, he was a homeless millionaire. After drifting for the past four years between the hotels and living out of a suitcase to a rented house in Holmdel and then back to living out of a suitcase, the lease on his house had run out. He hadn't yet purchased his Graceland, nor did he intend to. His harshest critics would later condemn him for being rich while singing about the working class and embracing their values…as if staying close to his roots made him a hypocrite. Once his politics were fleshed out, the political right would take aim at him regularly. For the time being, he was able to shrug everything off, and it was the first time in his career…in his life…that he was able to just sit back, exhale and not give a shit about anything. He'd just finished a massive tour of a commercially successful album, and for once, the record label wasn't on the edge anxiously expecting something. For once, he was in total control of what the future would be, and he'd make sure it stayed that way.

Springsteen immediately rented another house, this time on a reservoir in Colts Neck, New Jersey. He'd watch the seasons change from his window and he'd go out very little. At some point while in Colts Neck, he'd meet himself. Demons and emotional voids buried in years of playing until he dropped of exhaustion, too tired to think…would rise to the surface. Something was still missing. At night he'd go to bed to face his own thoughts, trapped in the prison of his own mind. There in the autumn 1981 chill, he'd write songs. But they'd be different kinds of songs. The topical direction he'd hinted at when he first premiered "The River" at the M.U.S.E. concerts two autumns earlier had come into full fruition. Was it his rotten mood that was going to dictate his next step? Whatever the case, he wasn't about to take it out on anyone or anything but his music. One day, in the quiet desolation of the lonely house, some 72 hours after the calendar flipped to 1982, he sat down in his bedroom with an acoustic guitar and a 4-track Tascam Portastudio, and he pressed the record button.

16

A MEANNESS IN THIS WORLD

Ronald Reagan's distaste for unions was well-known, and so was organized labor's dislike of Reagan. One of only two unions that did endorse him in 1980 was the Professional Air Traffic Controller's Organization (PATCO), which the President, soon after, showed his appreciation for with a resounding *fuck you*. Air traffic workers demanding increases in wages and benefits, decided to strike in early August 1981. Most thought the President was bluffing when he warned the workers they'd be fired if they didn't return to their jobs within two days. Over the next few weeks, half of PATCO's membership, some 11,000 workers were fired, and the union demolished. Reagan learned of the strike over the first weekend of August. The president took focus on the written oath each employee signs: *That he or she will not strike against the U.S. government or any of its agencies.*

Interestingly enough, Reagan, who was usually very thorough in the details of most days of his presidency in his White House journal, omitted an entire month from August 6-September 3, opting instead to address those

27 days in one written entry. This also conveniently coincides with the start of an extended vacation for the Reagan's in California. What he mentions of the few days leading to the strike is marked in numbers…percentages of workers who showed up each day, as if written in hindsight with the numbers already prepared for him, but that is nothing more than speculation.

Tax cuts were next.

During the same month, when the president signed the Economic Recovery Tax Act of 1981 into law on August 13, Democratic Speaker of the House, Tip O'Neill referred to it as "royal tax cuts." Democratic criticism suggested that the cuts would only benefit the rich. Little did they know that Reagan's actions would become the foundation of the GOP playbook for the remainder of the century and into the next millennium.

In Colts Neck, Bruce Springsteen wrote music reflective of the times. Picking up right where "The River" left off, the songs hinted at even darker places than the death of dreams. But the songs off *The River* album at heart were still about picking up broken pieces and carrying on. The new songs left nowhere to go.

The failing economy mentioned in "The River," was reflective of America during the Carter years. By the beginning of Reagan's second year in office, unemployment had skyrocketed to 10.8 percent. For decades, economists have hotly contested whether or not Reagan's tax cuts were responsible for any sort of improvement such as the slow but eventual drop in unemployment that began in 1983 and continued over the course of his two terms in office. Even David Stockman in a controversial move revealed to *The Atlantic* in 1981 that the tax cuts had been a Trojan horse tactic designed to bring down the top rate.

Regardless of what sparked the surge in job growth, Springsteen's new songs going into 1982 mirrored a country bottoming out. Early in January, he taped a new collection of acoustic demos in his bedroom. Originally intended as rough sketches for full-band rock arrangements, he carried the cassette around with him, playing it often and trying to figure out how the band would be incorporated into the desolate new material. But he couldn't. Studio work began that spring, and while some songs worked within the full-band dynamic of the E Street Band, the primary batch that he felt was cohesive enough in its gloomy and unsettling tone did not seem to fit the rock model. The material seemed almost too intimate for rock music, let alone other instruments. At some point, he decided to scrap the idea of integrating the band into his efforts. As a result, songs like "Downbound Train," "Murder Incorporated," "Glory Days," "Working on the Highway," "Wages of Sin" and "Born in the U.S.A.," songs that did work in band arrangements, got tossed aside in favor of the darkest and quietest recordings. When Springsteen penned "Born in the U.S.A," it was an acoustic ballad reminiscent of the old Dust Bowl-era recordings later unearthed and released by Harry Smith in 1952. "Born in the U.S.A" was completely contemporary, however, addressing the plight of the Vietnam Vet upon returning home to a hostile public, indifferent government and bleak future. Out of two dozen or so songs recorded both with and without the band, "Born in the U.S.A.," recorded in several versions, was not chosen, nor were any of the studio-recorded songs used for the next official release. Instead, Springsteen handed in the 4-track cassette demo as his album...and the record company obliged.

That Columbia released the demos in their stark and hollow condition and fully marketed it as the *new Bruce Springsteen album*, was a testament to two significant factors. One, the trust and faith the label had in the artist. And two, the clout Springsteen had earned in the music business. To the fans, the next album would be an unexpected shock...to critics, a bold and welcome move. Whereas Bob Dylan, two decades earlier, had stunned the acoustic folk world by "going electric," Bruce Springsteen, the biggest and most revered rock artist in the world was about to follow up his biggest success to date by going...acoustic.

Regarding the album that became *Nebraska*, Springsteen's mood was clearly ugly. On the flipside of *The River*'s life-affirming conclusion, the singer and narrator of *Nebraska*'s opening song goes out and murders ten people. On trial, he knows he's going to the electric chair and willfully accepts his fate, asking only for his girlfriend to be sitting on his lap when they pull the switch, so she fries too. In front of the judge, he addresses the question of why he did what he did and tells him simply that there is "a meanness" in the world. The mass murder in the title track is based on the true story of Charles Starkweather, who at 19 years old went on a rampage with his 14-year old girl friend, Caril Ann Fugate, and killed eleven people in Nebraska and Wyoming. The 1957 and '58 murders shook Lincoln and surrounding towns to their core, as law enforcement sent out house-by-house searches along with the governor calling for assistance from Nebraska's National Guard. The same story and characters had already been immortalized in Terrance Malick's 1973 film, *Badlands*. Sung in first-person, Springsteen's title track sets us up for a collection of stories and situations highlighted by people affected, often direly, by outside elements of society beyond their control...and often elements from within themselves that manifest in some dreadful ways. Let there be no mistake...*Nebraska* is a dark and dreary album.

Contrary to the characters on *The River* who have a sense of purpose, each playing their role in the wheel of American civil society, the characters on *Nebraska* have already become statistics in the harshest possible ways. The ones who haven't yet are barely hanging on. The album recognizes that it is easy to get to a point of complete nihilism where the laws and concerns of a functioning society become meaningless. Where *The River* was about looking for connection, *Nebraska* is about the invisibility of isolation. In "Johnny 99," a guy named Ralph who is out of work, desperate to find a job and faced with mounting debts that could never be paid by any honest man, has too much to drink one night and shoots a night clerk. Sometime earlier, the bank was about to take away his house, but Ralph, now known as Johnny 99 for his sentence of *98 and a year* will be residing some place much different than home. Johnny explains to the judge his situation and acknowledges that it by no means makes him an innocent man, nor does it excuse what he has done, yet he assures the court that it was far more than what could ever be recounted that put the gun in his hand in the first place…namely those outside forces and elements at work that often break the human spirit and can result in desperate and drastic measures.

Nebraska is as psychological as it is social. Characters perceive themselves as so low on the totem pole that they often address the listener as "sir." Someone always has the upper hand over the people in *Nebraska*'s songs. The album came at a time when Springsteen was still struggling to make peace with his father. Whereas an artist like John Lennon yearned for a relationship of some sort, or just the mere presence of his mother in his life, almost pleading for her, Springsteen is scarred by the tumultuous lifelong baggage that such presence can leave behind. "My Father's House" is marked by guilt, longing and a sense of being excruciatingly haunted by an unresolved past. As always, the artist is conflicted by the archetype of the father/son relationship. There is no distinction between artist and character, as the first-person narrative paints a depressive psychological landscape. The sense of regret against the passage and distortion of time is Bergmanesque in a *Wild Strawberries* kind of way. "Mansion on the Hill," in its warm summery yet foreboding imagery recalls that of an Edward Hopper painting. It is a still moment on the album reminiscent of present consciousness that gets briefly interrupted by a past memory, only to be shaken awake back into the now. "Used Cars" is a softer look at his father as provider and protector. Written from the eyes of a child, or as an adult somehow seeing his past through vivid memory, the voice of the song is a witness to his father's plight. He sees and feels his humiliation in front of the car salesman and carries the same rage his father must feel. The people on *Nebraska* are not all losers and murderers, however. Not all have fallen through the cracks of society, and would gladly contribute to the rat race if they could only get hold of their own little piece of it. In the case of the *Nebraska* album, the people in its grooves would be much better served if they were able to find the most basic necessity for a life of purpose and dignity… a job. "Atlantic City" perhaps sums up the overall atmosphere with a couple coming up against hard times and looking for a little bit of luck in a gambling city that is barely surviving the economy itself. The ever-present pressing on in the face of dying dreams still inevitably triumphs by the end of the album. Despite it all, the tough will survive, and even the weak who have not turned to crime manage to scrape up enough faith in each passing day by finding some reason to believe.

Springsteen spent the next year and a half in the studio working on the next proper rock album…an effort he originally began for the project that became *Nebraska*. When it was all over, the end result was *Born in the U.S.A.*, an album that went on to sell over 30 million copies. During his peak wave of popularity and celebrity in 1985, Springsteen would get married, and like Reagan and Lennon, he'd fuck it up the first time. The second time, in 1991, he'd get it right, marrying backup singer and musician, Patti Scialfa and raising three children together. Much can be written about regarding those emotional voids and missing parts of himself mentioned in the previous chapter. These things come into full realization in the early Nineties when Bruce addresses relationships, commitment, family, children and the fears that kept him in a very dark place for many years despite his artistic success. That said, these parts of his story are inevitably for another book, and not this one, as they bear no significance or consequence to this particular study of Springsteen's work and evolution as an artist.

For the next three decades, Springsteen maintained his status as the biggest rock recording artist in the world, getting ever-increasingly active in politics and social justice causes.

As we near the conclusion of our assessment of this brief period in time, it becomes necessary to look into the future…the 1990s and beyond, and deep into the consequential twenty-first century…the first decade of which deified Ronald Reagan upon his death in 2004 in the middle of a decade that saw George W. Bush as President of the United States. The second Bush presidency…the son of George Herbert Walker, would lead an administration under the hovering shadow of the Reagan presidency. No matter what the forty-third president achieved, tried to achieve or thought he could achieve, the presence and memory of the fortieth was always near. Reagan, in the eyes of the new century GOP was the shining example, and had set the gold standard for a Republican presidency. He was the nation's backbone and strength. He was a military man and a self-made man who didn't take any shit. He preached bootstrapping and saw government benefits to the poor and underprivileged as counterproductive. He bitch-slapped the Soviets and ended the Cold War, they said. Suddenly his likeness and memory were propelled into a fond nostalgia and reverence much like liberals of generations past reserved for FDR. Years into the new century, conservatives from the richest CEOs to politicians in Washington to poor and middle class suburban slobs on social media all posted the same mantra…

We need a president like Reagan again!
Bring Back Ronald Reagan!
Now there was a real President!

And thus also began the myth of the Reagan Era.

Was it really a myth though? Did it not really happen? Was Ronald Reagan really not a towering figure both during and after his presidency? Was he really the evil villain liberals make him out to be? Do we maybe exaggerate his accomplishments while downplaying or ignoring how destructive his actions as president have been over time? Or do we exaggerate how destructive he was? Wasn't he kind of tame compared to the shit going on in modern America? But should that be an excuse to let him off the hook? Should we just objectively take some of these things apart a little bit? Let's talk about that thing conservatives always love to mention…the economy.

While the economy would eventually bounce back by Reagan's second term, federal outlays were averaging 21.7 percent of gross domestic product (GDP) compared to the 21.1 percent of GDP average during the Carter years and the far more significant 19.3 percent during Lyndon Johnson's presidency. Federal spending averaged some 22 percent of GDP during the years of George H.W. Bush's presidency. What is significant about this number is that it came on the heels of the ending of the Cold War and a 15 percent reduction in defense spending. This is not to disrupt the flow of this book with dry numerical figures, but to provide some factual examples in areas that this publication has not fully explored, and thank God, because it would scare away a lot of the John Lennon and Bruce Springsteen fans who are attracted to this book for its musical aspects.

Some historians judge the success of revolutions based on whether they are built from the top down or from the ground up. One could only speculate what his father's reaction to the post-Tea Party/Trump-era division in America would be, but Michael Reagan's assertion of a grassroots electorate is consistent with the overwhelming victory in the 1980 election in that the Reagan brand appealed to a changing populist sentiment. Paying taxes has always been the biggest collective gripe of what became of the New Right in the late Seventies, and tax cuts for millionaires and above became the GOP's number one mantra through the next three decades alongside the long-range influence of Ronald Reagan. A massive tax revolt was part of the circumstances under which the country was born. While many were wary at best over the basic fundamentals of supply-side economics, it breathed new life into the conservative world as a whole, giving it a new language. It was a vocabulary that the populist movement found refreshing compared to all the talk of sacrifice, limitations and buckling down in self-denial to save the country. Instead, it was a welcome mat to a world of growth where everybody was promised they would win. Of the future, Jack Kemp predicted a tidal wave of Republican voters, many of which would not normally vote Republican but would do so simply because they saw a better chance at the

American Dream.[254] The so-called Reagan Revolution was effectively and cumulatively felt through three terms between the Reagan and George H.W. Bush presidencies over a 12-year period, and by the end of it, the federal deficit reached an unprecedented $2.4 trillion with federal red ink amounting to 70 percent of GDP growth. Yet, the tenets of Reaganism were completely dismantled and sealed into the eternity of debunked American mythology by George W. Bush as federal spending rose to 25 percent of GDP, which after measured for inflation amounted to 50 percent…an increase from $2.1 trillion to $3.2 trillion in the space of his two terms. Some apologists for the entire era like to isolate what they see as the positive effects of Reaganism on a very specific and limited time frame…Reagan's actual eight years as President of the United States, claiming that regardless of the post-presidential years, the Reagan Revolution did what it was supposed to do *at the time,* thus reviving the economy. And even if that were true, how do we account for and apply it to the presidency of George W. Bush whose tax cuts for the rich and resulting economic disasters were right out of Reagan's playbook?

Another part of the Reagan legacy, significant for both the right and the left, is the death of labor unions. Depending on which side of the aisle we stand, Reagan largely gets the credit or the blame for destroying the power and existence of labor unions in America. Well into the twenty-first century, struggles from the previous century that were fought over and became either law or just a commonly-accepted agreement out of human decency between workers and employers morphed into issues again. Things Americans didn't have to worry about for decades…labor laws and workers' rights that were fought for during a version of America that desperately needed to modernize in its treatment of people in perhaps the same manner as it modernized through industry and technology…these things were suddenly being fought for by modern day twenty-first century Americans. People found themselves fighting for a higher minimum wage after decades of conservative obstruction. Public workers fought for collective bargaining rights as conservatives aggressively tried to have them stripped while movements were put in place to make teachers public enemy number one for the simple fact that they were protected by strong unions. The lasting imprint of Ronald Reagan was always felt by those who had a little something but were still struggling just to live a modest and honest life. And his imprint indeed remained on the wealthy, whose trickle-down theory had duped the middle class and poor into believing it was for the greater good, and their own good…to feed the rich and wait gullibly and obediently for the crumbs to fall their way. Reagan did have an understanding of the needs and fears of the working people, and he found a way through his charm, eloquence and sagely tone to connect with them, even as his party was conspiring against their very interest. And that right there was the genius of Ronald Reagan and his era of conservatism…the ability to turn the working class of America against its own interests.

On the subject of Reagan, Bruce Springsteen never spoke out again with concern or criticism in front of an audience, although *Rolling Stone's* Kurt Loder asked him about the president during the opening leg of the Born in the U.S.A. Tour in 1984. *Born in the U.S.A.* had become the biggest-selling album of his career, and it completed the era of worldwide rock and roll dominance that began in the autumn of 1980 with *The River*. Four autumns later, Springsteen found himself crossing America again during another presidential election season with the Reagan re-election campaign declaring that it was "Morning in America." But Springsteen just couldn't see the dawning of a new morning in the midst of American inequity, criticizing economic policy as being rooted in an indirect racism where black people at the lower end of the economic spectrum were always affected the worst. He believed people generally knew this, though many would never admit to it or dare talk about it on any honest level. That said, Springsteen did not believe Reagan to be a bad man, but he also didn't feel he was shrouded in anything resembling reality in America. He represented a mythical America, presenting a seductive image that appealed to a form of nostalgia for a certain Normal Rockwellesque version of the country that had not only passed, but may never have really existed. Springsteen's view of America was one of a compassionate place, and he just didn't see it as that place anymore. At the very least, the social consciousness of the Sixties counterculture suddenly seemed outdated. And so, he could easily understand Reagan's appeal even though he didn't support him.[255]

Social conscience and left wing causes such as labor unions became an underlying concern and effort throughout the Born in the U.S.A. Tour, when during the intermission of each of Springsteen's lengthy shows audiences could find tables set up in the lobby, representing local unions and community food banks. Given the historical nature of this publication, it is unfortunate that we have to refer to labor unions as a "left wing cause" when they are really an American cause.

While Springsteen was clearly with the unions wherever he travelled on tour, it was gradually becoming evident over time that Reagan had singlehandedly sown the seeds for the end of days for unions as a powerful presence in American labor. The end result of the PATCO strike was not that the president fired thousands of people, but a gradual deterioration of the strength of unions across the workforce. Once businesses and corporations saw Reagan manhandle the entire body of air traffic controllers protected by PATCO, they decided they were giving away the store in dealing with the unions in their own lives and saw fit to do likewise. Workers in all walks of trade and profession could now be fired, as union protection and the threat and leverage of striking no longer meant anything. Employers got as bold as Reagan had, and over a period of time, the Republican Party began to flip the narrative on strike-breaking. Whereas strikers were once looked upon with sympathy and support, they were now portrayed as selfish lawbreakers who were not reflective or representative of regular Americans. In much the same twisted way that Reagan was able to take the credit for the release of the hostages upon his inauguration, he managed to become a hero to the unscrupulous side of businesses and corporations, while crossing a picket line, once a taboo act of betrayal, became a patriotic action, as did strikebreaking in general. In one simple action, Reagan managed to start the slow inevitable reversal of a century's worth of progress in American labor.

Reagan's handling of PATCO became standard procedure that began to be pushed in business school curriculum almost immediately. As early as 1982, the Wharton School drew up a manual that encouraged business leaders to take their cue from the PATCO strike. A sure sign of success and survival for future chief executives would be taking on and fighting the unions. Strikebreaking was in vogue as a result of Reagan, and employers were emboldened because of his treatment of the air traffic workers. As a direct result, firings spread across the workforce including striking copper miners in Arizona, paper workers in Maine, as well as meat packers and bus drivers all losing their jobs as a result of striking during Reagan's 1980s. Employers more or less *wanted* union employees to strike so they could fire and replace them with non-union workers. Striking, once the ultimate leverage for workers in America became a lost cause during the 1980s.

At a stop in Hammonton, New Jersey during his re-election campaign, Reagan strayed from his usual standard stump speech with a transparent and hollow attempt at co-opting Springsteen.

"America's future," he told the local crowd, "rests in a thousand dreams inside your hearts. It rests in the message of hope in the songs of a man so many young Americans admire…New Jersey's own, Bruce Springsteen."[256]

A relentless media sought out a response from Springsteen, who second only to Michael Jackson and Reagan himself, was possibly the most famous man in America in 1984. The artist avoided commenting until he was onstage a few days later in Pittsburgh.

"Well, the president was mentioning my name in his speech the other day, and I kind of got to wondering what his favorite album of mine must've been, you know? I don't think it was the *Nebraska* album."

And then he launched into the tragic and harrowing "Johnny 99."

"I don't think he's been listening to this one."[257]

17

REVOLUTION FROM THE TOP DOWN

It is at this juncture that we wrap up our narrative of a very particular timeline of simultaneous historic and artistic events, while assessing the long-term impact they had on America and consequently the world.

In the end, the success of a presidency and its influence on the future has very little to do with how good or bad the president was. Polls and histories are and will always remain subjective, so we define good and bad by nothing concrete. Good and successful are not always synonymous. Success is most effectively measured by whether or not the person in question has reached and completed his or her goals, despite the effect they may or may not have. And so, when we assess the goals of the Reagan presidency, we do so knowing that the goals were to control inflation, deregulate the economy and cut taxes along with the size of government. But the reality of Washington is, it is virtually impossible for politicians to resist their constituencies when it comes to money and government favors. In a nutshell, with the tax cuts of 1981 and the Tax Reform Act of 1986, Ronald Reagan accomplished much of what he'd come to Washington to do, regardless of the effects. Reagan's 1981 tax cuts helped bring in the era of deregulation along with CEO and Wall Street greed. The result of the Reagan presidency was the beginnings of American government as the enemy in the eyes of conservatives, and the foundation of their rhetoric for the next thirty years and well into the twenty-first century. *Big government* became a household term. It became the biggest scapegoat for slashing federal funding for education, health care, social programs, public services, environmental protections, the arts and anything that didn't have the sole intention of feeding Wall Street and the Military Industrial Complex. Regardless of taxes, spending became the biggest factor in the disaster that post-Eighties America would inherit...a debt that tripled under Reagan...unprecedented at the time, and small in comparison to what future Republican presidents would create...but nonetheless a catalyst in a new era of Americans and Washington itself not having a handle on spending, thus running up astronomical levels of debt, and so circling back to the government for help. The government only grew bigger under Ronald Reagan.

Well into the twenty-first century, the continued tired and washed up mantra of the GOP calling for a reduction of *big government* persists. It remains perplexing and hypocritical when Republicans talk to Democrats about balancing the budget while simultaneously vowing further tax breaks for the rich and expanded military spending, which was precisely what ran up a nearly three trillion dollar debt during Reagan's presidency. In a way, it is comparable to a group of arsonists lecturing a fire department on putting out fires. It might, however, be unfair to suggest Reagan himself as a hypocrite on certain issues considering he had gone through legitimate transformations due to his own personal experiences, or some would say misconceptions and distortions of those issues, over a period of decades. For example, his hostility toward unions would be answered by the fact that he served as president of his own union, the Screen Actors Guild, in 1947. The next decade would shape his skills as a negotiator and bargainer as he'd be re-elected four times as SAG President, and in 1959, lead a strike against the producers. His years of dealing with the old Hollywood movie bosses no doubt molded his negotiating etiquette as a politician. He would later remark how dealing with guys like Mikhail Gorbachev was nothing compared to sparring with the studio moguls.

But Hollywood had changed since Ronald Reagan left for a career in politics. Over the course of his three decades in political life, the industry was restructured by way of corporate takeover and then consolidation as several film companies were swallowed up. Mergers of Warner Communications with Time Inc. and Rupert Murdoch's purchase of Twentieth Century Fox marked a new era of pressure in Hollywood for meeting target quarterly numbers imposed by corporate suits. The marker of a film's success became measured by its box office numbers on opening weekend. After unprecedented blockbusters in the 1970s like *Star Wars* and *Jaws* hinted at the possibilities, think tanks and strategists determined a new model under which the mega success of those films would no longer be the exception, but the rule. Every film could be a *Star Wars*! The Reagan Eighties saw *Raiders of the Lost Ark, ET, Top Gun, Ghostbusters, The Terminator, Rambo: First Blood, Part II* all released at first to hype, and then delivery on the hype. The monstrous success of these films with profit as the bottom line factor in well with the symbolism of a decade synonymous with greed. None reflected that greed more so than Oliver Stone's *Wall Street*...a film that so accurately mirrored an age of *get rich quick/screw the little guy* sentiment, that its antagonist Gordon Gecko uttered for all intents and purposes what is perhaps the definitive characterization of the Reagan Era: "Greed is good."[758]

Whether or not greed really was good, the Reagan years seemed to validate it for a while. But rather than watching that greed dissipate into the ether of embarrassing historical blemishes, it became the model for the GOP in subsequent decades...their very starting point where rewarding the rich became the bottom line, as was working hand-in-hand with a conservative media structure serving as its propaganda ministry, shaping a narrative of the poor being the blame for the nation's problems. The radical shift bred a new contempt for any thoughts or ideas that so much as questioned the unruly inequitable downside of free markets and the ancient laissez-faire approach.

In music, while bands like U2 and R.E.M. stayed close to social issues, the symptoms of superficial excess were seen in the world of hard rock and heavy metal. Acts that would later become known as *hair bands* rose to the top of the arena circuit, propelled more by MTV popularity than radio air play. In terms of criteria for popularity, it was a visual decade more than anything else…big hair, lots of makeup and hairspray, denim, leather, sequins and lace, and mindless songs about sex, partying, sex, partying, partying, sex and sex and sex. It was a mindless good time for those who indulged and lived to tell about it. It was also the decade of AIDS, where by the second half of Reagan's second term, the president was being criticized for not so much as mentioning the alarming disease that the world still knew very little about, but at the time was being attributed to gay men and those who blindly fucked their way through the debauchery of the Seventies.

In addition to Gordon Gecko, the Eighties were most profoundly and effectively characterized by Alex P. Keaton, the main character in *Family Ties*, a sitcom that ran from 1982-1989. Alex was a Young Republican in high school with a love for President Reagan and a joking disdain for the 1960s counterculture that is still near and dear to his hippie parents whose sentimentality for the age is marked by fondness, unbending principles and lament over something lost. The family unit was a staple to Eighties television in shows like *Family Ties*, *Growing Pains*, *The Cosby Show* and *Who's the Boss* among countless others that had kids and parents alike tuning in weekly long before the idea of streaming and binge-watching entire seasons in one sitting were ever conceived of. Though artists like Michael Jackson, Madonna, Prince and Boy George shocked and influenced pop culture in mainstream suburbia, the times, compared to the present day, were still fairly tame with clear visible lines that had not yet been crossed. Artistically, the decade was still a wealth of social and political activism in the form of musicians lending their voices and talent often to Amnesty International, a worldwide organization focused on Human Rights that saw benefits in the form of the *Secret Policeman's Other Ball*, the *Conspiracy of Hope* concerts, and the *Human Rights Now* Tour. Musical projects such as *Band Aid* and *USA for Africa* took on starvation in Ethiopia, culminating with the massively unprecedented *Live Aid* concerts taking place simultaneously on two continents, the latest satellite technology connecting it all together and the entire world watching. Projects like Steve Van Zandt's *Sun City* took on apartheid and had the support and involvement of Bruce Springsteen, Bob Dylan, Jackson Browne, Bono, Miles Davis, David Ruffin, Eddie Kendricks, Joey Ramone, Darryl Hall, John Oates, Lou Reed, Gil Scott Heron, Afrika Bambaata, Peter Wolf, Kurtis Blow, Peter Gabriel, Bonnie Raitt, Grandmaster Melle Mel, George Clinton, Run DMC, Pat Benatar, Peter Garret, Darlene Love, Ringo Star and at least a dozen other names. Music was often overtly political during the Eighties if not just simply reflective of the times. Two landmark New York City albums from Grandmaster Flash and Lou Reed, from opposite ends of the decade, *The Message* and *New York,* showcased where the most potent and significant work in both rap and rock were rooted in holding a mirror to the ills of society. Whether it music, film, literature or painting, the arts flourished in the Age of Reagan. Reed's 1989 album along with director, Spike Lee's brilliant and devastating masterpiece film *Do the Right Thing*, both released in the same year, not only serve as the two greatest artistic documents of New York City during the late Eighties, but as an overall temperature gauge for political and social climate across the country by the end of the decade. Yet, there were no real threatening figures in the arts that scared the shit out of Republicans. Nevertheless, conscientious and provocative art, present as it was, still took a pop cultural backseat to the fun-filled wholesome good times that television and video music provided, as well as the nonstop excess of materialism. Without the over-the-top superficiality of the Reagan Eighties, the conditions would not have been ripe for an explosion of music with a rebellious spirit, led by bands like Nirvana. Such a music scene had already existed to great effect through bands like Sonic Youth and Black Flag, but whereas Eighties punk remained underground, what became known as grunge in the Nineties would take that spirit to the mainstream...not that grunge ever had a political/activist bone in its body...though it would be the last rock-related explosion of its kind. Not only would rock music cease to exist as the center of pop culture, reflecting the state of the world and informing politics and fashion trends, but the role of rock in activism would no longer be a commonly-accepted given.

But let's backtrack.

In the late autumn of 1980, with John Lennon gone and a new Republican administration coming into the White House, the political right had nobody in the music world to take aim at. Let us clarify that statement to ensure that we do not equate politicians taking aim at artists such as Lennon in the same way that the Parents Music Resource Center (PMRC), co-founded by a liberal senator's wife, took aim at artists later in the decade for content that was considered sexual or violent. But this wasn't Lennon. Lennon, conservatives feared, was more powerful than he ever came close to being. And so, at least to Richard Nixon's paranoia, he was a threat. This is not to suggest that Lennon was an everyday public target in the same manner in which musical artists and Hollywood celebrities are subjected to ridicule and hatred in the twenty-first century by those who have literally turned on their favorite artists and actors simply for using their First Amendment rights... just as they always have. While artists weren't always endorsing politicians by name, they made it clear which side of the fence they were on by the work that they did, and nobody complained.

What changed?

Suddenly, we're not living in the same universe anymore where artists used their platform and were not only celebrated for it, but in some cases, counted on for it. It is difficult to imagine Bob Dylan being told to *shut up and sing* in 1963. It's hard to wrap one's head around the idea of fans complaining about "Masters of War" or "The Lonesome Death of Hattie Carroll" because they *paid to be entertained*. But that is exactly what artists face in current times. Dylan's first years in music came out of the early 1960s folk revival that accompanied the Civil Rights Movement. Considering the climate in present-day America, it is tempting to imagine a media propaganda structure like FOX News existing in 1964. Things may have turned out much differently for Dylan had pundits like Sean Hannity and Bill O'Reilly been around to rile up the conservative base against Dylan for speaking his mind, much like they've repeatedly done to Bruce Springsteen over the years. It is frightening to imagine how such bias against artists and activists might have escalated already-existing racial tensions and possibly jeopardized the Civil Rights Movement itself. Would FOX have referred to it as a terrorist movement? But thankfully, for the sake of the progress of humanity, no such channel or TV personalities existed in 1964. But the hypothetical doesn't end with Civil Rights. It's extremely unlikely that humanitarian crises such as in Bangladesh and Kampuchea would have sparked mainstream interest in the West without artists like George Harrison and Paul McCartney helping raise that awareness. *Live Aid* would not have happened without the concern of artists, nor would have entire tours dedicated to Human Rights and fighting against Apartheid. Suburban kids in America may not have known about the plights of people like Nelson Mandela or Rubin "Hurricane" Carter without the efforts of rock stars speaking out against social injustice. In 2020, such efforts would be dismissed as left-wing propaganda and millionaire stars patting themselves on the back with the publicity they receive. Sure, we get that Old World bootstrapping philosophy that many Americans hold where poor people and the unemployed amount to lazy liberals sitting on the couch looking for handouts. As irresponsible, offensive and insulting as that is to the intelligence of Americans who know different, we can almost forgive the Archie Bunker-like mentality due to the fact that Archie Bunker was very real and still lives amongst the collective body of those who don't know any better due to several generations of ignorance where the old karma of angry ghosts now spills over like waterfalls into modern times. Playing devil's advocate, we could almost see and understand why social and economic conservative thought might attribute necessity as a *liberal thing*. But humanitarian crises and catastrophic occurrences such as global pandemics...acts of God, for lack of better description in current times have been politicized into *liberal things* as well, where wearing a mask during a pandemic indicates that you must be a Democrat. How did one side become so defiled and warped in their views toward humanity that they would actually attribute social consciousness as a *liberal* thing? How did pop culture arrive at a point where artists using their platform for anything other than entertainment, was treated as treacherous? How did artists go from being hailed as voices of their generations to the collective conservative ridicule of *shut up and sing*? Believe it or not, it has its seeds planted in the Reagan years, but it wasn't until deep into the Reagan Era following his presidency that the results of those seeds began to surface. That said, Ronald Reagan himself did not completely plant the seeds for the adversity America suffers from in the twenty-first century. That division was cultivated by the people who have largely made up the GOP from 1995 onward and have shamelessly tried to link themselves time and again *to* Reagan.

When William Jefferson Clinton became the forty-second President of the United States in January 1993, he was not only the first Democrat in office since Reagan defeated Carter in 1980, but he was also the first Baby Boomer president. That meant he was much closer to John Lennon's side of the Sixties than Ronald Reagan's side of the Sixties, and it was imperative that the Republicans figure out a way to not lose what they saw as a long-term cultural war. From the moment Bill Clinton took office, Republicans vowed to take him down however they possibly could. It wasn't anything remotely like the happenstance of Watergate where it was eventually stumbled upon that Richard Nixon was involved. Yet, it was where Republicans would get their revenge somehow someway. TV and radio host Rush Limbaugh helped usher in and assure the beginning of a new division that helped transform the word *liberal* into something profane and vile. He rededicated his public existence to contributing to the downfall of the new Democratic president and actually insisted that America was being "held hostage." It was the first time in modern American history where one side of the political aisle abandoned its obligations to the American people and embarked on a full-scale agenda of destroying the other side. The GOP made that the priority over bi-partisan efforts that had been seen in past relations between Congress and the White House, namely the mutual respect between Tip O'Neil and Ronald Reagan.

Three major contributing factors leading to the current climate in America were rooted mostly in the 1990s. First, the Republicans saw their first majority in Congress in 40 years following the 1994 midterms. In early 1995, the controversial 104th Congress, led by Newt Gingrich and his *Contract with America*, swaggered arrogantly into Washington with a ruthless agenda, much like the rookie cops opposing Clint Eastwood in *Magnum Force*. It wasn't long before Clinton's second term was scarred by a government shutdown and an impeachment trial over the fact that he lied under oath concerning a blowjob he received in the Oval Office. With a 71 percent approval rating at the time of impeachment, it begged the question of what was more absurd...that he was impeached over a blowjob or the fact that he was under oath over a blowjob in the first place. But even this is unfair to just point to Clinton's second term. For the most part, presidential second terms have always been disastrous, even Reagan's which was tainted the same way by the Iran-Contra affair. Second, the Clinton presidency was also challenged by a rise in domestic right-wing terrorism in the form of mail bombs, car bombs, garbage can bombs and the simple use of gun fire. American citizens from innocent people opening their mail at home to doctors who performed abortions were targets, as were Federal buildings and the Summer Olympics. Anti-government sentiment, once harmless rhetoric just 15 years earlier, had turned hateful, violent and deadly. While Clinton had growing concern on his plate in the increasing influence and presence of Islamic terrorists who wanted to kill Americans, it certainly didn't help that he also had to deal with Americans, who out of hatred of their own government, also wanted to kill Americans, and did. The third factor was gradual and unfolded over time as a trend of consolidation and mergers resulted in the corporatization of media. When Reagan took office in 1981, the media, consisting of television and radio stations and networks were controlled by over 50 companies. By the turn of the century, that number was reduced to six. With corporate political agendas serving as the foundation and backbone of media, the once reliable everyday tradition of objective news reporting was replaced with the 24-hour cable news cycle that hired "personalities" rather than reporters and journalists. This had its roots in the United States Federal Communications Commission's repealing of the 1949 policy known as the Fairness Doctrine which prevented broadcasters from editorializing the news and ranting their opinions into the faces of viewers. It called for equal and balanced coverage of controversial topics and assured those innocent days that so many old souls like to fondly look back upon...when news anchors simply read the news. Consequences took several decades to be fully realized, but it was Ronald Reagan who vetoed the liberal congress's effort to stop the FCC's repeal of the Fairness Doctrine, thus creating the conditions that allowed for the beginning of partial and biased reporting. TV news and radio would never be the same again as politics dictated how news was presented and whether or not certain news was presented at all. In the case of biased reporting, it was FOX News that rose above the rest following the 9/11 terrorist attacks in 2001. As the nation mourned through a prolonged period of sadness, shock and anger, FOX fueled the already-present anti-Muslim sentiment, and benefitted from the growing division by rising to the top of the cable news ratings where it remained as the most-watched channel in America for the better part of the next several decades. From a distance, it is ironic and seems laughable that for years, FOX has continued to use the term *mainstream media* in a completely derogatory fashion as if it is separate from it. The fact remains that FOX *is* the mainstream media, and has been the biggest *part* of mainstream media since the new century began. The irony is everywhere we look on this matter. Opponents of the Fairness Doctrine argue that it violated First Amendment rights. They also insist that it is outdated and does not apply to cable news and that the anachronistic minds that put such laws into place back in the olden days just couldn't foresee the future of media, nor could they have anticipated how it evolved…an argument that comes from the same people who champion the Confederate flag, Electoral College and their dangerous misreading of the Second Amendment. But out of all dislocated vestiges of the past, it is the Fairness Doctrine that manages to remain dispelled. One more layer of hypocrisy deserves mention here, as we consider the right's tired indictment of what they call the "liberal media." In today's climate, if the media was as liberal as FOX claims it to be, it is highly unlikely that conservatives would oppose the Fairness Doctrine and they would probably be screaming to restore it.

And so, in short, the three seeds planted for the current division in America, again, were one, the re-emergence of Republican takeover of government with a vengeful agenda sparked by a backlash against the 1960s counterculture and everything it represented socially, as well as the eventual dismantling of landmark liberal and progressive accomplishments such as the New Deal and Great Society. Where the Great Society built on the New Deal and the post-war years spawned two decades of a booming economy and a thriving middle class, Republicans by the mid-1990s set out to ensure that the shining city on a hill reaching that kind of economic zenith would be short-lived and exclusive to the Baby Boom generation. Two, the rise of violent anti-government extremism, which occasionally reared its ugly head to remind America that there was an entire population of so-called patriots who were waiting to duke it out with the government. And three, the corporatization of media, which combined with a further-increasing cultural division, created the perfect storm for the rise and normalization of editorializing as news.

George W. Bush ran for president on the marketing strategy of restoring "honor and dignity" to the White House after Bill Clinton disgraced the office. As the FOX propaganda machine went to work on the minds of the American people who made it the most-watched channel in the country, the ministry did an exemplary job of continuing to see that the word *liberal* was synonymous with everything immoral, corrupt, cowardly and un-American. At the time, the GOP was still the self-professed party of morals, principles and family values. But restoring honor and dignity didn't just mean morals and family values. It was a restoration of inequity, hostility and fiscal irresponsibility. Reaganomics had been rolled back during the 1990s by Bill Clinton and to an extent, George H.W. Bush. America was carried through most of the decade by Clinton where liberal democracy triumphed much to the seething dismay of the other side representing the Congressional majority. Consequently, it sparked a conservative backlash designed to defeat the counterculture, as Gingrich often referred to Democrats. The backlash restored hegemony in Washington and resulted in war, bankrupt energy policies and generations of debt. The years of the second Bush presidency left the country in far worse condition than Ronald Reagan could ever have left it some 20 years earlier.

But what does any of this have to do with the political right's hatred of Hollywood and the music industry? What does the right's intolerance for artistic expression and activism have to do with the three major contributing factors to the cultural and political civil war that continues to grow in America? Well, for starters, it's just one more symptom of the divide, but to make it more interesting, let's add it as the fourth contributing factor. Let's be clear though. Celebrities have always to a certain degree endorsed and celebrated politicians, even if they didn't shout about it. Ronald Reagan had quite a few at his inaugural parties. But beginning with Clinton, it was the first time celebrities, musicians and youth en masse embraced an American president. And beginning with George W. Bush, it was the first time celebrities and musicians en masse spoke out against an American president. At one point during the 2004 election season, an entire itinerary of concerts were put together called the *Vote for Change* Tour, led by Bruce Springsteen and featuring artists like Jackson Browne, R.E.M., Pearl Jam, the Dave Matthews Band and the Dixie Chicks. Natalie Maines of the Dixie Chicks had been in the news prior to that tour for making her opposition to the actions of the Bush Administration known. While her anti-war sentiment was shared by much of the world, FOX News called her out as anti-American, and within hours, she was receiving death threats. Such was the division instigated by right-wing media that showed no signs of slowing down. Years later, when Springsteen stood in front of his audience in Australia shortly after Donald Trump became President of the United States, he told the crowd, "We stand before you, embarrassed Americans tonight."[259] Once FOX reshaped it as "Bruce Springsteen is embarrassed to be an American," the vitriol across cable and social media spread quickly from ocean to ocean, just as it had and would continue to every time Springsteen opened his mouth publically on any number of topics.[260] The same people who spewed poison for eight years about Barrack Obama were acting as if Springsteen were attacking a member of their own families through his criticism of Trump. Their identification in relating to the outlandish and embarrassing manner in which the demagogue as both candidate and president conducted himself was frightening. Still, Springsteen did not judge. For example, when asked if he thought all Trump supporters were racists, he dismissed the question with a stern *no*. It was irresponsible to generalize. It also wasn't very difficult to understand why people who may have struggled for the past thirty years were lured by Trump and attracted to him. He provided simple answers to complex questions, and it was that simplicity and bare bones approach to the system that they felt America needed. Springsteen was not apologizing for the voting actions of Trump supporters, nor condoning them. He was merely stating that he could understand them. His own personal views were known as he made clear in 2016 just before the presidential election.

"This is a man whose vision is limited to little beyond himself…who has the profound lack of decency that would allow him to prioritize his own interests and ego before American democracy itself…somebody who would be willing to damage our long-cherished and admired system rather than look to himself for the reasons behind his own epic failure. That's unforgivable."[261]

Given the constant turmoil imposed on the American presidency as well as the continued assault on America's democratic institutions by Donald Trump, Springsteen's words have proven prophetic and could not have been more accurate. Still, he is the artist whom the right still loves to hate.

It wasn't always like this though, at least not before the age of corporate media.

Let's put it in perspective.

Springsteen has always had a massive audience. In America, his audience comprised both sides of the political aisle, both Republicans and Democrats. Neither side took issue with him speaking out on anything during the first three decades of his career. Granted, bandwagon fans that hopped onboard thinking "Born in the U.S.A." was a feel-good aerobics stomp never paid much attention to its lyrics, but for the most part, fans of his music know that the sentiment behind his songs is not rooted in conservatism… because if it were, then, as some critic once pointed out, we would have a tough time explaining the phenomenon of stadiums full of mostly white middle class fans pumping their fists in the air while screaming at the top of their lungs that they believe in a Promised Land. His politics were always in plain sight. While Reagan was hurting labor unions, Springsteen was doing whatever he could to help them. His conservative fans didn't seem to take issue or complain that they only paid to be entertained. Even during the first Bush presidency, Springsteen's show did not shy away from artistic commentary on the first Persian Gulf War and the 1992 Los Angeles riots. He'd often introduce "Souls of the Departed" as a "prayer for peace," while his

Van Zandt-produced live arrangement of "57 Channels" sampled chants of "No Justice, No Peace." Nobody was telling him to shut up and sing.

Then came "American Skin."

When Springsteen unveiled the controversial ballad "American Skin" (41 Shots) in June 2000, he presented his new song, as he so often has done, within the framework of characters in a story he was telling. The problem with the song was that it was based on the shooting of an unarmed man named Amadou Diallo by New York City police officers, where a case of mistaken identity resulted in a tragedy of 41 shots being fired. The devastating event for all involved was a hotbed of division from day one. The first verse is written from the point of view of a police officer, as Springsteen imagines the horrific ordeal of split-second decisions that being in such a situation can entail. The second verse is from the point of view of a mother pleading with her young son to respect police officers while terrified that one day he may not return home. Springsteen does not mention race, though what subtlety implies is unquestionable.

"American Skin" was premiered in Atlanta, and by the time Springsteen got to New York City for his next run of shows later in the week, conservative media was calling for boycotts of his Madison Square Garden concerts after reshaping the content of the song into something that was anti-cop without having heard a single note of it. The sudden hate that was spewed against the artist was something completely new. Once conservative media was telling the country what a scumbag Springsteen was, the uproar began. When the concerts at the Garden finally happened, there were boos. But the boos were drowned out every night by cheers of approval. While those who booed chose not to listen, they completely missed the fact that the song is far from *anti-cop* as they were suggesting, and instead humanizes police officers in an age where people were demonizing them, especially under the antagonistic

Giuliani Administration. While Springsteen's lyrics portray a mother's fear every time her young son leaves the house, they also honor the confusion and horror experienced by the police officers in such a situation that no decent individual who courageously puts that uniform on would ever wish on anyone let alone his or herself. People's disapproval of the song came from the fact that they were only paying attention to the repeated chorus of "41 shots"…most likely the same fans that 15 years earlier approved of the chorus of "Born in the U.S.A." because they believed it to be a patriotic anthem when it was the furthest thing from it. From the outset of the new millennium, conservative media did not let up on Bruce Springsteen, nor was vilification exclusive to him. Anyone who showed support for the anti-war movement, social justice causes or support of Democratic candidates were deemed *anti-American* with boycotts urged against them. So, one can imagine the level of contempt that conservatives had for performing artists by the time of Barrack Obama's presidency. No mistake should be made…Cancel Culture begins with the right and FOX News.

But the hypocrisy stretched even further when it came to artists getting opinionated. When conservative rocker, Ted Nugent waved multiple guns onstage in front of a paying audience and expressed his violent fantasies toward then presidential candidate, Barrack Obama and former First Lady Hillary Clinton, he was praised by the political right, and defended viciously by pundit Sean Hannity who stressed that Nugent was a friend of FOX who would continue to be invited on as a guest. As for Nugent's advances toward Obama to come and suck on the barrel of his machine gun, Hannity dismissed the comments and told FOX contributor, Bob Beckel not to go see Nugent in concert if he didn't like it.[262]

Nugent did not let up.

A year later, he made comments that seemed to be suggesting death threats toward President Obama and was promptly questioned by the Secret Service, after which he was cleared of being any sort of real threat. Soon after, in one of the more symbolically hostile gestures by any member of Congress toward an American President, Republican congressman and convicted felon, Steve Stockman invited Nugent to attend President Obama's State of the Union Address as his own personal guest. Nugent's fanatical support of the NRA was enough validation for Stockman, an unapologetic opponent of gun control. Deep into the president's second term, the lunatic fringe of so-called Second Amendment experts was still waiting at the front doors of their compounds for Obama to come for their guns. Needless to say, Obama never came for their guns.

In addition to propaganda from the Second Amendment fanatics who seemed to be using the most misunderstood and misinterpreted document in American history as an excuse to stockpile weapons in their basements and living rooms, came the repetitive conditioning of vast stretches of the American population into believing that President Obama had a radical Islamic socialist agenda. Seemingly ignorant of the left-to-right political spectrum, some pundits would refer to him as a communist on one night and a fascist the next night as did keyboard warriors all over social media.

But how do we connect this paranoia back to Ronald Reagan?

Or can we?

In retrospect, Reagan was indeed of an era that made far too much out of the threat of communism. Contrasting the fear of nuclear weapons in connection with communist regimes halfway through the twentieth century, however, does not equate with the sense of beating a dead horse with talk of socialism in the twenty-first century. Historian, Will Durant once said that there is nothing in socialism that a little money won't cure, and it is precisely for that same reason that America was never at any time threatened by communism, nor will it ever be a communist country. The same applies to socialism.

While Reagan was focused on fighting communism, Islamic radicalism grew and flourished, marking its presence and territory well into the present. America went to war several times to deal with situations created during the Reagan years, the first of which was the alliance with Iraqi dictator, Saddam Hussein. Further problems ahead had their roots elsewhere, preceding the Iran/Iraq War. The secret sale of weapons to the Afghan rebels in their war against the Soviets continued throughout the Reagan years and ultimately became known to the public. When Mikhail Gorbachev withdrew troops from Afghanistan between 1988 and 1989, the country and its people were completely abandoned by the United States and other Western nations. With no assistance in the rebuilding of Afghanistan, the country was marked by a political and economic vacuum that was filled by militants who soon evolved into the Taliban, and welcomed financial assistance from terrorists such as Osama bin Laden and Al Qaeda, all but guaranteeing the subsequent crisis that followed internationally. To be fair, and to reiterate, weapons sold to rebels in Afghanistan went as far back as Carter's last year in office, though continued American support for the jihad against the Soviets ensured the rise of Al Qaeda while the U.S. CIA secretly sent billions of dollars in military aid to the mujahedeen throughout Reagan's two terms. We know the result of those consequences and do not need to rehash history, not even for the sake of recap. While Reagan may not in his heart of hearts have wanted to go to war at any time during his presidency, he was surrounded by people who did, and the consequences of actions taken by the United States during the Reagan years were often delivered in the form of war by those in succeeding Republican administrations much more willing to drop bombs. When the first airplane arrived over New York City on that Tuesday morning in September 2001, most were thinking accident. After the second, it was pretty clear what was taking place.

Reagan, during and after his White House years, was often the beneficiary of a wealth of lies, untruths and distorted assessments of Carter's presidency, especially with respect to the military. He would claim that Carter left the armed forces "in a state of shambles."²⁶³ He insisted Carter gutted the military when in fact defense spending actually increased during his one term. Reagan would take credit for the MX and Trident missile programs that had both been developed under the previous administration. Carter would later call him out on all of these claims as well as other instances where Reagan lied to the American people or was blatantly disingenuous at the expense of his predecessor, such as blaming the deregulation of intelligence during the Carter years for the deaths of 241 U.S. Marines in Lebanon, or lying about the Contras in Nicaragua and trying to undermine the Sandinistas…events that come well after the period in which this book focuses on.

Following the Reagan years, the GOP not only decided it had a monopoly on God and morality, but now it had one on the military. Before Reagan, it wasn't very common for presidents to flaunt their achievements related to military service, keeping in the tradition of civilian control over the military.²⁶⁴ The Reagan years, however, saw the beginning of the presidential image being militarized along with "commander in chief" being an alternate title for the President of the United States, which before Reagan, was not common.²⁶⁵ Although the U.S. was not particularly at war during the Reagan years, small operations like Urgent Fury brought in a new era of jingoistic patriotism that was suddenly synonymous with militarism…and two decades into the twenty-first century, it hasn't gone away. It wasn't so much the "my country right or wrong" that returned after 9/11, but rather the accompanying monosyllabic grunting of male locker room mentality that was expressed and somehow passed off as national pride. Historian David Sirota put it most eloquently when he stressed the gradual shift away from humility toward the more modern American militarism that is synonymous with the braggadocio of muscle flexing, fist pumping and measuring how big one's penis is.²⁶⁶

Reagan's image in the eyes of those who saw him as someone dangerous was largely contributed to by Reagan himself in his philosophy toward his opponents. In 1980, he elaborated on such ideas in conversation with William F. Buckley.

"I think one of the foolish things we've done going back to the Vietnamese War, is telling potential enemies things we would not do. For example, when President Johnson repeated over and over again that of course we would never use nuclear weapons there. I don't think we should have used nuclear weapons there. But I think the North Vietnamese should have gone to sleep every night worrying about whether we would."[267]

But Reagan, despite popular opinion on the left, was not a warmonger. He knew the horrors of war. He did not personally experience combat, but through the return of Signal Corps films from the liberation of Hitler's concentration camps, he was among the first to witness the horrors, seeing firsthand the darkest depths of what humans were capable of, with enough of an impression to last the rest of his life. Reagan knew that although rules of war were violated throughout history, rules still existed in warfare in which armies didn't wage war on civilians. Soldiers fought soldiers. In World War 2, however, the rules were thrown out when Hitler declared total war and bombed not only the opposing soldiers, but factories producing weapons, as well as surrounding communities and the population living in them. Reagan knew that attacking civilians became part of military strategy. Of nuclear weapons, Reagan also knew even as his buildup proceeded, that America was placing its entire faith in a weapon that would wipe out entire populations…its primary target being civilians. The entire concept of a nuclear war was not to simply destroy other missiles. A nuclear war was intended to kill people, and that was the plain fucking reality. He knew, as the Pentagon would inform him that at least 150 million American lives would be lost in a nuclear war against the Soviets. In addition, he knew that the planet would be so poisoned that anyone left alive would not be able to survive much longer, nor would they have a place to live. He knew that nobody "won" a nuclear war and he also knew that as long as these weapons existed, there was always the chance that they would be used. In his memoirs, the sentiment he paints is one of uncomfortable uncertainty about the risks of that first attack and then the inevitable second in retaliation, assuring certain death on a mathematical scale. Reagan had obviously not considered Hiroshima and Nagasaki and that his own country had already unleashed the first one. But his intentions were in the right place, and it is highly likely and believable that his concerns about nuclear weapons in relation to the Soviets were genuine.

But Reagan's advisors as well as a significant number of people at the Pentagon did not share his view of arms reduction. They couldn't conceive of a world free of nuclear weapons and tried convincing him that nuclear war was inevitable, and that they had to prepare for it, throwing around phrases such as *throw weights* and *kill ratios* as if talking about baseball statistics. Whereas Carter wanted to comply with SALT, Reagan imposed the over-bloated and grotesquely expensive Strategic Defense Initiative, dubbed the Star Wars program by critics such as Ted Kennedy and later the media. As SDI became as close to arms reduction as the United States was going to get under the Reagan Administration, Carter remained outspoken and critical of the program long after his presidency and into Reagan's second term. The Soviets agreed that SDI had to be thrown out, which Caspar Weinberger was not going to allow Reagan to do, nor would he allow the president to agree to the terms of SALT II. The bottom line was that once Carter was out of the picture, détente was scrapped, as Reagan embarked on a concerning buildup of nuclear weapons through advanced technology, doubling the Pentagon budget as well as the national debt in his first term, more or less forcing Russia into parity, thus spending them into the ground. Russia wanted diplomatic talks with Reagan during his first term but there wasn't much room for talks given the hostile nature of which his White House disrupted the peace process that went back over a decade, referred to Russia as an "evil empire" and initiated the Cold War back into a threatening reality. It was only after the U.S. had successfully completed its massive rearmament when he began to change his mind on talking to Russia. Needless to say, all things fell into place as Mikhail Gorbachev emerged on the world stage shortly after Reagan's re-election. Reagan's gradual shift toward diplomacy marked an evolution in his presidency whereby he went from opposing any sort of dialog with the Soviets to very specific foreign policy goals. By his second term, it seems in retrospect that he becomes painfully aware of what his legacy will be, and in the face of the warmonger reputation of the past, becomes more accommodating, adopting a far less harsh political image in favor of that of a peacemaker.

Ronald Reagan and the Reagan Era seem to be two different things. The extent of the long range effects and consequences of the Reagan years often seem to be at odds with Reagan the man. For even despite his change of political ideology, he appears to be uncomfortable in his actual decision making…so much so, that he often leaves it to his dysfunctional administration to influence the outcome. He is more akin to the very things he later saw as a detriment to society, and humanly more relatable to the other two men we've paralleled his story with. John Lennon and Bruce Springsteen may have represented aspects of the American story and American freedom itself that conservatives now hold in contempt. But each man, like Reagan, *is* the American story…and all three, like America, were deeply flawed. While the obvious similarities between Reagan and Lennon reveal two co-dependent men whose spouses set the agenda, both were often estranged from the children of their first marriage as well. It is for this reason that the childhoods of Michael Reagan and Julian Lennon were probably not unlike each other in terms of attention from their fathers or lack thereof at times. John himself experienced an entire childhood of neglect, growing up without his father and only having his mother for a very brief period. In Mimi Smith, Nelle Reagan and Adele Springsteen, all three men had strong female figures in their lives providing the soft useful wisdom and counterbalance to the abrasiveness and instability of the male figures or lack thereof. All three, however, seem to be much more profoundly marked by their fathers.

From the paternal side of family life, Lennon is quite different from Reagan and Springsteen. Lennon's father, Alfred Lennon, also known as Freddie or Fred, disappeared very early in John's life and then came back after John was successful, only to be viciously rebuked and rejected by his son, never seeing him again after an explosive and scarring reunion in 1971. The two briefly reconciled and made their peace by phone shortly before Freddie's death in 1976. In the case of Springsteen, anyone who has followed his music and attended his concerts, especially in the Seventies and Eighties, knows that Bruce's relationship with his father has been well-documented. Douglas Springsteen was described by his son as a domineering and frightening figure. One of the strongest images that he retained in his mind's eye of growing up was of his dad sitting at the kitchen table late at night. Bruce in his late teens would stand in front of the driveway preparing to sneak into the house after hours. In the event he got caught he'd tuck his hair down into his collar so his father wouldn't be able to tell how long it was getting. As he'd tip toe through the darkened house and toward the stairs, his father would call out to him. From the entrance into the kitchen, all Bruce could see was the light of his father's cigarette as he sat quietly at the table. Then he'd call Bruce to sit down, and the conversation always inevitably ended up on what he was doing with his life before it often became combative. Realistically, the relationship between Bruce and his father was not at all uncommon when it came to parents and alienated teens in the rock and roll era. But there was mental illness…depression that ran in the family that apparently was undiagnosed in Douglas Springsteen. Bruce would suffer from the same depression even long into a successful career as the biggest rock star in the world. Soon after the birth of Bruce's first son, Evan, Douglas would knock on his son's front door on a Sunday morning, and over several beers the two would hold one pivotal healing conversation that would change the course of their relationship until Douglas's passing in 1998. Springsteen's audience has had a front seat to his recollections and recreations of father and son encounters over the years which manifest themselves in songs, the spoken word of his beautifully-crafted Broadway show and in the introduction stories that preceded live performances of "Independence Day" and "The River" during the 1980s…those stories set to the gorgeous dramatic keyboards of Roy Bittan and Danny Federici often serving as little pieces of art themselves. Springsteen spent years trying to get to the bottom of his own psychology, ending up with a much clearer understanding of the *whys* and *whats* of his life, as well as a balanced approach to accepting it all and translating it to his audience, which through performance or written text was in its own way cathartic and therapeutic. Lennon, who only lived to 40, was a fucking mess, caught up much more in the language of spirituality and new age trends that treated the mechanics of mind as opposed to the content of mind. Had he lived long enough, he might have gotten much closer to dealing with his demons. That is not to suggest that psychology is any more helpful than spirituality. The thing about psychologists is that they often believe their own bullshit, but if it is useful for the individual, then who is to judge? Reagan was altogether from a different school, much closer to that of Douglas Springsteen, where men toughed it out, didn't talk about things, and if there was anything clinically undiagnosed in his personality, it still remains a mystery…just as it did when he was alive.

Whether we can reconcile the beautifully homespun folk portrait of America that Reagan painted as "Morning in America" in the 1980s with the uptight scowling man that served as foil to 1960s youth has yet to be seen. His personality, though still somewhat undefined, often clashes with his politics, and his politics with his actions. It is difficult to determine whether Reagan's positions on any number of issues were moral, psychological or merely political in the hopes of luring voters. What seems plausible here is politics and how they play into the fact that the presidency is much bigger than the individual occupying the office. While critics of politicians can always claim hypocrisy, and it certainly holds true as we've seen, there is also something called reality when it comes to the presidency. The arrogant and openly corrupt leadership of the Republican Party by the year 2020 was more than enough to prove this as true. Yet, the intentions of the GOP were stripped of all reality under the Trump presidency. In the past, the reality of the presidency was to work for the good of the country and defend the Constitution in the process. It meant bi-partisanship and compromise and being a president to all Americans and not just the ones who will bow to you. The reality that Ronald Reagan exhibited was that even though he was in theory a conservative, in practice he was what H.W. Brands called a "flexible" pragmatist.[268] This is seen time and time again throughout not just his presidency, but his political life as a whole, relaxing the state of California's abortion laws as a pro-life Governor, negotiating tax increases in order to attain the best political deals with Congress, embracing the communist leader of America's evil villain in order to forge an alliance.[269] He even supported a Clinton-era ban on assault weapons when he was no longer being steered by politics, but by his own conscience. Serious discussion of Reagan today inevitably dredges up many of these often pleasant contradictions that arise when we assess his personality, presidency and even his influence. And for that reason among countless others, we are no closer today to understanding Ronald Reagan than those who were around him during the course of his life.

18

LAST GASPS (AFTERMATH)

Historians suggest the late 1970s gas crisis was a goldmine for the populist imagination. Polls were showing that most of the public thought the crisis was manufactured by the oil companies and there was no actual energy shortage. It is nothing short of ironic then, that the populist movement championed and supported Republican policies that favored those very oil companies. It is that same sabotaging sentiment that has continued to lend itself to Republicans being elected long into the twenty-first century where corporate greed is alive and well. Even the populist portion of the left maintained, rather stubbornly and ignorant to history, that there were no fundamental differences to either of the major parties, and thus would rather run the risk of Donald Trump as president rather than vote for a Democrat.

Would Ronald Reagan be horrified at what became of his party in the present century? Ron Reagan said his father wouldn't take the state of the GOP so easily. Although he appealed reverently to the extremist faction of the right that eventually took over the Republican Party during the Obama years, he still acted in an often bi-partisan manner, governing and presiding in ways that could irritate his most ardent supporters. As the youngest of Reagan's children reminded Christiane Amanpour in a 2011 interview, "After all, he did raise taxes. He cut taxes, but then he raised taxes when he was president. The deficit certainly grew under his administration. He would blame the Democrats for that, of course, but nevertheless, it did grow. When he was Governor of California, he signed into law one of the most liberal abortion policies in the country and also an amnesty program for illegal immigrants. So I'm not sure that today's Republican Party or Tea Party would be all that thrilled with him."[270] Michael Reagan, on the other hand, spoke to the opposite, suggesting his father would have embraced the Tea Party. "He would have endorsed what they're doing," he told Amanpour. "The fact is Ronald Reagan was the original Tea Party. He understood that the electorate lived in the grass roots of this country…It was grassroots America that supported Ronald Reagan back in 1980. That's why he became the President of the United States of America."[271] That, however, was in 2010, six years before Donald Trump happened. What Michael Reagan did not consider in his comparison of his father to the Tea Party were the obvious racial implications that were so painfully evident from the movement's sudden appearance at the outset of Barrack Obama's presidency.

Barack Obama entered his presidency with more simultaneous national crises than any American President since FDR. The problem with electing the first black president in the United States is that the Civil Rights Act of 1964 didn't change a damn thing when it came to racism. The staples of bigotry simply went underground once it became clear that the cultural zeitgeist had changed, and opponents of Civil Rights also went underground once they knew their platform was no longer tolerable and socially acceptable, and so they remained silent. And waited.

For four and a half decades, they waited.

In the weeks before Barrack Obama even took office, with not a single day of presidential activity behind him, armed protesters were already taking to the streets screaming that they wanted their country back. By the time of his inauguration, the Tea Party movement had already formed. Such a movement under any other president would have remained inconsequential, and compared to Ronald Reagan's era of conservatism, this group would likely have been dismissed as the lunatic fringe of the right. Images of prop puppets simulating lynchings were alarming to see, as were pictures of Hitler next to the face of the new black president. This is not to suggest that the Tea Party was completely a racist movement, though racist sentiment certainly found a place in the protests. It wouldn't be until after the 2016 election and long after the Tea Party was even on the radar, when bigotry and racism were up front and center and given their biggest platform since pre-Civil Rights America. But while fringe publications on both the right and the left might give attention to extremist movements, it was FOX News, already the most-watched channel in mainstream media, that in 2009, gave full coverage to the Tea Party, thus spreading the alarmist rage and igniting fears over the idea that Obama was a Muslim terrorist who was going to turn America into a socialist place. The influence of FOX on the psyche of the country, especially as the number one channel in America, began to normalize the constant propaganda about socialism, while glorifying the abhorrent behavior of armed extremists showing up in front of government buildings. The round-the-clock coverage and praise of Tea Party protests against the new Democratic president became the standard at FOX in the early days of Obama's presidency. That it was legitimizing and giving credibility to the Tea Party movement was testament to the channel's true agenda, which was fully realized by the midterms when Tea Party members managed to get elected as Republicans in Washington, thus infiltrating the very government that it was against, once again illuminating the longstanding political hypocrisy of the GOP. The unsettling presence of armed vigilantes storming government buildings and undermining local law enforcement later became a regular occurrence encouraged by Donald Trump during his singular focus of getting re-elected while America lost hundreds of thousands of lives during the Covid-19 pandemic in 2020.

Regarding those seeds that were inadvertently sewn during the Reagan years, and the irreparable long-term harm that came from those years, the Reagan presidency needs to be somewhat defended in this case. The Reagan Era didn't last very long, as it was replaced with an era of conservative extremism and obstruction on every level in yet another cultural divide. But unlike the 1960s, the rift wasn't generational, but rather based on identity politics. Ronald Reagan and the Democratic majority had a mutually respectful discourse and dialogue. It was a taken-for-granted era, but nonetheless, an era of decency. The two parties acknowledged their political differences but still worked together to find common ground wherever possible in order to accomplish something in the interest of America. As much as liberals can criticize the actions and dissect the intentions of Republican presidents, Reagan-Era Republicans were at least conciliatory in their rhetoric. They acknowledged how they were viewed and at least tried to calm the fears of the other side, and more importantly, the American people. George H.W. Bush spoke of a *kinder, gentler nation*, while George W. Bush talked about a *compassionate conservatism*, even if the two words together seemed like an oxymoron. Their tone and their intentions were to be presidents to every American, and when they spoke, it was to one America. With future Republicans, it turned into a game of "gotcha." In Donald Trump, America got someone who even after entering the presidency never stopped campaigning and holding rallies for himself while maintaining his *us vs. them* approach to America. To Trump, America entailed only those who showed him loyalty, while the rest of the population was made the enemy.

In 2009, just prior to Barack Obama taking the office of President of the United States, Speaker John Boehner unashamedly declared on *60 Minutes* that compromise was not an option and not even in his vocabulary. The only objective of the Republicans, as Rush Limbaugh suggested, should be to commit themselves to the complete failure of Barack Obama in order to assure that he was a one-term president. The controversial statement paled in comparison to years of racist and misogynistic comments that had oozed out of Limbaugh's mouth over a period of decades, so much so, that his advertisers began to abandon him by 2013. But what proved most reprehensible about deliberate Republican obstruction was that it became their modus operandi at a time when the country was suffering from multiple crises and needed bi-partisan unity more than ever. Instead, the Republican Party became the party of "no" at the expense of government shutdowns, threats to crash the economy on purpose and the deliberate sabotaging of a government's commitment to its citizens…all in the interest of achieving what they intended as the failure of a Democrat. By that time, the identity politics of defining someone's character, validity and value based on their politics was already sealed into permanence. It had clearly become a deep-seated division, and by the time of the 2016 election, a civil war. Incidentally, in a deliberate act of political vengeance on Democrats, Donald Trump, as President of the United States, would use a State of the Union Address to award Limbaugh the Presidential Medal of Freedom.

The differences between the Reagan Era and the extremities of the Republican Party that followed deep into the present day while partisan neo-cons desperately and shamefully attempted to link themselves to Reagan's lineage, again, are precisely why we must call it out. For as critical as we are of Reagan, the cultish demagoguery of Trump was a completely different monster, and the two have very little to nothing to do with each other. For Reagan, like him or not, one got the sense that it truly was America first… not Ronald Reagan's personal interests and vendettas first. And he certainly wasn't using the Department of Justice and the Supreme Court to fight his personal battles. Granted, the issue of communism never left him and he made it a focal point of his presidency, taking it all the way up to the last smoldering embers of the Cold War. But he remained diplomatic aside from strong throughout the entire process. From the outset of his meetings with Mikhail Gorbachev, the first of which took place in November 1985, Reagan maintained optimism in the Soviet leader, believing in the possibility that he was different from his predecessors. He recognized that they were both idealists and neither subscribed to the status quo or the pessimism that such relations were pointless and not forgeable. This optimism came just two years after his "evil empire" comment.

The distance between Reagan and Trump is just how long it took for the Republican Party, ever self-righteously boastful of their family values and moral decency, to bottom out in the most profound manner. The pendulum, in the face of naturally-occurring progress at the will of the American people, was taken hold of and forced in the opposite direction. When we consider the racism and bigotry that was given voice as a result of Donald Trump being elected, it almost seems logical and inevitable that the election of a black president would result in such a backlash. It is important to note, however, that not every supporter of Donald Trump is a racist...far from it. Which is why it can be mind-numbing trying to understand why those who do not fall into that category would associate and align themselves with a cultist wannabe authoritarian that white supremacists and dictators have clearly been empowered by...a president who referred to anti-fascists as terrorists and white supremacists as good people...a divider whose racial insensitivity and deliberately inflammatory language on a daily basis both lowered the morale of America and awakened the wounds of its past by ripping them wide open. Even the evangelicals put aside their traditional Christian morals to maintain their support of the pussy-grabbing president. The grandiose narcissistic antics of nearly every single move by Donald Trump as President of the United States has been by design predicated upon honor and praise of himself, and any deviation from such obedience has resulted in the discard of just about everyone in his administration, often several times over. The Republican Party, with blinders has accepted it all, knowing its agenda is being implemented one act at a time, especially as they salivate at the prospects of the much-coveted Supreme Court seat held by Ruth Bader Ginsberg whose well-known health issues they watch closely as this book goes to publication. There is no shame on the part of Republicans either as this has transpired over the years. This is because they have been the beneficiaries of America's corrupt electoral process, whereby state governors impose dishonest electoral boundaries which have allowed for Republicans to be incorrectly represented in Congress compared to the actual vote, as well as win the presidency twice in recent years despite losing the election. It is, in essence, the living embodiment of minority rule. In summation, the Republican Party and its voters crossed a frightening line by putting blind allegiance in one man over their allegiance to America. They signed over their democracy to Donald Trump, and have let the world know unapologetically that he is above the law, with no checks on him whatsoever. Never before in American history was one figure shown loyalty on such a messianic level. It is also significant to note at this juncture that Michael Reagan has stated clearly more than once since 2016 that his father, Ronald Reagan, fortieth President of the United States, would never have had anything to do with Donald Trump or the current Republican Party.

The final months of 1980 symbolically mark the end of one era and the beginning of another. If political assassinations coupled with Manson and Altamont put holes in the hippie dream, thus deflating the collective hopes of those who fought for a better America, the murder of John Lennon was the last gasp of a decade that had reverberated defiantly for another ten years after the murders of four kids at Kent State who happened to oppose the war in Vietnam. Those last months of 1980 were a conduit to a much larger channel through which policies were established and alliances forged that would alter the course of American history, and as a result, the rest of the world. Music would play a role too, though many would look the other way as the Eighties became nothing but a good time, and yet the pulse of America was still gauged most accurately by artists who were slightly more reflective. Bruce Springsteen not only became the voice of that era, but he has become the last gasp of the Baby Boomers voice in pop culture, even as he continues to be the favorite target for right-wing disdain once reserved for John Lennon. The era ran its course though, comprising the whole of both Reagan terms, the terms of George H.W. Bush and Bill Clinton, and to a certain degree, both terms of George W. Bush, although the flags of division and foundations for another culture war were already in place through corporate media in the aftermath of 9/11.

It is safe to suggest then, that the Reagan Era ends with the election of Barack Obama. Of course, the long-lasting legacy of trickle-down economics and tax cuts for the rich are still the main objective for the GOP while a devastating portion of the American middle class and poor still vote against their own interests. Republican greed aside, the Reagan Era ends in January 2009 when Barack Obama takes the Oath of Office. It does not end because of Obama himself, but because of the Republican Party's *reaction* to Obama and the manner in which it lowered itself time and again to ultimately reveal by 2016 exactly the kind of deplorable outcomes critics of the party were long afraid it was capable of achieving. Apologists for the party's extremism seem to believe its actions come with some delusional territory of divine right or entitlement that falls into their laps as part of the Reagan mythology that also states that America is a conservative/center-right country. On top of such unsupported claims are efforts by post-Reagan Era conservatives emboldened by social media to hijack the history of political ideologies by rather ignorantly confusing them with the names of the two major political parties. When conservatives claim a direct lineage to Abraham Lincoln and Theodore Roosevelt for the simple fact that they were Republicans in their own time, those who know better can clearly see through the bullshit. When they say Democrats were in favor of slavery while the Republicans were not, it is because they are either ignoring or just unaware that the ideologies of the major parties shifted during the early part of the twentieth century, and that the Democratic slave-holding South was actually dominated by conservatives. While it is true that some conservative Democrats and liberal Republicans still exist, this fact is neither here nor there. The point remains that the core of division in America is rooted in ideology, not party…and conservatives have proven masterful in confusing the two. It is difficult to fathom for some that liberals like Lincoln and progressives like Roosevelt would never have anything to do with the present-day Republican Party or any version of the Republican Party of the past 100 years. In other words, they were Republicans in name only during a period of American history when Republicans were the liberals and the conservatives were the Democrats. Perhaps one day they will come up with something substantial in support of this cockamamie idea that modern America is a conservative country, but until then, the country's history remains on the side of liberalism and progressivism.

And yet, even in present-day with the American presidency and democracy itself badly in need of restoration in 2020, the counterculture of the 1960s is everywhere we look. While artists like Neil Young mourn the loss of something they feel evaporated a long, long time ago, most notably in his 2012 album, *Psychedelic Pill*, it is evident across the span of the big picture that the hippie dream has been fully realized despite continuous efforts over the decades to thwart progress. We see the counterculture in the fights against the social injustices that in spite of Civil Rights persist deep into the twenty-first century. We see it in feminism, whether in Gloria Steinem's wing or Camille Paglia's. We see it in the LGBTQ movements and gay rights coming into full fruition. We see it in the Western embrace of Eastern spirituality and culture in increasing interest in Buddhism and Taoism, and through the incorporation of yoga and meditation into Western fitness and overall daily life. We see it in the trends of healthy eating and consciousness toward diet. We see it in the armies of youth who mobilize nationwide to fight for gun control. Whether it for sensible regulations on assault weapons or working to get a handle on climate change, we see increasing numbers of socially and politically-conscious teenagers taking up the fight beginning with social media and reaching large numbers, utilizing their resources in ways that previous generations never had access to. Frontline activists like Emma Gonzalez and Greta Thunberg, two high school students from different countries with the same role that each has reluctantly assumed while facing the usual predicted ridicule and scorn from the American right wing. We see it in the popularity of Bernie Sanders and Alexandria Ocasio-Cortez, and the overwhelming waves of support for progressive agendas and progressive candidates from young voters all over America who have in no uncertain terms put the moderate Democratic Party on notice. We see it in the legalization of marijuana. And we see it in youth all over the world who still flock to Central Park West to visit the Dakota and Strawberry Fields as pilgrimage sites. John Lennon's "Imagine" prevails, and the counterculture, rooted in liberal and progressive values, is everywhere. And so, if we consider the concentrated period of time that this publication focuses on as symbolic of the end of one era and the beginning of another, it is also beneficial to acknowledge that history is cyclical as well as linear.

At present time, as I wrap up some final thoughts in this book during the consequential summer of 2020, American voices as well as voices around the world have been raised and heard in protest, American cities have burned in riots, a pandemic rages, the death toll rises daily and America is without leadership. The world watches in horror as America seemingly crumbles under the weight of its own history. The lines of cultural division are now marked by who wears a mask during a pandemic versus who doesn't wear a mask during a pandemic, and even those decisions have been informed by politics. Bruce Springsteen, from lockdown, at the age of 70, does an occasional radio show from his own channel on Sirius XM. It serves as a refuge, keeping him creative and communicative with his audience. And his audience finds refuge in that as well. Forty years past the election of Reagan, he is well-oiled, razor sharp and seething. The right still doesn't like him. And he still doesn't give a fuck.

"I had another show prepared for broadcast this week on this strange and eventful summer, but with 100,000-plus Americans dying over the last few months and the empty, shamed response from our leaders, I've been simply pissed off," he tells his listeners. "Those lives deserved better than just being inconvenient statistics for our president's re-election efforts. It's a national disgrace."[272]

Springsteen cues up Bob Dylan's "Disease of Conceit" as his first record for the hour.

"I'm going to start out by sending one to the man sitting behind the resolute desk," he said. "With all respect, sir, show some consideration and care for your countrymen and your country. Put on a fucking mask."[273]

History-making news events of the present continue to move so fast that this very book publication struggles to keep up. We are traveling at warp speed where the pendulum has once again swung in the opposite direction, as voices around the world have collectively risen up with the United States in a universal rejection of racism, bigotry, misogyny, homophobia, xenophobia and all of those elements that crept back into normalcy ever since the 2016 election. What began as protests against police brutality after the violent murder of a man named George Floyd, ended up capturing the attention and support of much of the world with demonstrations taking place in Sweden, England, Japan, Brazil, Spain, Senegal, Denmark, Scotland, South Korea, Belgium, Hungary, Italy, Australia, Poland, Turkey, France, Switzerland, Portugal, Canada and Germany. What continues to happen worldwide is not only a backlash against racism, but a full-scale global rejection of Trumpism on every level. It is hopeful in anticipating the last gasps of the ugliest elements of the American character that the cult of Trumpism represents. It lets us know that the counterculture is alive and well, that the hippies did in fact win, and that current conservatism is an anachronism whereby the Republican Party on its own merits has no place in the twenty-first century because it never came to terms with the twentieth, and so would rather take America back to the nineteenth. This was the true essence of Trump's distortion of "Make America Great Again" when he stole it from Ronald Reagan who could never himself have envisioned what would happen in his own country just 36 years after he used those same words. All of this taken into account, it conjures up reminders of Reagan's Farewell Address and his humble acknowledgement of his presidential legacy, along with a hopeful yet uncertain glimpse into America's future where his prophetic last words as President of the United States are what continue to haunt us...

"Your mandate will make it possible not just to continue, but to build upon the achievements of the past eight years. This is not the end of an era, but a time to refresh and strengthen our new beginning. To those who sometimes flatter me with talk of a Reagan Revolution, today my hope is this...you ain't seen nothing yet."[274]

BIBLIOGRAPHY

BOOKS

Beatles. *The Beatles Anthology*. San Francisco: Chronicle Books, 2000.

Birmingham, Stephen. *Life at the Dakota: New York's Most Unusual Address*. New York: RandomHouse, 1979.

Brands, H.W. *Reagan: The Life*. New York: Anchor Books, 2015.

Brinkley, Douglass. *The Unfinished Presidency: Jimmy Carter Beyond the White House*. New York: Viking, 1998.

Brown, Mary Beth. *Hand of Providence: The Strong and Quiet Faith of Ronald Reagan*. Nashville: Thomas Nelson, 2004.

Buckley, William F. *The Reagan I Knew*. New York: Basic Books, 2008.

Bunch, Will. *Tear Down this Myth: How the Reagan Legacy Has Distorted Our Politics and Haunts Our Future*. Free Press, 2009.

Cannon, Lou. *Governor Reagan: His Rise to Power*. New York: Public Affairs, 2002.

Carter, Jimmy. *Keeping Faith: Memoirs of a President*. New York: Bantam Books, 1982.

Carter, Jimmy. *White House Diary*. New York: Ferrar, Straus, and Giroux, 2010.

Colacello, Bob. *Ronnie & Nancy: The Path to the White House 1911-1980*. New York: Warner Books, 2004.

Coll, Steve. Ghost Wars: *The Secret History of the CIA, Afghanistan and Bin Laden, From the Soviet Invasion to September 10*. New York: The Penguin Press, 2004.

Crunden, Robert M. *A Brief History of American Culture*. London and New York: Routledge Taylor and Francis Group, 1996.

Dickenson, Mollie. *Thumbs Up: The Life and Courageous Comeback of White House Press Secretary, Jim Brady*. New York: William Morrow and Company, 1987.

Diggins, John Patrick. *Ronald Reagan: Fate, Freedom, and the Making of History*. New York: W.W. Norton and Company, 2007.

Dobrynin, Anatoly. *In Confidence: Moscow's Ambassador to America's Six Cold War Presidents*. Times Books, 1995.

Edwards, Anne. *The Reagan's: Portrait of a Marriage*. New York: St. Martin's Press, 2003.

Eizenstat, Stuart E. *President Carter: The White House Years*. New York: Thomas Dunne Books, St. Martin's Press, 2018.

Freeman, Joshua B. *American Empire 1945-2000: The Rise of Global Power, the Democratic Revolution at Home*. New York: Viking, 2012.

Frum, David. *How We Got Here: The 70s: The Decade that Brought You Modern Life (For Better or Worse)*. New York: Basic Books, 2000.

Glad, Betty. *An Outsider in the White House: Jimmy Carter, His Advisors, and the Making of Foreign Policy*. Ithaca and London: Cornell University Press, 2009.

Greenberg, Keith Elliot. *December 8, 1980: The Day John Lennon Died*. Backbeat Books, 2012.

Haig, Alexander, with Charles McCurry. *Inner Circles: How America Changed the World, a Memoir*. New York: Warner Books, 1992.

Hillen, Andreas. *1973 Nervous Breakdown: Watergate, Warhol, and the Birth of Post-Sixties America*. London: Bloomsbury, 2006.

Hine, Thomas. *The Great Funk: Falling Apart and Coming Together (on a Shag Rug) in the Seventies*. New York: Sarah Crichton Books, Farrar Straus, and Giroux, 2009.

Hopkins, Jerry. *Yoko Ono*. New York: Macmillan Publishing Co., 1986.

Hunt, C. & Humphries, P. *Blinded By the Light*. New York: Henry Holt and Co., 1986.

Jenkins, Philip. *Decade of Nightmares: The End of the Sixties and the Makings of Eighties America*. New York: Oxford University Press, 2006.

Johnson, Haynes. *The Age of Anxiety: McCarthyism to Terrorism*. Orlando: Harcourt, Inc., 2005.

Kalman, Laura. *Right Star Rising: A New Politics 1974-1980*. New York: W.W. Norton & Company, 2010.

Kelley, Kitty. *Nancy Reagan: The Unauthorized Biography*. New York: Simon and Schuster, 1991.

Kline, Dr. Ray S. *The CIA Under Reagan, Bush & Casey*. Washington D.C.: Acropolis Books, 1981.

Kleinknecht, William. *The Man Who Sold the World: Ronald Reagan and the Betrayal of Main Street America*. New York: Nation Books, 2009.

Loyn, David. *In Afghanistan: Two Hundred Years of British, Russian, and American Occupation*. London, New York: Palgrave Macmillan, 2009.

Marsh, Dave. *Glory Days: Bruce Springsteen in the 1980s*. New York: Pantheon Books, 1987.

Madrick, Jeff. *Age of Greed: The Triumph of Finance and the Decline of America, 1970 to the Present*. New York: Alfred A. Knopf, 2011.

Martin, Branford. *The Other Eighties: A Secret History of America in the Age of Reagan*. New York: Hill and Wang, 2011

McFaul, Michael. *From Cold War to Hot Peace, An American Ambassador in Putin's Russia*. Boston:Houghton Mifflin Harcourt, 2018.

Medved, Michael. *Hollywood vs. America: Popular Culture and the War on Traditional Values*. New York: Harper Collins, 1992.

Morehouse, Ward. Inside the Plaza Hotel: An Intimate Portrait of the Ultimate Hotel. New York: Applause, 2001.

Morgan, Iwan. *Reagan: American Icon*. London: I.B. Tauris, 2016.

Navasky, Victor. *Naming Names*. New York: Viking Press, 1980.

Noonan, Peggy. *When Character Was King: A Story of Ronald Reagan*. New York: Viking Press, 2001.

Norman, Philip. *John Lennon: The Life*. New York: Harper Collins, 2008.

Partridge, Elizabeth. *All I Want is the Truth: A Photographic Biography*. New York: Penguin, 2005.

Patterson, James T. *Restless Giant: The United States from Watergate to Bush v. Gore*. Oxford, United Kingdom: Oxford University Press, 2005.

Reagan, Michael, with Joe Hyams. *On the Outside Looking In*. New York: Zebra Books, Kensington Publishing Company, 1988.

Reagan, Michael, with Jim Denney. *The New Reagan Revolution: How Ronald Reagan's Principles Can Restore America's Greatness*. New York: Thomas Dunne Books, St. Martin's Press, 2011.

Reagan, Nancy, with William Novak. *My Turn*. New York: Random House, 1989.

Reagan, Ron. *My Father at 100*. New York: Viking, 2011.

Reagan, Ronald. *Where's the Rest of Me: The Ronald Reagan Story*. New York: Duell, Sloan, and Pearce, 1965.

Reagan, Ronald. *Ronald Reagan, An American Life: The Autobiography*. New York: Simon and Schuster, 1990.

Reeves, Richard. *President Reagan: The Triumph of Imagination*. New York: Simon and Schuster, 2005.

Riley, Tim. *Lennon: The Man, the Myth, the Music, the Definitive Life*. New York: Hyperion, 2011.

Rosebush, James. *True Reagan: What Made Ronald Reagan Great and Why it Matters*. New York: Hachette Book Group, 2016.

Rosen, Robert. *Nowhere Man: The Final Days of John Lennon*. Soft Shell Press, Inc., 2000.

Sandbrook, Dominic. *Mad As Hell: The Crisis of the 1970s and the Rise of the Populist Right*. New York: Alfred A. Knopf, 2011.

Schatz, Thomas, Editor. Hollywood: Critical Concepts in Media and Cultural Studies. London: Routledge, 2004.

Shapiro, Ira. *The Last Great Senate: Courage and Statesmanship in Times of Crisis*. New York: Public Affairs, 2012.

Shirley, Craig. *Last Act: The Final Years and Emerging Legacy of Ronald Reagan*. Nashville: Nelson Books, 2015.

———. *Reagan Rising: The Decisive Years 1976-1980*. New York: Harper Collins, 2017.

Sirota, David. *Back to Our Future: How the 1980s Explains the World We Live in Now*. New York: Ballantine Books, 2011.

Speakes, Larry, with Robert Pack. *Speaking Out: Inside the Reagan White House*. New York: Charles Scribner's Sons, 1988.

Stockman, David. *The Great Deformation: The Corruption of Capitalism in America*. New York: Public Affairs, 2013.

Thomas, Helen. *Thanks for the Memories, Mr. President: Wit and Wisdom from the Front Row at the White House*. New York: Scribner, 2002.

Thornton, Richard C. The Reagan Revolution: The Politics of U.S. Foreign Policy. Victoria, B.C.: 2003.

Wheen, Francis. *Strange Days Indeed: The 1970s: The Golden Age of Paranoia*. New York: Public Affairs, 2009.

Wilbur, Del Quentin. *Rawhide Down: The Near Assassination of Ronald Reagan*. New York: Henry Holt and Company, 2011.

Wilentz, Sean. *The Age of Reagan: A History 1974-2008*. New York: Harper, 2008.

Woodward, Bob. *Veil: The Secret Wars of the CIA 1981-1987*. New York: Simon and Schuster, 1987.

Yager, Edward M. *Ronald Reagan's Journey: Democrat to Republican*. New York: Rowman and Littlefield Publishers Inc., 2006.

PERIODICALS

Ambinder, Marc. "Full Secret Service Transcript: The Moment Reagan Was Shot." *The Atlantic*, March 11, 2011.

Bangs, Lester. "Greetings from Asbury Park, N.J." review. *Rolling Stone*, July 5, 1973.

Bonner, Raymond. "Time for a U.S. Apology to El Salvador. *The Nation*, April 16, 2016 (May 9-16, 2016 Issue).

Bowden, Mark. "The Desert One Debacle." *The Atlantic*, May 2006.

Breslin, Jimmy. "Are You John Lennon?" *Daily News*, December 9, 1980.

Bummiller, Elizabeth. "The Brief Sojourn of Robin Orr." *Washington Post*, December 17, 1980

Cannon, Lou. "A Day of Fine Rituals, Rites of Passage." *Washington Post*, November 5, 1980.

Carroll, Maurice. "Reagan, Visiting New York, Talks With the Cardinal and Top Blacks." New York Times, December 10, 1980.

Cherub, Sandra. "Special Collection Showcases Friendship Between Paul Laxalt, Ronald Reagan." *Las Vegas Review Journal*, March 7, 2016.

Clines, Francis. "The Reagan Play-By-Play Still Plays." *New York Times*, March 31, 1985.

Clymer, Adam. "Michael Deaver, 69, Dies; Shaped Reagan's Image." New York Times, August 21, 2007.

Collins, Denis. "TV Evangelist Snags Reagan, But Not Everyone Down Home." *Washington Post*, October 4, 1980.

Corasaniti, Nick. "Coroner Said to Rule James Brady's Death a Homicide, 33 Years After a Shooting." *New York Times*, August 8, 2014.

Cott, Jonathan. "John Lennon: The Last Interview." *Rolling Stone*, December 23, 2010.

Cytowic, Richard E. "The Long Ordeal of James Brady. *New York Times Magazine*, September 27, 1981.

Davis, Patti. "My Father, Ronald Reagan, Would Never Have Stood For This." *Washington Post*, August 15, 2018.

Dolan, Marc. "How Ronald Reagan Changed Bruce Springsteen's Politics." *Politico Magazine*, June 4, 2014.

Doyle, Jack. "Watching the Wheels." *The Pop History Dig*, October 19, 2010.

FitzGerald, Frances. "A Disciplined, Charging Army." *The New Yorker*, May 18, 1981.

Fowler, Glenn. "Loyal Davis, Neurosurgeon, Dies; President Reagan's Father-In-Law." *New York Times*, August 20, 1982.

Gaines, James R. "Descent into Madness." *People*, June 22, 1981.

Geyelin, Philip. "When Reagan Was Being Reagan." *New York Times*, April 22, 1984.

Gilmore, Mikal. "Beatles Acid Test: How LSD Opened the Door to Revolver." *Rolling Stone*, August 25, 2016.

Grad, Shelby, and David Colker. "Nancy Reagan Turned to Astrology in the White House to Protect Husband." *Los Angeles Times*, March 6, 2016.

Gwertzman, Bernard. "Solzhenitsyn Says Ford Joins in Eastern Betrayal." *New York Times*, July 22, 1975.

Hamill, Pete. "The Death and Life of John Lennon." *New York Magazine*, March 18, 2008.

Heller, Billy, and Michael Kane. "We Were There on the Awful Night John Lennon Was Shot." *New York Post*, December 4, 2005.

Hersh, Seymour M. "U.S. Secretly Gave Aid to Iraq Early in its War with Iran." *New York Times*, January 26, 1992.

Hess, Stephen. "Jimmy Carter: Why He Failed." *Brookings Institution*, June 1978.

Hillburn, Robert. "John Lennon: He Doesn't Believe in Magic or Beatles." *Los Angeles Times,* November 16, 1980

Hilton, Als. "This Lonesome Place: Flannery O'Connor on Race and Religion in the Unreconstructed South." *The New Yorker*, January 29, 2001.

Hinckley, David. "Night That City Stopped Cold: John Lennon's Death Still Haunts New Yorkers." *Daily News*, December 4, 2005.

Hojnicki, Carrie. "Inside New York's Most Famous Apartment Building." *Architectural Digest*, April 24, 2017.

Hornblower, Margot. "Sears Details Disorder in Reagan Camp." *Washington Post*, February 29, 1980.

Infusino, Divina. "Springsteen Mesmerizes With Pure Rock." *Milwaukee Journal*, October 15, 1980.

Karr, Gary. "The Boss Stuns L.A. in Four Concerts." *Daily Trojan*, USC, November 5, 1980.

Kaye, Ken. "A Rough Flight for Fired Air Traffic Controllers." *Sun Sentinel*, July 31, 2001.

Kelley, Jeremy P. "John Hinckley Stalked Carter in Dayton Before Shooting Reagan." *Dayton Daily News*, July 27, 2016.

Kneeland, Douglas E. "Reagan Says U.S. Should Meet Khomeini's Demands on Hostages," *New York Times*, September 14, 1980.

Knott, Jack. & Aaron Wildavsky. "Jimmy Carter's Theory of Governing." *Wilson Quarterly*, Winter 1977.

Knutsen, Torbjorn L. "The Reagan Doctrine and the Lessons from the Afghan War." *Australian Journal of Politics and History*, August 1992.

Kopel, David B. "Gun Foes Should Tell the Whole Story." *Chicago Tribune*, March 30, 1991.

Kreitner, Richard. "July 7, 1981: Reagan Nominates Sandra Day O'Connor for the Supreme Court." *The Nation*, July 7, 2015.

Lewis, Neil A. "New Report Say 1980 Reagan Campaign Tried to Delay Hostage Release." *New York Times*, April 15, 1991.

Loder, Kurt. "The Rolling Stone Interview: Bruce Springsteen on Born in the U.S.A." *Rolling Stone*, December 7, 1984.

Michaelson, Judith. "The Blacklist Legacy: A New Generation in Hollywood Takes Political Sides Again, But Remembers the Witchhunt." *Los Angeles Times*, October 18, 1987.

Mohr, Charles. "Guns Traced in 16 Minutes to Pawn Shop in Dallas." *New York Times*, April 1, 1981.

BIBLIOGRAPHY

O'Sullivan, Sibbie. "It's Been 37 Years Since John Lennon Was Shot. Can We Find the Real Lennon in Books?" *Washington Post*, December 6, 2017.

Pont, Jonathan. "A Night for the Vietnam Veteran: A Backstreets Retrospective." Interview with Bobby Muller, *Backstreets Magazine*, Fall 2001, Issue No. 72,

Rockwell, John. "Rock Stars Are Into Politics Again." *New York Times*, September 16, 1979.

_____. "Springsteen Makes Biggest Impact at Antinuclear Benefit." *New York Times*, September, 24, 1979.

Rosellini, Lynn. "Honey I Forgot to Duck, Injured Reagan Tells Wife," *New York Times*, March 31, 1981.

Rosen, Jane, and Paul Keel. "A Vigil But No Funeral for Lennon." *The Guardian*, December 10, 1980.

Rowes, Barbara. "The President-Elect Gains a Daughter-In-Law as Son Ron Makes His Pas De Deux Permanent," *People*, December 8, 1980.

Sheff, David. "John Lennon Interview." *Playboy*, January 1981

Schruers, Fred. "Bruce Springsteen: The Boss is Back." *Rolling Stone*, November 27, 1980.

_____. "Bruce Springsteen and the Secret of the World." *Rolling Stone*, February 5, 1981.

Severo, Richard. "Donald Regan, 84, Financier and Tope Reagan Aide, Dies." *New York Times*, June 11, 2003.

Shef, Vicki. "The Day the Music Died," *People*, December 10, 1990.

Sick, Gary. "The Election Story of the Decade." *New York Times*, April 15, 1991.

Soloman, Jay. & Carol E. Lee. "Inside the 37-Year Standoff Over Iran's Frozen U.S. Dollars." *Wall Street Journal,* December 28, 2016.

Strout, Richard L. "How John Got His Gun." *Christian Science Monitor*, September 4, 1981.

Taubman, Philip. "Suspect Was Arrested Last Year in Nashville on Weapons Charge." *New York Times*, March 31, 1981.

Taylor, Stuart. "Lloyd Cutler: The Last Superlawyer." *The Atlantic*, May 2005.

Troy, Gil. "The Example of Ronald Reagan." *New York Times*, November 9, 2016.

Wadler, Joyce. "A Farewell." *Washington Post*, December 15, 1980.

Wadler, Joyce. & Mike Sager. "I Just Shot John Lennon, He Said Cooly." Washington Post, December 10, 1980.

Walsh, Edward. and Lou Cannon. "Reagan and Carter Finally Brought Together." Washington Post, October 17, 1980.

Weiner, Jon. "Lennon NOT a Closet Republican." *The Nation*, June 29, 2011.

Weiner, Jon. "Nancy Reagan and the Problem of the Two Nancys." *The Nation*, March 6, 2016.

Weisman, Steven R. "Reagan is Angered at Tehran's Stand in Hostage Impasse." *New York Times*, December 25, 1980.

Whittle, Dan. "Hinckley Stalked Carter in Tennessee." *Murfreesboro Post*, January 1, 2012.

UN-CREDITED PERIODICALS

"Oath on the Bible Used by Reagan's Mother." *New York Times*, January 21, 1981. A36.

"Survey Finds Carter's Popularity Has Risen Sharply in Iran Crisis." *New York Times*, December 10, 1979. A22.

"It's Business as Usual at Shop in Dallas Where Hinckley Bought Gun." *New York Times*, April 14, 1981.

ELECTRONIC MEDIA

ARTICLES AND BLOGS

Allen, Jonathan. "Why Jimmy Carter is a Great American Leader." *Vox*, August 20, 1015. https://www.vox.com/2015/8/17/9163717/jimmy-carter-great-leader-outsider

Altamont Enterprise, "Lennon's death taught cop on the scene "life is tenuous." December 10, 2015.

BIBLIOGRAPHY

Brooks, Peter. "CIA Clash: The Left Assaults Langley-Again." *The Heritage Foundation*, November 4, 2009. https://www.heritage.org/homeland-security/commentary/cia-clash-the-left-assaults-langley-again

Day, Meagan. "Even Shooting the President Can't Get Lasting Gun Laws Passed." *Timeline*, timeline.com, August 1, 2016. https://timeline.com/hinckley-brady-gun-control-714b9759deba

Deriso, Nick. "When John Lennon and Harry Nilsson Got Tossed From the Troubadour For Heckling.
Ultimate Classic Rock, March 12, 2015. https://ultimateclassicrock.com/john-lennon-harry-nilsson-troubadour/

Douglass, William. "For Nancy Reagan, the White House was the role of a lifetime." March 6, 2016. https://www.mcclatchydc.com/news/politics-government/white-house/article64406977.html

Duffy, Peter. "Impresario Seaman." The Morning News, themorningnews.org, December 2, 2010. https://themorningnews.org/article/impresario-seaman

Estes, Adam Clark. "John Lennon wrote Come Together for Timothy Leary but pot ruined it." Gizmodo, August 8, 2014. https://gizmodo.com/john-lennon-wrote-come-together-for-timothy-leary-but-1618446177

Fox News. "Bruce Springsteen is 'embarrassed 'to be an American." February 3, 2017. https://www.foxnews.com/entertainment/bruce-springsteen-is-embarrassed-to-be-an-american

Gillespie, Nick. "The Triumph of Politics Over Economics." Interview with David Stockman, April 2011. https://reason.com/2011/03/21/the-triumph-of-politics-over-e/

Hagen, Carrie. "The Media Learned Nothing After Misreporting the Reagan Assassination Attempt." Smithsonian Magazine, August 11, 2016. https://www.smithsonianmag.com/history/media-learned-nothing-after-misreporting-reagan-assassination-attempt-180960091/

Hayden, Chaunce. "John Lennon's Other Lover: May Pang Talks to Chaunce Hayden." MN Magazine, December 2019. https://mnmagazine.com/2019/12/john-lennons-other-lover-may-pang/

Kamarch, Elaine. "The Iranian Hostage Crisis and its Effect on American Politics." Brookings, November 4, 2019. https://www.brookings.edu/blog/order-from-chaos/2019/11/04/the-iranian-hostage-crisis-and-its-effect-on-american-politics/

Knot, Stephen F. Fred Fielding Interview for Miller Center, August 17, 2004. https://millercenter.org/the-presidency/presidential-oral-histories/fred-fielding-oral-history-0

Leepson, Marc. "How Bruce Springsteen Rescued Vietnam Veterans of America, and the Vietnam Veterans Movement." *The VVA Veteran Online*, March/April 2016. http://vvaveteran.org/36-2/36-2_springsteen.html

London, Dr. Paul A. "Inflation: The Reagan Myth and Carter Record." *Huffington Post*, June 11, 2013. https://www.huffpost.com/entry/inflation-the-reagan-myth_b_3418868

McCarthy, John. "John Lennon's Bermuda." *The Telegraph*, November 1, 2013. https://www.telegraph.co.uk/travel/destinations/caribbean/bermuda/articles/John-Lennons-Bermuda/

Riedel, Bruce. "Lessons From America's First War With Iran." *Brookings*, May 23, 2013. https://www.brookings.edu/articles/lessons-from-americas-first-war-with-iran/

Schapiro, Jane. "My Friend and Bruce Springsteen." *The Sun*, January 2007. https://www.thesunmagazine.org/issues/373/my-friend-and-bruce-springsteen

Summers, Sue. "John Lennon's Last Day: A gripping NEW eyewitness account on the 30th anniversary of Beatle's murder." *Daily Mail*, December 5, 2010. https://www.dailymail.co.uk/tvshowbiz/article-1335829/John-Lennon-NEW-eyewitness-account-30th-anniversary-Beatles-murder.html

Taub, Amanda. "The Republican Myth of Ronald Reagan and the Iran Hostages." *Vox*, January 25, 2016. https://www.vox.com/2016/1/25/10826056/reagan-iran-hostage-negotiation

Van der Voort, Tom. "Memories of the Attempted Reagan Assassination."https://millercenter.org/issues-policy/the-first-year/the-attempted-reagan-assassination

Wischmann, Leslie. "The Killing Spree That Transfixed a Nation: Charles Starkweather and Caril Fugate, 1958." A project of the Wyoming State Historical Society, November 8, 2014. https://www.wyohistory.org/encyclopedia/killing-spree-transfixed-nation-charles-starkweather-and-caril-fugate-1958

Wosahla, Steve. "John Lennon's Been Shot: The Marshall Tucker Band's Ghosts of Christmas Past." *No Depression: The Journal of Roots Music*, December 6, 2015. (link no longer available at time of publication)

Young, James Sterling., Stephen F. Knott. and Erwin Hargrove. Michael Deaver Interview, University of Virginia. https://millercenter.org/the-presidency/presidential-oral-histories/michael-deaver-oral-history

TELEVISION

"The Election of 1980," *American Experience*, PBS.

"Meltdown at Three Mile Island," *American Experience*, PBS.

John Lennon in conversation with Howard Cosell,*ABC Monday Night Football*, December 9, 1974.

John Lennon interviewed by Tom Snyder, *The Tomorrow Show*, NBC. April 8, 1975.

Tom Petit, NBC News report, January 21, 1980.

Dick Cavett Show, May 11, 1972.

"Pertzborn's People," John Pertzborn, *KSDK Eyewitness News*, St. Louis, April 17, 1988.

With God on Our Side: The Rise of the Religious Right, PBS documentary, 1996.

The Day John Lennon Died, ITV1. 2010.

"Family Feud: Reagan's Children Debate the Legacy of their Father," *ABC News*, January 28, 2011.

Dr. David Halleran interviewed for CNY Central, Syracuse, New York. 2011.

Tim McCarthy interviewed for *American History TV*, CSPAN, May 2017.

"John Lennon's Last Day and Death in New York City," Sal Bono, *Inside Edition*. December 7, 2017.

RADIO AND PODCASTS

The World This Week, CBS Radio, November 9, 1980.

Vin Scelsa on-air comments, WNEW-FM, New York City. December 8, 1980.

Kevin Goldman news report, WNEW-FM, New York City. December 9, 1980.

John Lennon Interviewed by Howard Cosell, ABC Radio, June 1974.

"Ghost Wars: How Reagan Armed the Mujahadeen in Afghanistan." Steve Coll Interviewed by Amy Goodman, *Democracy Now*, June 10, 2004.

"U.S. Links to Saddam During the Iran-Iraq War," *Day to Day*, National Public Radio, September 22, 2005.

"PATCO: The Strike That Changed American Labor." *The Takeaway*, PRI, October 17, 2011.

May Pang Interviewed by Ed Opperman for the *Opperman Report*, November 6, 2015.

Rick Neilson / Cheap Trick interviewed by Howard Stern, April 6, 2016.

Bob Gruen Interviewed by Mike Derrico , *Rock Under Fire*, May 1, 2017.

"When Reagan Broke the Unions." *Planet Money*, National Public Radio, December 18, 2019.

Bruce Springsteen, E Street Radio, Sirius XM, June 17, 2020.

BIBLIOGRAPHY

ARCHIVED DOCUMENTS

Public Papers of Jimmy Carter, Office of the Federal Register National Archives and Records Service.

Public Papers of Ronald Reagan, Office of the Federal Register National Archives and Records Service.

Jimmy Carter Annual State of the Union Address, January 17, 1980.

Ronald Reagan Inaugural Address, January 20, 1981.

Jimmy Carter White House Diary

Ronald Reagan White House Diary

Jimmy Carter Presidential Library and Museum, www.jimmycarterlibrary.gov

Ronald Reagan Presidential Library and Museum, www.reaganlibrary.gov

National Security Archive, George Washington University nsaarchive2.gwu.edu

U.S. News and World Report, November 14, 1977 www.cia.gov

Reagan Foundation https://www.reaganfoundation.org/media/51313/red-scare.pdf

U.S. Congressional Serial Set.

John Hinckley Jr. personal journal entries

Transcripts of John Hinckley Trial

BRUCE SPRINGSTEEN CONCERT RECORDINGS

Cleveland Ohio, Richfield Coliseum, January 1, 1979
Chicago, Illinois, Uptown Theater, October 10, 1980
St. Paul, Minnesota, Civic Center, October 13, 1980
Los Angeles, California, Sports Arena, October 30, 1980
Tempe, Arizona, Arizona State University, November 5, 1980
New York City, New York, Madison Square Garden, November 27, 1980
Philadelphia, Pennsylvania, Spectrum, December 9, 1980
Providence, Rhode Island, Civic Center, December 11, 1980
Uniondale, New York, Nassau Coliseum, December 28, 1980
Paris, France, Palais Des Sports De Saint-Quen, April 19, 1981
Stockholm, Sweden, Johanneshov Isstadion, May 8, 1981
London, England, Wembley Arena, June 5, 1981
East Rutherford, New Jersey, Brendan Byrne Arena, July 5, 1981
Los Angeles, California, Sports Arena, August 20, 1981
Pittsburgh, Pennsylvania, Civic Arena, September 21, 1984.
Worcester, Massachusetts, Centrum, February 25, 1988
Harare, Zimbabwe, National Sports Stadium, October 7, 1988
Pittsburgh, Pennsylvania, Consol Energy Center, January 16, 2016

SPECIAL THANKS

Backstreets Magazine
Sal Calcaterra
Tom Dziedzic
Dr. Frank J. Esposito Ph.D.
Keith Elliot Greenberg
Bob Gruen
Dr. David Halleran (for coming out with the truth)
Divina Infusino
Shannon Jamieson
Philip Jenkins
Barbara Kammerer
Nicole LaForte
Michael Lee Nirenberg
Christopher Phillips
Rob Rosen
Deartra Sato
Laura Schilling
Fred Schruers
Paul Sisolak
Abbey Suchoski

CHAPTER NOTES

CHAPTER 1

The opening chapter outlines a brief overview of John Lennon and Ronald Reagan as two opposing figures of the cultural divide. My Lennon notes for this chapter are as follows: The information pertaining to the chance meeting between Lennon and Peter Fonda is documented in several places, much more in recent years. I used several articles, listed in Source Notes as well as John's own account in his 1980 interview for Playboy with David Scheff. Backgrounds on Timothy Leary, Ralph Metzner and Richard Alpert are well-documented over the years, as Leary and Alpert are well-known pop cultural/countercultural figures. The articles I drew from are listed in Source Notes. Details given on the Billboard pop charts were taken from the actual chart records for said weeks mentioned in the chapter's content. The accounts provided of the "Lost Weekend" and the Ono Lennon marriage come from a 2015 podcast interview with May Pang, details of which are listed in Source Notes, Yoko Ono's personal recollections in Phillip Norman's book on Lennon, and assorted quotes of John's from over the years, publications listed in Source Notes.

The information and details given about Ronald Reagan's childhood with regard to his often unreachable personality were used with much consideration to the ideas about Reagan's character that HW Brands presents in his book, *Reagan: The Life*, a vital source overall for my Reagan notes. I also consulted Reagan's personal White House journals, which use direct quotes regarding his relationship with Nancy Reagan. Use of these journals is frequent throughout this book and they will appear repeatedly in these notes. My account of the random chance meeting of Reagan and Lennon on Monday Night Football come from sportscaster, Frank Gifford's personal recollection as shown in an ESPN showcase, details also listed in Source Notes.

CHAPTER 2

Details on the Unit 2 reactor at Three Mile Island came from the PBS documentary, *Meltdown at Three Mile Island* as well as the firsthand documentation of newspaper articles.

Regarding studio recording sessions and live performance history, Bruce Springsteen is one of the most widely-documented artists of modern pop music. With respect to personal knowledge that comes from decades of being an avid fan, the chronological timeline of Springsteen's work progress provided in this chapter are all supported by a rich variety of available sources…official websites, fan sites, book and magazine publications, and live recordings.

CHAPTER 3

Immediate details on the first weeks of the Iranian hostage crisis were culled from newspapers and television news reports that occurred in real time.

I worked closely with H.W. Brands's *Reagan: The Life* as a guide through two very important elements of my study of Ronald Reagan…first, Reagan's childhood and thorough history of Reagan's parents, Jack and Nelle Reagan.

More significantly, the assessment that Brands offers accounting for Reagan's often distant and enigmatic personality. Much of what Brands, as well as many other writers have noted with respect to Reagan's childhood has been confirmed by Ronald Reagan himself, as he addresses much of it in his autobiography. It should come as no surprise that Reagan's autobiography also served as one of my most important sources for this project. In this particular chapter, I consulted it for firsthand information pertaining to his military service during World War II. With respect to the Reagan children, Nancy Reagan's memoir was a primary source, as it highlighted sentiment and relationships within the family. A handful of additional publications were consulted for this chapter, as reflected in Source Notes.

CHAPTER 4

As with the third chapter, this chapter continues on trying to reconcile the public perception and persona of Ronald Reagan with the elusive core of his personality with those who actually knew him and/or were closest to him. My main sources for this chapter are the accounts that look closely at his friendships, particularly with Michael Deaver and Paul Laxalt. Some insight from his youngest child Ron, whose book *My Father at 100* proved extremely useful in our attempts at understanding the Reagan character through its lineage going back to Jack Reagan. Supplemental sources on Reagan, as always, include newspaper and magazine articles significant and critical to their time period, all listed under *Periodicals*.

CHAPTER 5

The details of John Lennon's life and progression through the early months of 1980 are provided through four key sources for this period...Tim Riley's book *Lennon: The Man, the Myth, the Music, the Definitive Life*, Philip Norman's book, *John Lennon: The Life*, *Yoko Ono* by Jerry Hopkins, and *Nowhere Man* by Rob Rosen. I also spoke at length to Rob Rosen about the content in his book, sourced directly from John Lennon's personal diaries, which Rob had access to for a period of time in 1981.

Studio sessions for *The River* are well-documented through various publications of *Backstreets* Magazine over the years.

CHAPTER 6

Sources are across-the-board for this chapter, spanning the entire bibliography comprising books, newspaper and magazine articles, TV interviews and news clips, and documentaries. The most useful publications where the bulk of the 1980 campaign season is explored are Jimmy Carter's White House Diary and Nancy Reagan's autobiography. Details between John Sears and Jack Kemp are sourced from Bob Colacello's *Ronnie and Nancy: The Path to the White House*. Michael Reagan's book, *Reagan: The New Revolution* was also valuable in recalling phone conversations and dialogue between Michael and his father.

CHAPTER 7

This chapter tracks Bruce Springsteen through the first months of his 1980 tour. All information and quotes are pulled from *Rolling Stone* reports, newspaper concert reviews corresponding to each individual show that is detailed in my pages, and transcripts from live recordings.

CHAPTER 8

Information concerning John Hinckley Jr. in October 1980 is sourced from newspaper articles written months later following his shooting of President Reagan. This chapter in general uses mostly articles from newspapers and scholarly journals documented in the Bibliography and Source Notes.

CHAPTER NOTES

CHAPTER 9

Information on John Lennon's schedule, whereabouts and personal thoughts was provided mostly by Rosen's *Nowhere Man* book, again, sourced directly from Lennon's personal diaries. Details of President Carter's meeting with President-elect Reagan come from Carter's White House Diary. Information on Springsteen's schedule and whereabouts is provided by Fred Schruer's interview/article in *Rolling Stone* magazine. Schruer's work in several articles during this period is largely a blueprint for my information on Springsteen during early December. Concert monologues and quotes, as always come from transcripts of live recordings during those weeks.

CHAPTER 10

The RKO interview is the main source in this chapter, along with recollections of Dave Sholin and Laurie Kaye featured in documentaries and television segments all noted in Source Notes and Bibliography under *Television*. Recollections of Bob Gruen are from my personal conversation with him on the *Rock Under Fire* podcast on May 1, 2017.

CHAPTER 11

Documentation on the murder of John Lennon is all over the place. A wide range of TV news and radio reports, eyewitness accounts and interviews with police officers, doctors and nurses have been sourced for this chapter. The details of the bullet wounds being entrance wounds in the chest as opposed to exit wounds were provided to me personally by Nurse Barbara Kammerer and confirmed by Nurse Dea Sato in the same phone conversation.

CHAPTER 12

Details of the immediate hours and days following Lennon's death are pulled from newspapers, mostly *New York Times* and *Washington Post* articles. This includes information regarding Nancy Reagan's press conference, the firing of Robin Orr and the initial responses of Ronald Reagan and Jimmy Carter toward the murder of John Lennon. The account of the Reagan's tour of the White House ending the chapter is sourced from Ronald Reagan's autobiography. Details of Springsteen's performances, as always, are sourced from live recordings.

CHAPTER 13

I worked closely with both Carter and Reagan's diaries in putting this chapter together. Transcriptions of Ronald Reagan's Inaugural Address are obviously a major element that went into this part of the book as well. The details of the limo ride and the Reagan's brief walk out onto the Truman Balcony before the Inaugural Ball are provided by Nancy Reagan's autobiography.

CHAPTER 14

The most comprehensive source for the assassination attempt on Ronald Reagan is Del Quentin Wilbur's *Rawhide Down* which was used to great extent here, as was Craig Shirley's *Last Act* and *Speaking Out* by Larry Speakes. The obvious source for direct quotes attributed to March 30, 1981 is TV news coverage of press conferences. Several Miller Center interviews are used as well...all are documented under *Electronic Media*.

CHAPTER 15

As with Chapter 7, this chapter, focusing on Bruce Springsteen's touring schedule is sourced directly from live recordings with onstage monologues transcribed by myself.

CHAPTER 16

Economic statistics are provided by David Stockman's *The Great Deformation* along with an interview with Stockman detailed under *Electronic Media*. With Stockman serving as Director of Management and Budget in the Reagan White House during the years of this publication's focus, I found no sources more valid than his own recollections and assessments. Information on the effects of the PATCO strike and firings are provided by segments on PRI's *The Takeway* and NPR's *Planet Money*...both documented by episode under *Radio and Podcasts*.

CHAPTER 17 / 18

These final two chapters tie up my arguments and are rooted mostly in my own observations and firsthand accounts of present unfolding history.

ENDNOTES

INTRODUCTION

1. Bruce Springsteen, Worcester, Massachusetts, February 25, 1988.
2. Bruce Springsteen, Pittsburgh, Pennsylvania, January 16, 2016.

CHAPTER 1

3. "I don't want to know": John Lennon interviewed by David Sheff, September 1980.
4. "I felt followed": *Dick Cavett Show*, May 1973.
5. Birmingham, *Life at the Dakota: New York's Most Unusual Address*, p. 16
6. Norman, *John Lennon: The Life*, p. 704.
7. May Pang interviewed by Ed Opperman, The Opperman Report, November, 2015
8. Chaunce Hayden, "John Lennon's Other Lover: May Pang Talks to Chaunce Hayden." *MN Magazine*, December 2019.
9. "There was some girl": Nick Deriso, "How John Lennon and Harry Nilsson Got Tossed from the Troubadour for Heckling." *Ultimate Classic Rock*, March 12, 2015.
10. "I was planted": John Lennon interviewed by Tom Snyder for *The Tomorrow Show*, April 8, 1975.

AUTUMN AND EVERYTHING AFTER

11. "You take": Frank Gifford in conversation with Brent Musburger for ABC's Monday Night Football, November 20, 1995.
12. "Saw Mommie": Ronald Reagan White House Diary, July 23, 1981.

CHAPTER 2

13. "The core": PBS documentary, *Meltdown at Three Mile Island*, 1999.
14. "I didn't buy it": Ibid,
15. Lester Bangs, "Greetings From Asbury Park, NJ" review, *Rolling Stone*, July 5, 1973.
16. "I saw the future": Jon Landau, The Real Paper, May, 1974.
17. "Well I almost": Bruce Springsteen, Cleveland, Ohio, Richfield Coliseum January 1, 1979.
18. "It's a good thing": Bonnie Raitt, *No Nukes*, 1980
19. "Well what's the difference": Tom Petty, *History of Rock and Roll*, TV series, 1995.
20. "were barely being tolerated": John Rockwell, "Springsteen Makes Biggest Impact at anti-Nuclear Benefit," New York Times, September 24, 1979.
21. "return to": John Rockwell, "Rock Stars Are into Politics Again," *New York Times*, September 16, 1979.
22. 'This is": *No Nukes* film, 1980.
23. "That's all": Ibid.
24. "I can't": Ibid.
25. "I can't go on": Ibid.
26. "Well dontcha know": Ibid.
27. "I'm just a prisoner": Ibid.

CHAPTER 3

28. "Blissfull": Patterson, *Restless Giant*, p. 108.
29. Hine, *The Great Funk*, p. 3.
30. "Newsweek said": Baily Smith, *Rise of the Religious Right* documentary.
31. "dominant force": Ronald Reagan, televised speech, November 13, 1979.

ENDNOTES

32. H.W. Brands, *Reagan: The Life*, p. 65.
33. Ibid., p. 10.
34. Ibid., p. 11.
35. Ronald Reagan, Ronald Reagan, An American Life: The Autobiography, p. 97
36. Ibid., p. 103.
37. Ibid., p. 106.
38. Brands, *Reagan: The Life*, p. 63
39. Victor Navasky, *Naming Names*, p. 27.
40. Ronald Reagan, *Reagan, An American Life*, p. 111.
41. Ibid., p. 111.
42. Reagan testimony before HUAC, 1947.

CHAPTER 4

43. "I have spent": *A Time for Choosing* speech.
44. Ronald Reagan, *Reagan, An American Life*, p. 145
45. Ibid., p. 155.
46. Ron Reagan, *My Father at 100*, p. 104.
47. Ibid., p. 66.
48. Brands, *Reagan: The Life*, p. 166.
49. "scaring": Sandbrook, *Mad as Hell*, p. 339.
50. Francis Clines, "The Reagan Play-By-Play Still Plays," *New York Times*, March 31, 1985.
51. "Those who do work": Ronald Reagan First Inaugural Address.
52. Madrick, *Age of Greed*, p. 115.
53. Brands, *Reagan: The Life*, p. 194.
54. "I am aware': Sandra Cherub, "Special Collection Showcases Friendship Between Paul Laxalt, Ronald Reagan," *Las Vegas Review Journal*, March 7, 2016.
55. "Always being": Michael Deaver Interview, Miller Center.
56. "Clark really was": Ibid.
57. "It was": Ibid.

CHAPTER 5

58. Norman, *John Lennon: The Life*, p. 783.
59. "Where are you": Rosen, *Nowhere Man*, p. 124.
60. Norman, *John Lennon: The Life*, p. 791.
61. "this new wave stuff": Hopkins, *Yoko Ono*, p. 212.
62. Spitz, Dylan: A Biography, p. 536.
63. "If I thought": Dave DiMartino, "The Boss Talks!" *Creem* Interview, January 1981.
64. Riley, *Lennon: The Myth, the Music, the Definitive Life*.
65. Rick Neilson interviewed by Howard Stern, April 6, 2016.
66. Riley, *Lennon: The Myth*, p. 632.
67. Ibid., p. 634. NE
68. Hopkins, *Yoko Ono*, p. 215.
69. Ibid., p.216.
70. Ibid., p. 216
71. David Sheff Interview, September, 1980.

CHAPTER 6

72. "It has never": Jimmy Carter, State of the Union Address, January 23, 1980.
73. "Our nation": Ibid.
74. "The unwarranted": Ibid.
75. "Since the end": Ibid.
76. "any means": Ibid.
77. "make Soviet involvement": Loyn, *In Afghanistan*, p.143.
78. Jimmy Carter White House Diary, p. 338.
79. Wilentz, *The Age of Reagan*, p. 52.
80. Michael Reagan, *The New Reagan Revolution*, p. 72.
81. "We have just": Tom Petit, NBC News. January 21, 1980.
82. Kelley, *Nancy Reagan: The Unauthorized Biography*, p. 263.
83. Colacello, *Ronnie and Nancy*, p. 485.
84. Reagan, *The New Reagan Revolution*, p. 73.

85. "You can examine": Margaret Hornblower, "Sears Details Disorder in Reagan Camp." *Washington Post*, February 29, 1980.
86. "Ronald Reagan is the kind of man": Ibid.
87. Reagan, *My Turn*, p. 217.
88. Colacello, *Ronnie and Nancy*, p. 486.
89. Ibid.
90. "If I go": Gerald Ford Interviewed by Walter Cronkite, CBS News, July 16, 1980.
91. Colacello, *Ronnie and Nancy*, p. 494.
92. Reagan, *My Turn*, p. 217.
93. Ibid.
94. Ibid.
95. "I happen to": *With God on Our Side: The Rise of the Religious Right*, PBS documentary, 1996.
96. "I was asked": Ibid.
97. "Reagan knew": Ibid.
98. "The Moral Majority": Ibid.
99. "We all made": Ibid.
100. "the marriage": Ibid.
101. "I know": Ibid.

CHAPTER 7

102. I wanna thank everybody": Springsteen, Chicago, October 10, 1980.
103. Fred Schruers, "Bruce Springsteen: The Boss is Back." Rolling Stone, November 27, 1980
104. "I met": Springsteen, St. Paul, October 13, 1980.
105. "I used to live": Ibid.
106. "Fans stood": Divina Infusino, "Springsteen Mesmerizes With Pure Rock." *Milwaukee Journal*, October 15, 1980.
107. "I don't want": Springsteen, Los Angeles, October 30, 1980.
108. "Devoted to": Gary Karr, "The Boss Stuns L.A. in Four Concerts." *Daily Trojan*, USC, November 5, 1980.

CHAPTER 8

109. "There are still": *Jimmy Carter*, Public Papers, September 1, 1980.
110. "In our zeal": Edward Walsh and Lou Cannon, "Reagan and Carter Finally Brought Together," *Washington Post*, October 17, 1980.
111. "terrible burden": Ibid.
112. "If you've got": Jimmy Carter, Public Papers, October 6, 1980.
113. Frum, *How We Got Here*, p. 344
114. Ibid.
115. "We should declare war": Philip Geyelin, "When Reagan Was Being Reagan," *Washington Post*, April 22, 1984.
116. Shirley, Last Act, p. 173.
117. "process president": Jack Knot & Aaron Wildavsky, "Jimmy Carter's Theory of Governing." *Wilson Quarterly*, Winter 1977.
118. "failures to set": Stephen Hess, "Jimmy Carter: Why He Failed." *Brookings Institution*, June 1978.
119. O'Neill, *Man of the House*, p. 297
120. "woefully unprepared": Marvin Stone, Presidential Debate, Cleveland, October 28, 1980.
121. "and now he's": Ronald Reagan, Presidential Debate, Cleveland, October 28, 1980.
122. "The Iranians": October 19, 1980 memo, U.S. Congressional Serial Set.
123. Brands, *Reagan: The Life*, p. 232.
124. "Nuclear weaponry": Jimmy Carter, Presidential Debate, Cleveland, October 28, 1980.
125. 'Are you": Ronald Reagan, Presidential Debate, Cleveland, October 28, 1980.
126. Wilbur, Rawhide Down, p. 37.

CHAPTER 9

127. Rosen, Nowhere Man, p. 153.
128. Ibid.
129. "I don't know": Bruce Springsteen, Arizona State University, November 5, 1980.

130. "You guys": Ibid.
131. John Weiner, "John Lennon: Not a Closet Republican," *The Nation*, June 29, 2011.
132. Rosen, Nowhere Man, p. 152
133. "Saturday night special": John Lennon interviewed by David Sheff, *Playboy*, September, 1980.
134. Carter White House Diary, November 20, 1980.
135. "How could it": Barbara Rowes. "The President-Elect Gains a Daughter-In-Law as Son Ron Makes His Pas De Deux Permanent," *People*, December 8, 1980.
136. "Hello, I'm Vin Scelsa": Vin Scelsa, Madison Square Garden, November 27, 1980.
137. "You've got": Rosen, *Nowhere Man*. 180
138. Ibid., p. 155.
139. Fred Schruers, "Bruce Springsteen and the Secret of the World." *Rolling Stone*, February 5, 1981.
140. John Lennon interviewed by Jonathan Cott, December 5, 1980.
141. "God help": Ibid.
142. "Do you like": Mark Snyder interviewed for *Mughots: Death of a Beatle*.
143. James R. Gaines, "Descent into Madness." *People*, June 22, 1981.

CHAPTER 10

144. *The Beatles Anthology*, p. 56.
145. "survived": RKO interview, December 8, 1980.
146. "I was at the studio": Bob Gruen interviewed by Mike Derrico, Rock Under Fire podcast, May 1, 2017.
147. Birmingham, *Life at the Dakota: New York's Most Unusual Address*.
148. "You want that": Paul Goresh account, Vicki Sheff, "The Day the Music Died," *People*, December 10, 1990.
149. "Send us": Personal interview with Rob Rosen
150. "Well our car": Paul Goresh account, Sue Summers, :"John Lennon's Last Day, Daily Mail, December 5, 2010.

151. "Did you": Laurie Kaye interviewed by John Roberts for CNN.
152. 'Well he's like a brother': Dave Sholin interviewed for *The Day John Lennon Died*.

CHAPTER 11

153. "Do you know": Joyce Wadler and Mike Sager, "I Just Shot John Lennon, He Said Cooly," Washington Post, December 10, 1980.
154. "Yes": Ibid.
155. "That's the one": Steve Spiro interviewed for *The Day John Lennon Died*.
156. "He just": Ibid.
157. "You what": Ibid.
158. "Please": Ibid.
159. "I think": Herb Frauenberger interviewed for the Altamont Enterprise, December 10, 2015.
160. "You better": Peter Cullen interviewed for Inside Edition, December 7, 2017.
161. "Don't let": Steve Spiro interviewed for *The Day John Lennon Died*.
162. "Are you John Lennon": Jimmy Breslin, *Daily News*, December 9, 1980.
163. "We have": Alan Weiss interviewed for *The Day John Lennon Died*.
164. "He just left": Jack Douglas interviewed for *The Day John Lennon Died*.
165. "Can you": Alan Weiss interviewed for *Outside the Lines*, ESPN, December, 8, 2010.
166. "This is not": David Halleran interviewed for CNY Central, 2011.
167. "You're covered": Personal interview with Barbara Kammerer
168. "Fellas": dialogue from ABC Sports, recorded December 8, 1980, as heard in *Outside the Lines*, ESPN.
169. "Three seconds": Frank Gifford, ABC Monday Night Football, December 8, 1980.
170. "Yes we have": Howard Cosell, ABC Monday Night Football, December 8, 1980.
171. "This is WNEW": Vin Scelsa, WNEW-FM, New York City, December 8, 1980.
172. "John Lennon was": Vin Scelsa, WNEW-FM, New York City, December 8, 1980.

CHAPTER 12

173. "Well, what": Ronald Reagan, New York City, December 9, 1980.
174. "What would I have to say": Maurice Carroll, "Reagan, Visiting New York, Talks With Cardinal and Top Blacks," *New York Times*, December 10, 1980.
175. "John Lennon helped": Jimmy Carter, Washington DC, December 9, 1980.
176. "pray for John's soul": Joyce Wadler, "A Farewell," *Washington Post*, December 15, 1980.
177. Fred Schruers, "Bruce Springsteen and the Secret of the World," *Rolling Stone*, February 5, 1981.
178. "Um..I'd just": Bruce Springsteen, Philadelphia, December 9, 1980.
179. "little gun": Thomas. *Thanks for the Memories, Mr. President*, p.134.
180. "Sure it bothers me": Steve Grahovac, NBC Nightly News, December 9, 1980.
181. "This past week": Bruce Springsteen, Providence, Rhode Island, December 11, 1980.
182. "countercultural void": Riley, *Lennon: The Myth, the Man, the Music*, p. 646.
183. "three for five dollars": Joyce Wadler, A Farewell," *Washington Post*, December 15, 1980.
184. "There's a book": Bruce Springsteen, Uniondale, New York, December 28, 1980.
185. "There's another Christmas": Steven R. Weisman, "Reagan is Angered at Tehran's Stand in Hostage Impasse,' *New York Times*, December 25, 1980.

CHAPTER 13

186. "We can and should agree": Douglas E. Kneeland, "Reagan Says U.S. Should Meet Khomeini's Demands on Hostages," *New York Times*, September 14, 1980.
187. "Are you serious": Jimmy Carter White House Diary, January 20, 1981.
188. "I looked": Ibid.
189. "I consider him": Ibid.
190. "Word is that": Ronald Reagan White House Diary, February 8, 1981.
191. Edwards, *The Reagan's: Portrait of a Marriage*, p. 174
192. "You can be": "Oath on the Bible Used by Reagan's Mother," *New York Times*, January 21, 1981.

193. "In this": Ronald Reagan Inaugural Address, January 20, 1980.
194. "We're not": Ibid.
195. "Those who say": Ibid.
196. "I'm told": Ibid.
197. "We are": Ibid.
198. Reagan, *My Turn*, p. 236.
199. Wilbur, *Rawhide Down*, p. 27.
200. Crunden, *A Brief History of American Culture*, p. 297.
201. "with Jerry Falwell": Jenkins, *Decade of Nightmares*, p. 106.
202. "transferring hundreds": Ronald Reagan White House Diary, January 31, 1981.
203. Reagan, *An American Life*, p. 547
204. Reagan White House Diary, March 24, 1981.
205. Ibid. February 14, 1981.
206. Ibid. March 13, 1981.

CHAPTER 14

207. "We've been left": Ronald Reagan speech to AFL-CIO, Washington Hilton, March 30, 1981.
208. "Together": Ibid.
209. "Mr. President": Edwards, *The Reagan's: Portrait of a Marriage*, p. 208.
210. "What the hell's that": Ibid.
211. "Rawhide's okay": Wilbur, *Rawhide Down*, p. 82.
212. Richard E. Cytowic, "The Long Ordeal of James Brady," *New York Times Magazine*, September 27, 1981.
213. Speakes, *Speaking Out*, p. 5.
214. "Honey I forgot to duck": Lynn Rosellini, "Honey I Forgot to Duck, Injured Reagan Tells Wife," New York Times, March 31, 1981.
215. Edwards, *The Reagan's: Portrait of a Marriage*, p. 212.
216. "Good afternoon": David Gergen, White House press announcement, March 30, 1981

ENDNOTES

217. "What's the note say": Leslie Stahl, White House press conference, March 30, 1981
218. "Constitutionally, gentlemen": Alexander Haig, White House press conference, March 30, 1981.
219. "You better read": Wilbur, *Rawhide Down*, p. 177.
220. "Right, Fred": Fred Fielding interviewed for Miller Center, August 17, 2004.
221. "Well, I have a very brief": George H.W. Bush, White House press announcement, March 30, 1981.
222. "He was wounded": Frank Reynolds, *ABC News Special Report*, March 30, 1981.
223. "Speak up": Ibid.
224. "All of this": Ibid.
225. "You find out": Tom Van der Voort, "Memories of the Attempted Reagan Assassination," The Miller Center.
226. "It is amazing": Ibid.
227. Ibid.
228. Johnson, *Sleepwalking Through History*, p. 162.
229. "I appreciate you coming down": Tom Van der Voort, "Memories of the Attempted Reagan Assassination," The Miller Center.
230. "Ya know": Tim McCarthy C-SPAN interview, May 2017.
231. "rake me over the coals": Reagan White House Diay, April 19, 1980.
232. "decent, deeply religious people" Ibid.
233. "rambunctious": Speakes, *Speaking Out*, p. 63.
234. Reagan, *My Turn*, p. 44.
235. "Twelve years ago": Nick Corasanti, "Coroner Said to Rule James Brady's Death a Homicde, 33 Years After a Shooting," *New York Times*, August 8, 2014.

CHAPTER 15

236. "could lose so big": Bruce Springsteen, London, England, June 5, 1981.
237. "I'm 31 now": Bruce Springsteen, Paris, France, April 19, 1981.
238. "could get you killed": Bruce Springsteen, Los Angeles, California, September 30, 1985.

AUTUMN AND EVERYTHING AFTER

239. "In America there's a promise": Bruce Springsteen, Stockholm, Sweden May 8, 1991.
240. "But it's hard": Ibid.
241. "This song I wrote": Ibid.
242. "I guess that's why we're here tonight": Ibid.
243. "It's in a bunch of little things": Ibid.
244. "I'd just like to make": Bruce Springsteen, East Rutherford, New Jersey, July 5, 1981.
245. "We just spent": Ibid.
246. "When I was over in Europe": Ibid.
247. "What do you do": Jonathan Pont, "A Night for the Vietnam Veteran: Interview with Bobby Muller," Backstreets Magazine, Fall 2001.
248. "older with these": Ibid.
249. "because their government": Bruce Springsteen, Harare, Zimbabwe, October 7, 1988.
250. "They were sensitive": Jonathan Pont, "A Night for the Vietnam Veteran: Interview with Bobby Muller," Backstreets Magazine, Fall 2001.
251. "If you think they're booing you": Ibid.
252. "Tonight we're here": Bruce Springsteen, Los Angeles, August 20, 1981.
253. "Thank you": Bobby Muller, Los Angeles, August 20, 1981.

CHAPTER 16

254. Sandbrook, *Mad as Hell*, p. 290.
255. Bruce Springsteen interviewed by Kurt Loder, October 1984.
256. "America's future rests": Ronald Reagan, Hammontown, New Jersey, September 19, 1984.
257. "Well the President": Bruce Springsteen, Pittsburgh, Pennsylvania, September 21, 1984.

CHAPTER 17

258. "Greed is good": Michael Douglas as Gordon Gecko, *Wall Street*, 1986,
259. "We stand": Bruce Springsteen, Melbourne, Australia, February 2, 2017.
260. "Bruce Springsteen is": FOX News Website, February 3, 2017.
261. "This is a man": Bruce Springsteen speaking at Hillary Clinton campaign rally, November 7, 2016.
262. Hannity and Colmes, May 12, 2011.
263. "in a state of shambles": Brinkley, *The Unfinished Presidency*, p. 141.
264. Sirota, *Back to Our Future*, p. 122.
265. "commander in chief": Ibid.
266. Ibid. p. 123.
267. "I think one of the foolish things": Ronald Reagan in conversation with William F. Buckley, *Firing Line*, January 14, 1980.
268. Brands, Reagan: The Life, p. 435-436.
269. Ibid.

CHAPTER 18

270. 'After all': Ron Reagan Jr. Interview with Christiane Amanpour, *ABC News*, January 28, 2011.
271. "He would have endorsed": Michael Reagan interview with Christiane Amanpour, ABC News, January 28, 2011.
272. "I had another show": Bruce Springsteen, Sirius XM, June 17, 2020.
273. "I'm going to start": Ibid.
274. "Your mandate": Ronald Reagan Farewell Address, January 11, 1989.

www.ingramcontent.com/pod-product-compliance
Lightning Source LLC
Chambersburg PA
CBHW071330080526
44587CB00017B/2784